SAIL PLAN—YACHT FIGARO

ACROSS THE WESTERN OCEAN

Oh, the times are hard and the wages low,

You sailor, where you bound to?

The Western Ocean is my home,

Across the Western Ocean.

A song of the American sailormen. The oldest of the
capstan shanties (the origins of which go back to the Atlantic
packet ships), and the one sung at the close of the voyage.

ACROSS THE WEST

ERN OCEAN

WILLIAM SNAITH

HARCOURT,
BRACE &
WORLD, INC.

NEW YORK

Photograph on the title page shows FIGARO *racing in the Solent.*
Courtesy Beken & Son, Cowes

ACKNOWLEDGMENTS

Writing a book may be a lonely task. Living this one certainly was not. To my companion-crews, who have made this record possible while sharing many wonderful sailing adventures, all my thanks. My apologies, as well as thanks, are in order to the sailing photographers who had to put up with my grudging approval while they were taking pictures (I thought, aloud, that they could more usefully employ their time trimming sails).

My special thanks to Dr. Norris Hoyt, a great shipmate, ocean sailor, raconteur, and photographer, who produced the lion's share of the photographs used in this book.

CONTENTS

I. SOME BACKGROUND   3

II. AN INTRODUCTION TO FIGARO   10

CRUISING: Trans-Atlantic 1961

III. SOME FOREGROUND   17

IV. THE PASSAGE BEGINS

    June 30—The First Day   20

    July 1—The Second Day   29

V. SAILING THE OCEAN AT NIGHT   35

VI. THE GRAND BANKS

    July 2—The Third Day   39

    July 3—The Fourth Day   47

    The Glorious Fourth of July—The Fifth Day   52

VII. NAVIGATION   59

VIII. MID-ATLANTIC

    July 5—The Sixth Day   65

    July 6—The Seventh Day   70

    July 7—The Eighth Day   74

IX. PASSAGE ROUTINE   81

X. A BREWER'S DRAY

    July 8—The Ninth Day   83

    July 9—The Tenth Day   86

    July 10—The Eleventh Day   90

    July 11—The Twelfth Day   95

XI. LANDFALLS AND ARRIVALS   101

XII.   IN THE CHANNEL

       July 12—The Thirteenth Day   104

       July 13—The Fourteenth Day   106

RACING: Trans-Atlantic 1963

XIII.   CRUISING AND RACING   111

XIV.   BEFORE THE RACE   118

XV.   THE FIRST TWO DAYS

       Sunday, June 30   124

       Monday, July 1   130

XVI.   THE THIRD AND FOURTH DAYS

       Tuesday, July 2   134

       Wednesday, July 3   137

XVII.   THURSDAY, THE (GLORIOUS)
FOURTH OF JULY   145

XVIII.   A SERIES OF INGLORIOUS DAYS

       Friday, July 5   155

       Saturday, the Inglorious July 6   158

       Sunday, the Even Less Glorious July 7   161

       Monday, July 8   163

XIX.   THAT OLD BLACK MAGIC

       Tuesday, July 9   167

       Wednesday, July 10   170

       Thursday, July 11   173

XX.   WE HOLD THE BREEZE

       Friday, July 12   176

       Saturday, July 13   178

       Bastille Day—Sunday, July 14   183

XXI.   SOME FINE RUNS

       Monday, July 15   186

       Tuesday, July 16   188

       Wednesday, July 17   192

XXII.   *ANOTHER HIGH?*

         Thursday, July 18   *196*

         Friday, July 19   *201*

XXIII.   *WHERE'S EDDYSTONE?*

         Saturday, July 20   *203*

         Sunday, July 21   *206*

         The Next Day   *208*

LIST OF ILLUSTRATIONS

FIGARO *racing in the Solent*   Title page

FIGARO *in the English Channel*   9

Jocko   14

The crew that took her from Newport   16

The Portuguee   18

Sometimes you have an easy time   26

Some days it blows hard on a reach   30

Or on the wind   31

Nearing a landfall at night   37

Skip keeps dry under the dodger   38

The scullery   41

Skip in the big sea   44

A hazy sky and bad horizon   48

The pastry chef   55

The Fourth of July party   57

Norry hears the clash of palm fronds   72

Passage routine above decks   75

The break of the watch during a Fastnet Race   79

How we look to the masthead man   89

Near the end of the passage   96

Land Ho!   98

An Old World port—Falmouth   103

Fastnet Rock   105

Running back from the Rock   108

Keeping cool in the Needles Channel   114

We win the Admiral's Cup   117

The fleet is ready to race   119

Jon Rohde and Cleody   *120*

Skip Snaith   *120*

Cleody Snaith   *120*

Buz Knowlton   *120*

Freddy Hibberd   *122*

Mike Richey   *122*

Conn Findlay   *122*

WTS, the Skipper   *122*

Clearing a pennant for the helmsman   *127*

Taking a sun shadow on the compass   *128*

Creaming along   *140*

Dragging the main boom   *147*

The main boom with splints and bandage   *149*

The spinnaker was breaking   *152*

Coming back from the Rock   *171*

Getting the jib off   *181*

Taking out a wrap in the halyards   *190*

Big seas ran down upon us   *193*

Eddystone at last   *207*

Conn gives his shorts the deep 6   *209*

ACROSS THE WESTERN OCEAN

I

SOME BACKGROUND

Just imagine yourself, one dark night, on board a 47-foot centerboard yawl, banging into a head sea somewhere south of Fastnet Rock in the southern approaches to Ireland.

You are there, working out your watch on deck. You sit, wet and weary, thinking only of your approaching turn in the sack. Trickles of salt water thrust impudent icy fingers between your oilies and your neck and armpit. You are locked into your misery, holding fast to the remaining glimmer of the only true happiness—*your feet are still warm and dry.* Then that unfeeling bastard, the skipper, thinks it's time to change jibs. So you go forward, get new-wet to the navel, fill your boots, and with eyes stinging with salt you come gasping back to the cockpit.

"She feels better," he says. "Balls," you think and, man, the time has come when you have joined a gallant company. You are with Ulysses at Scylla and Charybdis, Leif Ericson in the Davis Strait, and Magellan in straits of his own. They, too, at one time or another, must have asked themselves: "What am I doing out here?"

That's the question each sailor answers for himself. You do not even have to be on deck for the question to arise. The sanctuary below decks is such only by comparison. Try sleeping inside a bass drum while the band is playing the "1812 Overture." That's what that little wooden island sounds like as she shoots off the top of a long green wave and falls into the hollow at the back side. You swear you can hear the heel of the mast grinding through the mast step. You pulse with each whack of the centerboard as it bangs from side to side in the trunk. With the disengagement of a somnambulist, you wonder how long this marvelous arrangement of wood, bronze, stainless-steel wire, and dacron can hold together. But, like Scarlett O'Hara, you'll think about that tomorrow.

Your bunk is no retreat. You are a vagrant chunk of ice in a cocktail shaker. You hold on to the berth with your toes and the muscles of your derriere, all the time scrounging out of the way of the Chinese torture-drop coming off the overhead. (Damn that shipyard man, you told him about that leak.) You don't feel like eating, but that damned fool Cookie (showing off) has fired up the alcohol stove. The cabin slowly fills with unconsumed alcohol fumes which make your eyes smart and which go right to the pit of your stomach before his miserable scrambled egg can get there.

My friend, you are ocean sailing: which, as a sport, can provide more concentrated discomfort than anything—short of bronco riding—and what it loses in vehemence, it makes up for in duration.

And still, the Corinthians* fight for a berth on a yacht going to sea. They can't all be masochists. There must be something more than that. Despite the opinion held in some quarters that anyone who would go to sea for a pastime would go to hell for his pleasure, the men who go out in small boats show more or less rational attitudes to most other aspects of living. There must be a reason for such an unseasonable madness.

And so there is, but to each his own. To one, it is the kinetic loveliness of a sailboat working its way through the seas. To another, it is the challenge of the unruly elements. To one man it may be the competitive zest of a race, while to his shipmate it could be the landfall after days at sea. To my late friend Judge Curtis Bok, it was the sea itself, "which has no memory and shows no compassion and which shows an indifference so vast as to make man go silent in its presence." To all, it is a unifying love for the sea, the love of ships and the wonders of things nautical—natural, man-created, and historical. They are part of a new and growing fellowship of the sea—those who go out upon the ocean in small boats for the enjoyment of this peculiar form of pleasure.

Now imagine yourself in another time and setting. You are in the snug saloon of a straight-stemmed, black-hulled P & O steamer, black coal smoke pouring from her high stacks as she plows down the Bay of Biscay. You are in the company of seafarers of another generation. In the Victorian snuggery of the cabin are the artifacts of a statelier tradition and on every hand the signs of good ship-keeping can be seen. A sea-coal fire burns in the grate. The oil lamps, which fill the cabin with a soft golden light, burn steady in their gimbals; the lamp trimmer has done a conscientious job. Dinner over, the table cleared, and Sumatra cigars aglow, the claret bottle is passing from hand to hand. The mahogany table, rubbed up like a mirror, gleams with crystal and ruby reflections. It is a warm and friendly atmosphere.

It is also time for ruminative talk. For in this imagined setting are men who have earned the right to a backward appraisal. Among them are Joseph Conrad and Marlow, his creation, observer and commentator on human events. It is Marlow who is speaking. His story is told in "Youth"—how, at the age of twenty, he set sail for Bangkok, going as second in the aging barque JUDEA OF LONDON. In speaking for the writer of the sea and of men, he holds a contrary opinion as to the make-up of the fellowship of those who follow the sea, for he says: "There is a fellowship of the craft which no amount of enthusiasm for yachting, cruising and so on can give, since one is the amusement of life and the other is life itself."

Well, life itself has become unlike anything that Marlow or the others in that cabin could have imagined. They may have had justification for that opinion

* Yachting name for amateur sailors, borrowed from the ancient city whose sailors probably went out on shares.

then, but now a deck officer distributes his skill between handling the dissident shop steward from a seamen's union and meeting the rigors of an unfriendly sea in a ship equipped with automatic gyro steering and anti-roll equipment. Now that the voyage to and from ports of call in such a streamlined container of mechanical marvels normally is as eventful as bringing the 8:10 A.M. daily commuter safely from Westport, Connecticut to New York City, I wonder if the fellowship of the craft does not lie with the other side.

Yachtsmen probably are the only supporters left in this Western world of that lovely old relic of the past, the sailing ship. With the exception of a few official sail training ships, the age of the lofty windjammers is gone. Today, the wind sailor goes to sea in a small sailing boat which, as a sport and a means of transportation, has been called the most vexing, expensive, slow, and frustrating means of getting from one unimportant place to another. And yet, men keep going out in these small boats for the sheer joy of sailing—a joy which mysteriously hovers between rapture and misery. They sail to enjoy active physical discomforts, loss of privacy, and most of the cherished props to one's *amour-propre*. Yet these are the very same men who, while on land, will complain if the toast is cold, or if there are insufficient towels in the bathroom, or if the headwaiter keeps avoiding their eye.

But at sea, and especially at the start of a long ocean race, they set out for their inevitable share of misery with foreknowledge of trials to come, but with spirit expanded and with wide-eyed contentment. It is the look of one who has found the way. For, despite all the discomforts to be, there will come great pleasures—pleasures in their own skills at a time when individual skills are disappearing into a mass, man-automated complex; a sense of victory in contest with powerful elementals; and the companionship of their fellows in the midst of a shared adventure. Surely, Marlow and Conrad notwithstanding, the great fellowship of the craft now must be with the yachtsman and cruiser.

I suppose that an important part of what makes it life itself for the professional is economics. He earns his living that way. In addition to the mysterious compulsion of the sea, he is motivated by the pragmatic compulsion of economic necessity. But for the yachtsman, there is an obverse side to that coin. Considerable economic sacrifice is made to indulge the passion for sailing. Far from being a means of earning a living, it is rather a costly indulgence. A fellow I know says ocean racing is like standing in an icy shower while tearing up $1000 bills. That's one owner's description of the price for fun in a specialized form of discomfort. But consider the Corinthians who sail with him. There is nothing more apt to defeat a schedule than a long yacht race. A race may start on Friday night at 1830 hours, but it can finish on Sunday or Tuesday—the gods of wind and wave willing. The Corinthian must be prepared to defend his loss of time on the job to a boss whose enthusiasm may be golf or his business, or have so ravishing a story to tell that his absence is glossed over.

And then there are social pressures. For instance, there is the married fellow whose wife was sympathetic and understood his passion for the sea in the first years of marriage. Now that sympathy and understanding is eroding with time.

An ocean-racing sailor is absent from home and hearth on occasions when all other families are practicing togetherness. At least a golf widow's club-swinger gets home to his cave toward evening—not so the ocean-racing widow's helmsman. Her man is off somewhere glorying in that all-male world which is an affront to any reasonable marriage.

What of the miseries? They are real enough. And yet the ocean-racing buff and his fellows keep going to sea, happily, ardently, and in ever-growing numbers. Each of the fraternity has a principal reason for his enthusiasm and shares a bit of the other man's. But Marlow was right in one regard—while it is a way of life, it is not to be confused with the business of living.

The pleasures and adventures of deep-sea racing are separate and treasured by each man who sails. They are kept in a sort of memory bank—to be drawn against when there is no sailing at hand. One form of memory bank is the ship's log, an active record of happenings which turn into memories. The memories not only are treasured, but must seemingly be shared. The tradition of sea tales and yarns is as old as sailing itself. The sailor's compulsion to tell yarns undoubtedly comes from the fact that to him a sea story is essentially a love story, the story of his love. In the telling, he warms himself in the memories of that love.

A word about logs. A ship's log is a privileged document, a fact evident even to the least technically informed readers of the life and times of Horatio Hornblower. A log must be sacrosanct, it cannot be altered. An attempt to tamper with it at times amounts to illegality, if not downright sacrilege. Yet its privilege is not that of the confessional to doctor, priest, or lawyer. That sort of privilege amounts to a secret between teller and hearer, not to be revealed outside of the confessional. A ship's log, conversely, is a professional document which, on occasion, becomes public and acts as a mute witness to events and phenomena experienced on board ship while at sea. Its testimony has hanged men and saved others from obloquy. It becomes public only if necessary to a maritime court of enquiry, at which time it reaches a level of credibility equal, if not superior to, any human witness. Its revelations are unchallenged, unless it can be proven that the entries were falsified from the outset with some desperate plan in mind. It also becomes public when it is published, so that others can share the sense of adventure, excitement, and magic of a voyage at sea.

At such a time, there is a permissible amount of wandering from the direct record into expansions in order to enrich the telling. These are not untruthful embroideries—the employment of any such artifices would attack the total credibility of an experience and make it a work of fiction, another sort of story. Additions and interpolations to straight reporting from a log usually are based on memories drawn from experiences of other times. They are introduced to explain or illuminate an event in order to provide greater clarity and understanding than the dry record can produce. An abstract out of a ship's log can be a simple narration of events during a voyage, or can be directed toward a specific purpose. Thus, when Richard Hakluyt set down "The Principal Navigations, Voyages, Traffiques, and Discoveries of the English Nation," his purpose was to bring public recognition and glory to the maritime enterprises of the English. He therefore took great pains to collect accurate accounts from the participants and survivors of various expeditions. He was fortunate in that he was a friend to Drake, Hawkins, and Frobisher, among other glorious captains. Because of his personal friendships, and through the judicial editing and selection of his material, he was able—within the framework of truth—to give his record a sense of adventure and heroism which by the nature of its contents fulfilled his purpose.

On the other hand, the bare account drawn from the log and evidences found on board the MARY CELESTE turns out to be one of the great cliff-hangers of all time. As a true mystery story, it is unparalleled. No one knows how the mysterious disappearance of the whole crew came about. We just know it happened.

But all accounts of voyages do not, of necessity, contain great gobs of adventure, hair-raising experiences of dangers past. Most voyages are calm, prosperous, and uneventful. Ploddingly kept, such a log is simply a dull record of weather, wind speed, sea conditions, and distance run. But yacht logs are different. If kept at all, their purpose must be to provide future pleasure through being read at a distant time. Therefore, in addition to a record of the sailings, the log contains reminiscences and ideas exchanged during the voyage. It reflects reactions to events at the time of their occurrence. The logs of FIGARO are maintained in that way and for that reason. A calculating eye is kept on the pleasure of future recollections rather than the edification of a marine review board. While yacht logs are not usually meant for an outside reader, a writer like Hilaire Belloc has drawn a delightful group of stories from a series of impossible boats, which happen to have been invested with his love.

However, in the case of certain wonderful stories of circumnavigation of our world, I find them filled so chock-a-block with adventure that I have sometimes wondered whether there was a dividing line between fact and fancy. For instance, I have often wondered whether Captain Joshua Slocum really spread those carpet tacks on his deck as a hedgehog defense against the hostile aborigines while lying off Tierra del Fuego. Was it, perhaps, the result of stepping on one himself and, by an exercise of imagination, turned into a great story? As an anecdote, it does so much to heighten the sense of loneliness, high peril, and wild nature found in the Straits of Magellan. I only wonder, I do not disbelieve. It is a secret the captain carried to his watery grave.

Since most voyages are not completed in the midst of terrors and torments, the logs often lack accounts of suspense and drama. This is nowhere so true as in a normal yacht log. Most skilled yachtsmen pride themselves on their ability to take their boat out and return with a minimum of fuss and trouble. They have pride in their ability to prepare for and to anticipate the trials which inevitably beset them when at sea. And yet, no amount of preparation can anticipate the sea. The sea is an elemental adversary which follows no rules but its own. It can be counted on for one surprise or another. In spite of great care I have had several serious mishaps. I have lost my mainmast overside as the result of a broken fitting. The main boom has been broken during a vicious roll down in the sea. Once I lost three-fourths of my fresh-water stores during the first night out of a 3500-mile trans-Atlantic race to Sweden, and still we finished the race and, for that matter, won it.

The fact that a log generally is written up a short time after the event, when the danger is over or almost past and it is clearly evident that all will survive, tends to flatten out a story. It is difficult, in a log, to convey the belly-griping sense of danger at the moment of a happening and during the protracted period immediately after while awaiting the outcome.

The same sort of qualities are often missing in a photograph of mountainous seas taken from the deck of a small boat. The height of eye from the deck and the camera perspective at the moment the picture is taken, whether from the crest or the trough of a wave, tend to reduce and flatten the actuality. Not only is the sense of awesome height and power lacking, but the attendant impact on the face and body of the wind-blown scud as it is torn from the wave tops, the sound and thrust of the sea as it rushes under the boat and foams over the transom, the sense of power when the boat hurtles on the downward slope of a wave, the scream of the wind in the rigging as it blows up and down some mad scale of its own—all of these are frozen into a jagged still life, unheard and unfelt in a photograph.

So it is with a yacht log. By the time it gets to be written, the danger, if any, has been frozen into the past tense or an accommodation has been made with the situation. The intense excitement is over and the adrenalin has slowed its mad coursing. But in the retelling a surge of remembered experience comes back and details omitted from the log come to the forefront of remembrance. So strong are these feelings that they sometimes come through in the rereading by those who have shared the experience. Such are the sweet uses and failings of a yacht log. It really is a basis for telling the story of love—a love for a boat, for the sea, and for what Marlow called the fellowship of the craft.

The story of love that I tell is drawn from logs kept during two trans-Atlantic passages made in my yacht, FIGARO III. The first was a cruise to England, the second a race to the same country. The sea, uninvolved with the petty plans of men, was the same majestic element in both crossings. The weather, while producing an average of the same conditions, had many variations in pattern. The significant difference, however, in one crossing from the other was the yachtsmen's attitudes. The fact that one was a race made it another kind of experience.

Since the fellowship of the craft is not based solely on experiences in sailing, but also is involved with some technical knowledge of boats, of sails, and of navigation, I have included a few brief discussions on aspects of these arts, pleasures, and sciences. They are meant to serve only as an introduction to this side of yachting. There is no intention to provide anything in them but an understanding of the passions and problems of the craft. These discussions are addressed to those who have sailed the sea and to those whose boating, until now, has been restrained to liners, ferries, and the smaller subdivisions of powered craft, and especially for those who have not had the treasured experience of sailing across a great sea.

And finally, there is included some gratuitous unburdening of stray bits of lore, of things nautical, which by this time must be old hat to anyone with a passing interest in the sea, but still fill me with a wonder equaled only by the delight with sailing itself.

FIGARO *in the English Channel—Ed Raymond at the wheel, crew on weather rail*

II

AN INTRODUCTION TO FIGARO

The proper heroine for a sea story is a ship, and FIGARO is the proper little ship to be such a heroine. As you think of it, you become aware that there are very few bad boats. Some are misconceived and do not perform exactly as the designer, builder, or owner had originally hoped, but eventually even these misfit craft find somebody who loves them. On rare occasions, we hear of a rogue ship. We are told how she killed or maimed a man at the launch and then went on into a cranky, stubborn existence, quite apart from the best interests of the men who sailed in her. Fortunately, such ships are few and far between. On the other hand, some ships are paragons, equaling, or even exceeding, the fondest dreams of their designers and owners. FIGARO is such a ship.

To begin with, she is very pretty. Just as beauty in woman creates allure and inspires affection, so it does in a boat. In a boat, that beauty also rests in a rare combination of form and proportion. In this case it is the shape and relationship of her bow to her transom; in the spring of her sheer; the height and rake of her spars; and in the placement and size of her deckhouses. In FIGARO, these all come out to mean beauty.

To top all this, she is sea kindly, taking rough seas softly and nimbly, except when she is jammed on the wind into a head sea. Even then, beyond a few complaining creaks and groans, she goes gallantly on. Downwind and on a broad reach, there are few boats near her size that can hold her. On the wind she needs care and understanding, and in light headwinds, forebearance. But then, you can't have everything.

Below, in this lovely, graceful boat, the quarters for her passengers provide space and opportunity for reasonable communal living. These accommodations have been the setting for many great times, especially when we were being borne to foreign ports and wonderful victories. Unhappily, there were times when our efforts were ingloriously rewarded. But then, it was clearly the fault of her guides and handlers, through mismanagement and bad judgment. You can't blame a boat for that.

On deck, she provides a good working platform. Her gear is fairly well placed, which makes sailing her an easy task. Her helm is a delight. Such is this man's biased opinion, and one shared by all who have sailed in her. Now for the particulars.

FIGARO is teak-decked, double planked of Honduras mahogany over white cedar. Her frame and keel are white oak. She was designed by the magician Olin Stephens, who has designed every kind of boat from a stock production sloop to the last word in perfection of a cup defender. She was built in Black Rock, Connecticut, not far from my home, so that I could watch her grow. Joel Johnson, her builder, was a craftsman of the old school. He was not one to monkey around with new-fangled things. In this age of miracle epoxies, Joel used air-stiffened orange shellac as a bonding agent buttered between the two skins of planking. "That's what we used on Henry Nevins' OLD POLLY," he said, "and she is still around and in good shape."

FIGARO was planked by one man. He used very long boards in order to keep end butts at a minimum. Louis Larsen, a Norwegian shipwright, did that solo job. Louis was nearly deaf, an affliction which he converted to a virtue. The first thing in the morning, he would turn off his hearing aid and then in splendid, quiet isolation go about his craft. At lunchtime, someone would tug at his arm and make signs of eating. Louis would turn on his hearing aid and, for a short time, rejoin the world of others. The level of all craftsmanship was fine, down to Malcolm Bryant, an apprentice boy, who kept the bilges free from shavings as the work progressed. It was he who built the accurate scale model which stands in its glass case in my trophy corner. These were the men who joined in the building of FIGARO, a centerboard yawl, 47½ feet long, on a designed waterline of 32½ feet. She floats a little over 33 feet now, what with all of the gear she carries. She has a generous beam of 12 feet 1 inch to hold up her rig of 1090 square feet of sail.

I like a yawl, although it is a rig of questionable value for going around the buoys. On the wind the mizzen probably creates more loss by windage than any advantage of power which can possibly be gained by that after handkerchief. It is true that you can carry a mizzen staysail, but this sail is useful in such a narrow spectrum of wind direction and speed as to make one wonder at its value when measured against rating (handicap) penalties. It has always seemed to me that the major advantage of this sail is psychological. It scares skippers of sloops and cutters, who expect that a destroyer-like burst of speed will follow when they see one of these break out. Little do they know that it is really a monkey on the back. Once the sail is up, the helmsman worries more about keeping it drawing than he does about keeping his workhorses, the main and spinnaker, going at an optimum. That's because this is the only sail he can see, if he can see at all. For the sail is just as apt to be collapsed over his head, draping him in a shroud of impenetrable nylon. But in spite of these shortcomings, I think a yawl is a wonderful rig with which to go to sea. It can provide balance in the widest range of conditions so that the boat is under good control at all times. And as for the mizzenmast itself, where else can you fly a private signal or have something to lean against while being master of all you survey?

FIGARO has an optional double head rig. We can take out her forestay quickly with the throw of an ingenious lever, swing the stay back to the shrouds, and sail her with a single masthead rig. For this we use a series of dacron Genoa jibs made of from five- to eight-ounce cloth. The Number One is our largest, a full hoist jib with a 180 percent overlap of the forward triangle; that is, the foot overlaps the mainsail by 80 percent of the distance measured from the forward side of the mast to the tack fitting in the bow. As the wind picks up speed, we change to sails which are smaller and of heavier cloth. They are the Number Two and Number Three progressively.

When it really blows up at sea, we may go to our double head rig, which means exactly what it says. You can use two jibs in place of one in the forward triangle, one over and ahead of the other. The forward and outer one is called a jib and the inner one a staysail. As the wind increases in speed, you need less overlap to create the Venturi slot effect between jib and main. At such a time, wind trapped in the overlap of a large Genoa just succeeds in pressing down the boat. It is best then to let the air get out fast. For this purpose we use the Number One or Number Two jib topsails which can be carried over a working staysail or a Genoa staysail. For hard reaching at sea, we have a Yankee topsail, a high-cut sail with a long overlap which can be sheeted to the quarter or to the main boom. With this sail, we have the advantage of a Genoa without picking the bow wave up in the foot of the sail. (When the boat is close reaching in a seaway, the bow wave falls into the low-cut foot of a Genoa with such weight and power as to tear it. The foot of the Yankee is cut up on a long diagonal to avoid this.)

These then, along with her main, storm trysail, spitfire, storm jib, hard- and light-weather spinnakers, and a whole assortment of drifters and ghosters, make up her sail complement. Buying sails is like any other form of addiction or collecting. It also is a notorious form of conspicuous consumption. I always am stricken to the heart when I hear of a winning boat which goes through the season with a main, two jibs, and a spinnaker. As a matter of fact, I never have carried all of my sails on the boat at one time. If I did, there wouldn't be room for us.

There are four winches for handling these sails, paired on each side of the cockpit. Two are the Number Six Merrimans, and the others, Number Seven Nevins. This year we added a Number Thirty-five Barient winch out on the fantail. The well-engineered gearing of this larger winch gives us the power we need to flatten in the Genoas. Until now, we have been underpowered in winch strength. At times, in order to get a sail in, we needed to lead the sheet from one winch to another, grinding on both. Most times, in this situation, the sheet would be on the winches on the leeward side. When it blew hard, the weight of three men (two grinders and tailer) on the leeward side was too much. We then would lead the sheet from the leeward winch across the cockpit to its opposite number on the windward side. I had visions of the cockpit crushing like an eggshell one day with the strains set up. But it wasn't until I was somewhat crushed myself that I took the problem seriously.

During the Fastnet Race of 1957, on the morning of the second day, we were banging along—or perhaps our situation could be better described as being banged by the English Channel—in very dusty weather. I was huddled under the spray dodger after a dousing spell at the wheel when I noticed the mizzen runner was adrift. I got up to fix it. Footing was not of the best in that sea and I did not lift my leg enough to clear the line across the cockpit. I came down heavily, my back across the coaming. I thought I had broken my back. Carefully moving one leg, then the other, the same with my arms, hands, fingers, and finally my neck, I found everything moved, but it hurt like hell. For the next three and a half days my cup of joy was empty. After we finished, it finally turned out that we were one of twelve finishers out of an entry list of some seventy boats, and that we had won a prize. The pain seemed to go away. It didn't return until I went back to work. The doctor said I had broken four or five ribs. Since it was too late to do anything about the ribs, I bought a big winch instead.

Down below, FIGARO is a compromise between an out-and-out racer and a pleasure dome for the joys of cruising. If one were to put the major accent on long-distance ocean racing, then the first decision must be to put all sleeping accommodations in the after part of the boat. This is the part with the least motion. Sleeping forward is for trampolin acrobats or Indian fakirs. However, if you fill the after part with bunks, then the galley, perforce, must be forward and a forward galley is for masochists, as well as being a lonely limbo. When Dante cast Francesca da Rimini into the inferno, she at least had Paolo for company, and all that lush Tchaikovsky music to whirl to. But when the captain sends his wife up to a forward galley to cook while a sea is running, she goes alone. And while the burns may not be as searing as those of the inferno, falling against the stove or a hot pot raises equally painful blisters. So I like a galley aft, right next to the cockpit. When you go below to cook, you have not been cut off from the happy life, you still are part of the joyous world under the sky, conversationally anyway.

Then I like a big main cabin. Gamming when the hook is down and talking it over after a race is an important part of the total experience and it needs a proper, traditional setting. Besides, my wife likes to sail, and at times she is chatelaine of the domain below decks. In such a case, the cabin should be not only luxurious, but uxorious as well. With the exception of this kind of obeisance to the blessings of marriage, FIGARO's cruising and racing accommodations are fairly normal. Starting aft with the galley and navigation section, we next come to the main cabin which contains four berths. It is a beautiful cabin, paneled with Brazilian rosewood and with large-scale scrimshaw decorations over which I spent many weary hours. The cabin is separated from the forward stateroom (with its two berths), by the head to port and hanging lockers to starboard. The forecastle, with a pipe berth and head, is forward of the stateroom.

On deck, at the forward end of the cockpit, is a shelter or dodger. It is such a useful contrivance that I am surprised that it is not used on more boats. It serves as a spray, wind, and rain dodger. A modest-sized sailboat takes two and a half to three weeks to sail from New York or Newport to a European port. During that time a yachtsman can absorb a lot of punishment while sitting in the open cockpit of his boat. The North Atlantic can produce a variety of weathers, mostly bad or at least uncomfortable for anyone who must sit out in it for several hours at a stretch. The chilling cold, the rain and spray have a depressing effect on morale and energy. The dodger on FIGARO goes a long way to overcoming this hazard. It is not unlike the top of a convertible auto. Leading from a windshield at its forward end, an aluminum frame supports a waterproof orlon top and plexiglass sides. The after end is open and arches over a small bridge deck which, in effect, is a seat. It provides room for three men to find shelter. Since a normal watch is made up of four men, only the helmsman is exposed and he is soon relieved by a fresh man—not one who, in bad weather, is going from one seat of agony to another. The dodger also stretches over the main companionway so that this principal access for people and air can be left open in all weather. It makes all the difference below, in terms of ventilation. As a crew saver and extender, the dodger is unparalleled.

This, then, is FIGARO, about to take us trans-Atlantic for the third time: a lovely and able boat. She is a home away from home and a racing machine that has competed successfully with the best. She has the magic quality of becoming at one with those who sail in her, and evokes a feeling of assurance that she will see you through whatever may come. You take care of her, and she will take care of you, is the unspoken pact she makes with all who sail in her.

Jocko—it's cold on the Banks

CRUISING

TRANS-ATLANTIC 1961

St. John's, Newfoundland

to Cowes, Isle of Wight, England

The crew that took her from Newport (left to right: Skip, Jocko, Billy Walden, Norry Hoyt, Bucky Reardon, Cleody)

III

SOME FOREGROUND

The story of FIGARO's cruise to England in the summer of 1961 begins in St. John's, Newfoundland. This port cannot exactly be described as a yacht marina, but does have a splendid harbor entirely surrounded by amiable and helpful natives. It is the Canadian port closest to England along the great circle route from Westport, Connecticut.

FIGARO was sailing to England to be part of the United States Admiral's Cup team. We were one of three American boats on the team challenging for that prime English ocean-racing trophy. While in England we would race during Cowes Week, sail the Channel Race, and have still one more bash at the renowned Fastnet Race.

FIGARO had been sailed to St. John's without me. I could not take the time for this first stage of the trip. Ahead of us were several weeks of sailing and racing, about the limit that I could spare from the office.

This is no longer the age of large professional crews, so that not the least onerous of tasks for an ocean-racing skipper is to find amateur crews for his various bold enterprises. It is rare that the men you want can take off all of the necessary time. They have problems of their own. When not along, wives, sweethearts, bosses, and bank cashiers seem to have a blind eye for the beauties of the deep. A crew for a campaign, therefore, is made up of skilled amateurs who take over at various periods in the schedule.

My crew members for the voyage across, and for the summer's campaign, were to be: Dr. Norris Hoyt, schoolmaster at St. George's, Newport; James "Bucky" Reardon, student at Providence College; and my son Shepperd, "Skipper," who had just finished at the Putney School. These three were staying the distance. Coming on board at Halifax (to replace my eldest son, MacLeod, who had a sailing date in Finland and who would rejoin us in England) was Frank Crawford, business executive of New York who lives in Rowayton, Connecticut. He was to leave us after our arrival in England. Sailing as far as St. John's from Westport were two schoolboys, Billy Walden and my son Jonathan, "Jocko," and coming on board to replace them in St. John's was Jack Latham, advertising executive of New York, and myself. But that's not all. In England, in order to bring the crew up to full racing strength, FIGARO was to be joined by still other men. Sounds involved, doesn't it? You bet it is!

Most of the work of preparing her for sea had been done in the States. She was in St. John's to make the last changes in crew, to take on water and fuel, and to replace anything that had broken down or gone missing in the cruise up from Newport.

FIGARO was in grand shape. Nothing had broken down but the head. But even this was looked on as a good omen, for what if it had happened when we were out to sea? At least here we could have it repaired. Still it bugged me. I could not see why this should happen. I had given specific instructions to the yard to give it a complete overhaul, with all new parts, and here at the start of the season it was acting up. A metal linkage was broken and so out came the head. We marched with it to a local blacksmithery. The head was tightly clasped in the arms of one stalwart, the rest of us surrounding him in a phalanx—seagoing centurions marching with the spoils or casuals of war.

All repairs were made and supplies on board in the afternoon of the day before our departure. I moved onto the boat, giving my hotel room to Billy and Jocko. We had a farewell dinner for our departing mates. The senior members of the crew had a prowl around the town, making a survey of its alcoholic refreshment, and then to bed, ready for the next morning.

The Portuguee—St. John's

Twice before, we had raced across: once from Spain to Newport, Rhode Island, and again to Sweden from Bermuda. Now we were to cruise across. Races are exhilarating and sometimes tense. We were looking forward to a pleasurable cruise. The Atlantic generally can be counted on for at least one nasty spell on the way across, but this time we were not going to push during the blow. No one cared if we were a day late. We were going to lie back and enjoy it.

IV

THE PASSAGE BEGINS

JUNE 30—THE FIRST DAY

0530   I was awakened by the voices of Billy and Jocko, and in my early morning bugle tones I woke the others. Full of the proper sort of belief that the young should have in their elders, our young shipmates had taken us at our word about an 0600 departure and had come down to the dock to say farewell. Instead of a bustling ship, they had found the ship's company strewn in their individual contortions of sleep. Now they watched with the dispassionate fascination of the young as each, in his own way, came awake and crept from his warm nest into the crisp morning, a little the worse for wear after a night on the few tiles that St. John's had to offer. All, that is, but my son Skip, who was not much for tiles but is a hard waker.

We made a brief breakfast, deferring a larger meal to a time when we would be well under way, and saying some inadequate good-byes to our young homeward bound shipmates, turned on the iron mainsail and, under power, headed out. At that moment I wanted very much to take my son Jocko along, but we had both agreed that he was still too young and unready for such a passage. And so, touched by this fleeting regret, I steered past the quiet docks of St. John's, sprinkled with a few morning workers at early chores. At last, we were on our long lap and, with much taking of pictures, we pointed our bow toward England on the great circle course.

0600   We have cleared the harbor mouth with its two watching hills and thrust out into the cold gray-green Atlantic. Outside, we have found a brisk southerly of 15 to 18 knots. We are carrying a big sail combination; the main, mizzen, and Number One Genoa have been set. It is an exhilarating start. FIGARO, despite the fact that she is deeply laden with supplies for the crossing and for use in England, feels lively and responsive. The feeling transfers from the hull right up through the seat of your pants and through the wheel into your hands.

Newfoundland is disappearing behind us into the fog. There is no last lingering look at the land for us. The curtain is being pulled down in a hurry. It's better that way. No use in looking where you have been. Now, the immediate thing we have to look for is ice. The latest ice reports indicate nothing serious ahead, but then small pieces are beneath reporting. However, at 8 knots, a small piece can do our wooden racing hull considerable damage.

We are squared away for Cowes, the great English yachting center on the Isle of Wight. Our course is 096° at a stimulating 8 knots.

0730 A solid breakfast of bacon and eggs, toast and coffee has been tucked away—wash-up now going on—and we are moving well. Now that we are off and away, and the pressures of organization and preparation for the voyage are over, there is time to sort out the actions and decisions leading up to them. There is a lot of time for afterthoughts at sea. It's a great place for 20–20 hindsight.

To begin with, we have flouted a hoary sea tradition by this choice of departure day. I cherish most of the traditions and superstitions of the sea. It's all part of the game. As long as these take their proper place as one of the adornments of living, they deserve to be recognized. However, when they intrude on plans, then one is entitled to second thoughts. One of these superstitions (age and origin unknown) is that ill luck betides the ship which sails on Friday. I do not deride the potency of this hoodoo. Maybe it was on a Friday that Tristram took Iseult off sailing. Perhaps the Flying Dutchman and the Ancient Mariner made their departures on that day of the week. But it is difficult enough to make things leading up to departure mesh without indulging a passion for all nautical mysteries. Besides, I have taken even more daring risks with the mysteries and have so far escaped the notice of any resentful demigods of wind and wave. Amen and mea culpa.

An instance of daring to fly in the face of an established tabu was the choice of upholstery for this FIGARO, the third to bear the name of the cock-a-snook barber. During her building, and in order to make her cheery and bright below decks, I chose yellow upholstery. You may say: "So what? It's yellow." But it shakes one up when you hear a knowledgeable fellow in a low-pitched voice of doom say that you are courting disaster. This particular fellow was not a collateral descendant of the hags of the blasted heath or anything like that, he was just a respecter of sea tradition. I was told that yellow was an unlucky color on a boat. As a rule, I pay careful attention to advice put forward in such a friendly spirit, but in this case I was stubbornly set on yellow. It is the color of my private signal and of a favorite sailing shirt. I always have loved Van Gogh's sunflowers, and as a child of my generation I can never lose my admiration for a yellow Stutz Bearcat.

And so, for these and other subliminal reasons, I was quite set on yellow. Beyond this, I could find no statistical support for such a superstition. To begin with, most sailors wear yellow oilskins and most sailors return unscathed. Their choice of yellow is logical, since the color has the highest visibility and their chance of recovery, should they have the misfortune to go overside, is enhanced. And, if I remember, the ship GREAT HARRY was painted yellow and she was considered a breakthrough in naval circles in Tudor times.

There are some spurious liberated minds who spurn the Homeric Greek custom of opening a live chicken or lamb in order to read its entrails for the omens and portents inherent in them, and yet will timidly pussyfoot around the superstition surrounding yellow. These characters wear yellow oilskins, but try to blunt the hoodoo by wearing a black souwester. This really is trying to keep too much under the hat. It is a pusillanimous approach to the mysteries.

True, yellow is the color of the quarantine and plague-on-board flag, but the main reason I can see for giving any credence to the theory of ill luck and yellow is that on rare occasion a poor fellow will be lost overside. Since there is every likelihood that he was wearing yellow oilskins because of bad weather, it naturally follows that the disaster index for the color will be high. However, now that FIGARO has been happily wearing her yellow upholstery for some six years and turns out to be a lucky and sweet ship, I am willing to accept the superstition hanging over yellow as some unyielding atavistic fear that we who have emerged into the bright sun of enlightenment must be prepared to discard.

For these statistical and other less logical reasons, I have set aside a few of the other obtruding sailing tabus. For instance, I no longer recognize the menace in coiling a line down against the movement of the sun, or whistling below decks, or that the only lucky boats are those whose names contain seven letters and a double "o" such as Typhoon, Pootang, or Boomkin. More importantly, from observation I am quite prepared to abandon the idea that you invite disaster by having a woman aboard. This is a most hoary tabu, and yet a fellow I know is seen to be sailing regularly with a beauteous first mate, albeit not always the same one. As a racing man, he does very well and, what's more, generally seems to be pleased with life.

I trust such reasoning will quiet lingering doubts about sailing on Friday. So far, the crew have not even mentioned it, but then they have had little time for afterthoughts. One decision that I may have a little more trouble with is: Why the hell leave at 6:00 A.M.? There is little tidal current, nor is there a bar to cross at St. John's. Why, then, leave so early on the morning after a night before? It's precisely for that reason. An English friend of mine, Major Gerald Potter, a former guardsman who, come to think of it, is probably a questionable authority on the subject, always has held: "There is no better place to sober up than at sea." There is a germ of truth in what he says, but only a germ.

There are far better reasons. There is a strange magnetism in the shore that holds a ship fast to its sides. There are endless necessary chores that rarely are completed, for something always comes up to replace them in the order of priority. It's best to cut your shore lines and get started. And there are good physiological reasons for starting early as well. The movement of a small boat upon the open ocean is quite a change from the stable platform of land. It is a decided shock to the system, to say nothing of the psychological impact of finding oneself out on the great green sea. All men are braver in daylight. And the routine of settling down to a long sea voyage in heart, mind, and stomach is better accomplished in these daylight hours when spirits normally are brighter.

It is best to provide as many of these hours as is possible to help the normally shore-bound yachtsman adapt himself to such a violent change of environment. On land, he could count on a stable base from which to launch all operations. This is no longer the case; now he operates from a base which is not only in movement, but moving in a rather irregular sequence at that. Furthermore, it is at a constant angle of heel. One is no longer in an upright world. Clothes hang from hooks obliquely into space. One eats from a table which is constantly in motion and has a high side and a low side and which, unaccountably and without warning, tosses things onto your lap—irrespective of content—be this maple syrup, a bottle of Mouton Rothschild '53, or a can of peaches. When a locker door is opened, things you never dreamed were on board come tumbling out at you. Newton's world has been turned aslant.

It is not only gravitation which plays tricks. One's own personal time continuum is suddenly at ducks and drakes. For eleven months and a bit, one has been going to sleep, waking, and eating at regular periods. Now, suddenly, time's great order is torn to shreds. You are rudely awakened at 2:00 A.M. and told that it is your time on deck, that it is raining and cold, and would you like a cup of coffee or hot broth, or a cold beer. Magically, in a few days, this upset will become routine, but the first day of transition is the hard one, and I always have felt that the way into and through the transition is easier in daylight.

I have learned this lesson the hard way. Racing to Bermuda is exciting, the trip home an anticlimax. We used to delay the home journey in order to wring the last dregs of sensuous delight from that island pleasure dome. We would make our departure after a studied application to stirrup toasts and, in a radiant glow, leave the shelter of Hamilton Harbor in the afternoon. There would follow a smooth passage down the channel, tucked behind the outer reefs. The sparkling, clean, bright water would add to the feeling that all was well in a well-ordered world. Then, turning Kitchen Shoals' buoy late in the afternoon, we would find ourselves sticking our nose into a boisterous northwester. That first night at sea is best recorded as a *tabula rasa*.

And so, for a multitude of reasons assembled the hard way through the years, I like to get the business of going to sea accomplished betimes, the business of ship routine well established before nightfall.

As one piece of routine, the watches have been set as follows:

STARBOARD WATCH		PORT WATCH	
CAPTAIN	William Snaith	MATE	Dr. Norris Hoyt
NAVIGATOR	Frank Crawford	A.B.	Jack Latham
A.B.	James "Bucky" Reardon	A.B.	Shepperd "Skip" Snaith

The watch periods are to be from 0600 hours to 1200 hours, 1200 hours to 1800 hours, 1800 hours to 2200 hours, 2200 hours to 0200 hours, 0200 hours to 0600 hours.

This is a form of the Swedish watch system. To my mind, it has these advantages:

First, since there are five watch periods, they are automatically dogged (thought to be derived from dodged), the nautical term for alternating the watch period in order to create equal patterns of duty and to avoid a circumstance which would find, as an instance, one watch always on duty at 0200 hours. By dogging, each watch stands the 0200 watch on alternate days. Many boats sail under a system of six equal watch periods of four hours each. To avoid the repetition of duty hours, a single watch of four hours is broken into two periods such as, 1800 hours to 2000 hours, 2000 hours to 2200 hours. (This is called dogging the watches and hence this short watch is called the dog watch.)

A second advantage of the Swedish watch system is based on the belief that a man's endurance is better during daylight. We, therefore, set the six-hour periods from 0600 to 1800. This gives the watch below time enough to become well rested, as well as giving them time to do personal chores of mending, etc., for themselves. In a four-hour watch-and-watch pattern, when the time that it takes to get out of and into deck gear—performing ablutions and eating and digesting—is subtracted, it leaves precious little time for sleeping. Hence, the one extended sleeping off-watch.

This five-watch system also lends itself to a convenient pattern for mealtimes. Under the system used on FIGARO, the watch on deck prepares the meal which will be served to the oncoming watch approximately one half hour before they come on duty. The offgoing watch eats after they have been relieved, and finally the watch taking over does the wash-up. Thus, the meal preparation duty falls alternately from one watch to the other, both in time period and the nature of the meal.

We still are moving very well. The weather is overcast and foggy, but our speed still is such that whatever shortcomings are apparent in the weather are made up for by the tingling drive of the boat.

Wind, SW. Sea, moderate. Speed, 8 knots. Course, 096°.

1500   The wind, clear of the shore, has settled into an authoritative 18 to 20 knots, southwesterly. It is foggy, cold. The fog condenses on our oilies. We, in our oilskins, boots, souwesters, glisten with the wet. The sun occasionally tries to break through the fog, but at best achieves a bleak, brazen eye. The chill is penetrating after you have been on deck for a time and there is much idle talk about building a fire in our fireplace. Perhaps we will.

FIGARO is romping along under her large racing sails. She still carries her main, mizzen, and Number One Genoa. The speed is exhilarating. So much so, that Frank is talking of spending two days (and himself) in Soho before his appointment in Scotland. A constant speed of 8.5 knots does things to a man.

The barometer has been falling for the last twenty-four hours. We could find nothing of any consequence on the weather plot we saw before leaving to indicate any trouble ahead. It showed a few vagrant, small-size depressions which were going east behind a big high that had gone through two days before. For the moment, at least, we presume that the falling barometer reflects a descent to levels normal in these latitudes, especially after the fairly high readings of the past few days. The outside air is a zippy 49°. The cabin temperature is 54°. While the cabin is not exactly a solarium, it makes those on deck eye the bunks with anticipation.

It is a source of everlasting wonder to me how hard a Corinthian fights to get a berth on a long race and, once on board, can think of nothing but his bunk. It is a companion thought to one once expressed by a former shipmate, Jurgen Kok, who made the race to Spain with us in '57; his question has become part of the standard repertoire of comment now used on board my boat. On hearing the running complaint of a watch mate upon being doused with spray, Jurgen reasonably asked: "If you don't like water, why do you go to sea?"

The sea, while not heavy, is beginning to run a bit higher. When a wave gets under her quarter, steering becomes active. FIGARO has an easy motion. When quartering down a wave on a reach, she will heel to leeward as the wave comes under her quarter (the after quarter of her hull). As the wave passes under her, she comes out of her rush, tending up to windward. After a period of steering, following the onset of such a condition, the helmsman develops a rhythmic response, anticipates her movements, which in FIGARO's case are regular, and steers a sinuous course, swinging a few degrees left and right, but keeping the boat closely heading on her course while adapting her movement to the sea. It is an easy roll, with speed and without strain. It takes a very short time for a fresh helmsman to work into the rhythm.

Bucky has just poked his head down the companionway to inform me, in response to my query concerning the course, that it must be okay. In his own swinging style, Frank has threaded the course several times. From the sound of the water foaming in the waterway, he must have gone through the course broadside. But with the clarion cry ringing clear in the frosty air, "Soho, here we come!" FIGARO has straightened out and is off and galloping.

1700 We have enjoyed our first Happy Hour, an institution which was started on an earlier FIGARO many years ago. Its purpose is to provide harmony and reduce tension and, if possible, promote friendship between the watches on a long ocean passage. The watch system and the space on board a small boat combine in producing a situation in which the men in alternate watches will see one another to talk to only for that brief interval at the break of the watch and then generally to exchange some rough unpleasantry. Gradually, what starts out to be a benign rivalry between watches can (because of the physical strains encountered during a long passage) evolve into an acrimonious series of exchanges. Little things that ordinarily escape notice become, instead, a focus of tension. A pair of wet, dirty socks left in the wrong place can take on the dimensions of a Sarajevo.

Happy Hour is an ordained time for conviviality. The off-watch is roused one half hour before their dinner time and assembled in the after cabin. A long fruit-juice drink spiced with rum (in the fashion of a punch) is served to all hands, at least to those who have their I.D. cards. (It is our version of grog, and for the same purpose.) Stories, songs, and jokes are saved for this occasion. Incidents which took place on either watch are exchanged. Briefly, the boat takes on the characteristics of a smoking car. At 1730 the off-watch is fed, preparatory to taking over, and the ship's routine re-established, except for a

Sometimes you have an easy time

brief continuation of the fun while the offgoing watch is at dinner. It is extraordinary the degree to which this simple device keeps down tensions and acrimony. Unfortunately, unless this is accomplished, what starts out to be a pleasure cruise can turn into a disagreeable experience. It also increases and deepens the friendships and relationships of all those on board.

A story, to this point, that I always cherish is one that I heard in Honolulu after a trans-Pacific race. The schooner GOODWILL (one of the racers), 165 feet long, carried a crew of fifty. (Because of the size of the crew she was immediately dubbed "We, the People.") It seems that two men met in a bar in Waikiki and, over a few drinks, came to a mutual admiration of each other's point of view of things nautical, political, and heterosexual. The first one asked: "When did you get to the island?" The second replied: "After the race, on the schooner GOODWILL." The first: "The hell you say, so did I."

1800   Dinner over, the port watch takes over. The wind is still increasing. We take off Number One Genoa, put up the smaller Number Three Genoa. FIGARO rides a little easier, she no longer feels pressed, our speed is still the same after the change: 8.5 knots.

The barometer continues to fall. What gives?

2200   Starboard watch relieves. This is the first night watch, although it is not quite dark. It remains fairly light up in these latitudes, not enough to read by, but enough to see the big, black, moving hills thatched with broken gray at their top which come rushing down at us. They always look larger than life at night. The best thing is not to look at them.

In bad weather during the old square-rigger days, a canvas screen was rigged behind the helmsman. In part, its function was to break the wind, but also in part to make it impossible to see the huge following seas which, by their size and threat, might adversely affect his steering. It is a source of wonder when on a good sea-boat to watch a wave bearing down from behind, its crest threatening to come aboard and smash everything before it. And then, magically, as it comes upon the boat, she lifts, her transom perhaps picking up a fleck of foam, the sea passes under her, she settles into the trough. A new wave, with its threat, comes rushing out. Perhaps its shape is a little different, but it all seems part of an endless repetition. Sometimes the crest of an overly boisterous wave, in breaking on the boat's quarter wave, will send a jet of foaming suds down the waterway, but the boat shakes it off. The water gushes out of the freeing ports and she continues to scud across the great, moving, watery meadows.

The sea is heavy and FIGARO is charging along like a drunken fullback. Wind speed about 25 knots. We take off the mizzen to improve the steering and settle back to see out the watch. It is our first night at sea. We cleared the shore with dispatch. Everyone appears to be settled in and in good shape. We are off in great style.

JULY 1—THE SECOND DAY

0600   The day begins, gray, foggy, and damp. The outside temperature is a keen 46°, but the cabin is warm and dry. It's hard to tell which of us have fared worse, those who have been on deck in the last watch of this first night, or those who are easing themselves out of the rack. For those on deck, it has been a chilling sequence of sitting in the cold damp, alternating with turns at the wheel every half hour. In between times, there has been a tour of the deck with a flashlight to look for any signs of chafe or wear, and there has been an occasional foray into the galley to make a cup of hot broth or cocoa.

For those in the bunks it has, at best, been a fitful sleep as they tried to adjust themselves to their new home and to their new bed. The only thing the latter shares in common with a bed at home is that one reclines upon a mattress. In this case, four inches of foam rubber. And there, the resemblance stops. Sleeping becomes an active experience at sea, for on the boat, one is always conscious of movement as she lifts to a crest and swoops down the slope, and of the roll as she is heeled down by the wind and wave action.

FIGARO is heeled at about a 20° angle. Her movement is a pendulum one with this amount of heel as an average constant. It causes those who are in a leeward bunk to sleep in a V made up by the mattress as one leg and the side of the boat the other. Those in the windward bunks also recline in a V, but in this case made up of the mattress and, on the inboard side, a section of dacron cloth about one foot high. This is made fast along its bottom length to the bunk and is tied at intervals along the top to the overhead with lanyards. It is called a bunk board. The device keeps the sleeper from being rolled out of his berth. It is a friendlier version of the wooden bunk board, a little more giving and less abusive to the hip and shoulder bones than its older cousin, the wooden board. In fact, it is a bundling board—without benefit of a partner on the other side.

At the Mystic Seaport Museum in Mystic, Connecticut, one can see the sailors' berths on board the old whaler, CHARLES W. MORGAN. They look like coffins: narrow, to keep a man from rolling about, and deep, to keep him from being thrown out. They must have been hot and airless in tropical calms. There were hard ships in those days. Today a yacht berth is a compromise between the luxuries offered by one's bed at home and meeting the conditions to be found at sea.

A trick I have developed from the experiences of former voyages is to lightly upholster the side of the boat along the length of the berth. At sea, almost as much time is spent sleeping on this side as on the mattress. The result not only is softer and warmer than the bare side of the boat but, more importantly, it helps keep the berth as dry as is possible. When a boat is heeled over, her immersed side is in water whose temperatures can go down into the low forties. The moisture from exhalation, body respiration, and cooking strikes this cold side. The side becomes a giant condenser and it is soon beaded with droplets of water. These are rubbed off and absorbed by the blankets, sheets, and the mattress and, before long, the berth is soaking wet. The thin cushion on the side forms a moisture barrier which fends this condition off for a considerable period.

Nearly everyone has eaten breakfast, some a little less heartily than others, but we are all in relatively fine fettle.

The wind is still at about 25 knots from the SSW, the sea running moderately high and, forchrisake, the barometer is still falling! What the hell.

1030   Hot broth! Just like a bleedin' Cunard liner. It takes some of the chill out of the bones. So far everything has been routine. Into your foul-weather gear and onto the deck. Out of your foul-weather gear and into your bunk, with time out for eating, But FIGARO charges along, oblivious of the changing hands on the wheel which guide her.

Changing our personal gear in a pitching, heeling cabin is tougher than any duty on the deck so far. To insert yourself into these garments you find a corner where you can brace yourself against a fall as you alternately lift each foot in order to thrust it into a leg of the trousers. All this to the accompaniment of unexpected rolls and pitches. Getting inside the vinyl-covered nylon oilies is like crying to get yourself into a cold clam stew. Then you keep adamantly shov-

Some days it blows hard on a reach . . .

or on the wind

ing your toe northward into a soft boot, the toe of which spitefully insists on lying to the east. A man must be in top physical condition to dress in a small boat at sea. It is almost as if one were trying to get dressed while bouncing on a trampolin in which the period of bounce is irregular. The sheer task of putting on trousers, sweater, and oilies needs the muscular control of a gymnast. This is the time when anyone with a queasy stomach finds himself faced with the long-drawn-out anguish of oncoming *mal de mer*. You have to develop a precise sense of timing as to how long you dare spend below decks while in a cramped position, head down and struggling with your clothes. Suddenly, you absolutely must be on deck if your well-being is to be preserved. At such times, the personal warning signals which announce that time is running out become so clamorous that the final dressing must be done on deck. This is unfortunate if spray is coming on board, for then you get a preliminary wetting down which steams under the oilies, but not as bad as giving of yourself into the sea of despond.

On deck, with the cool air and a fixed horizon to look at, recovery can be made. It is the lack of a fixed horizon which is said to affect the inner ear when below; this, plus the exertion of dressing and the lack of fresh draughts of air, is what turns hearty mariners into bedraggled sports.

1500   All is peaceful. The ship's company act like passengers on a P & O steamer, straight out of Kipling, except that the temperature is much lower than he normally runs in his stories. Hoyt, with his genius for making himself comfortable at sea, is coiled up under the dodger in the region of the companionway, out of any chilling wind or unfriendly spray. All we need is a deck steward serving tea. Skip, the only presently working member of the duty watch, is steering. Of the watch below, Bucky and Frank are in their bunks sleeping, or trying to, and I am writing up the log. It is peaceful and serene.

But it was not ever thus. At 1130 hours, the heavens filled with lightning. Thunder crashed and rolled. It seemed to echo and re-echo as though in a fjord. The flashes of lightning, leaping out of a black sky, etched an angry, broken, and threatening sea. It was awesome, though more so in sound than fury. Then the rains fell, cold and unfriendly. The luck of the draw had the captain at the wheel. I keep assuring myself that the fates constantly put to test and try the spirit of those in whom they have a kindly interest. For, with the exception of Crawford, relatively dry under the dodger, all the others were below, yawning, stretching, and scratching themselves in gestures of sheer indolence. They were sheltered, silently congratulating themselves on the fact that they were some minutes away from their official presence on deck.

The dawdling seemed to be stretched out unnecessarily. It was more than flesh could bear and I reacted over-vigorously, saying: "Feed those bastards and get them on deck." No one took offense, knowing that the apparent harshness came from a vast personal discomfort and weariness. Their understanding, however, didn't hurry them. But comeuppance is rapid at sea. For, with a rush, a wild wind squall was on us and those below came pell-mell on deck only partially prepared for the weather. They handed the main, which meant a tussle with a flogging sail as it descended. All the time the sail was being tamed and furled on the boom, the rain pelted down. This duty finished, they scurried below somewhat dampened in body, clothes, and spirit.

Finally, the worst of the squall having passed and their luncheon eaten, they oozed back on deck to take over the watch while I went below, reassured that the fates will sometimes conspire to support authority and rank at sea.

The rain remained intermittent, finally settling down to a cold, drizzly fog. The barometer is at last beginning to rise. The center of the depression must be slowly passing to the north of us and we hope for better weather. The spirit of the crew rises with the line on the barograph, and they speak once more of worldly things.

There is much scholarly dissertation from various experts over the virtue (or lack of it) and other distinguishing merits of a tiger-eyed, small-titted nude, ruthlessly torn from her mother and a gentlemen's magazine. The magazine had been stolen from the steam room of the Yale Club. Crawford, the ship's librarian, bows to no man or institution in matters of taste and discernment. However, in the case of the official library for FIGARO (which is devoted solely to cheesecake —the men bring their own reading material and then swap), he thrust the niceties aside. He enlisted the aid of some disaffected Yale men and walked off with an armful of the journalistic treasures of the Club. We suspect that these may have been part of the equipment used by the Club servants in preparing some of the older members for a night on the town.

1515 (Entry by Navigator)   Main was reset at 1515 hours and shortly thereafter the watch on deck broke out the Number One Genoa and a case of beer. With the amazing accuracy of the steering, there are two places where I am reasonably sure we must have been.

    June 30   1200 D.R. Lat. 47° 52′ N Lon. 51° 37′ W
    July   1   1200 D.R. Lat. 48° 57′ N Lon. 46° 52′ W

1530   We have just had the odd experience of turning our engine on in gear at sea. I have often offered a golden doubloon to the man who could fall forward against the clutch handle unbeknownst to me. Application for the reward to be made, in my ignorance, to the ship's purser. In a long ocean race the engine cannot be used for propulsion. It is used to charge the batteries which run the lighting system of the boat. We restrain our use of these to just a few, such as the compass, instrument and navigation lights, the light in the galley and in the head. Our constant cabin light is a kerosene lamp. But even these lights usually run the batteries down in about two to three days. We generally wait for a lull in the wind to run the engine for battery charging. Then the boat is relatively upright, the cooling water intake is submerged, and the lubrication system functions. In calm air we experience the strange anomaly of wallowing in a sea, making very little forward progress while the engine runs merrily on. It is then that I would appreciate a secret engaging of the clutch. But, alas, I sail with sportsmen.

1700   Batteries are up and the engine is off. We had been doing 7.4 knots with the engine in gear and 7.0 knots without.

2300   The wind is increasing again and shifting to the quarter. It is clocking around. It must mean that the depression to the north of us has picked up speed and is moving eastward again.

The ship is quiet except for the rush of the bow wave. Below, a single oil lamp turned very low just barely outlines the bodies of the sleepers, dimly seen in the after berths. They are faceless, cocoons burrowed into their blankets. On deck, the helmsman's face can be seen from time to time as he leans over the binnacle. All others are swallowed up in the darkness of the night. Another day is gone, at times wet and cold, but withal it is grand sailing.

V

SAILING THE OCEAN AT NIGHT

In the range of men's activities, there are a few experiences which share the unique qualities of mystical and physical sensations. These are experiences which result from a vigorous action taken in the presence of an elemental force, a tumultuous event, or an epic manifestation of nature. They are sensations of danger, of loneliness, and the awareness of power and immensity beyond human scale. The extrasensory consciousness of mystery is created by the combined effect of these sensations, although the intensity and shading changes with the nature of the experience.

War, as an instance, is an extreme experience in which jeopardy and the sense of having been caught in the general callousness toward human life brings a man face to face with the meaning and resolution of his life, a resolution not of his own choosing. On the other hand, sport is filled with occasions in which a man chooses to expose himself to jeopardy for the sense of achievement and victory. Climbing mountains, diving into the sea, soaring in the sky, making a singlehanded ocean passage, and skiing on slopes of virgin snow, all share the quality of action touched by danger which takes place in a lonely immensity. All of these qualify to meet William James's "moral equivalent for war." But of all such experiences, few match sailing the ocean at night in the potential to evoke a metaphysical response. It is because of the darkness which masks the ever-changing sea. It leaves the sailor without forewarning of a break in the regularity of the sea's movement, a change which he can anticipate only by instinct and the memory of past experience.

It is not only darkness, but silence as well which shrouds the change. Those who stand upon a beach can hear the sea roar and feel it shake the earth as it crashes on the shore. But on the ocean, these powerful rolling hills, unimpeded, rush silently along. Only the occasional breaking crest of a wave hisses the hint of the power in them.

On the ocean it is the sea's companion, the unseen wind, which whispers, howls, or screams in the rigging as it piles the sea up into waves. Once started, they roll endlessly on to destroy themselves on a faraway shore. But the wind cannot be counted on to show the direction of an oncoming sea, for the sea is not always obedient to the wind. Forces stronger than the wind alter the direction of waves. The earth's rotation is a cosmological fact which we accept. We know it is the reason that the sun rises and sets. But beyond making night and day, its power to further influence us seems as remote as a distant star. And yet, the earth spinning on its axis helps create the great trade winds and, therefore, the vast ocean currents. It is also the cause for the Coriolis effect, a force which acts on bodies in motion and causes a deflection to the right in the northern hemisphere. It is the reason why water spins clockwise as it goes down the drain, and it makes the wind and sea direction differ.

At other times, beyond the disparity in direction of the wind and sea, they seem utterly out of phase. For at times, the sea may roll heavily, even though no wind is blowing. Waves, born in a distant sector of the ocean, will go through an area of calm leaving the boat helplessly rolling. Her spars swing in arcs and her rigging clashes and strains. Sometimes this stillness of the wind is the foreboding zone of calm between two weather systems; the lull before the storm. The waves which spring from the winds in the storm area outrace the forward movement of the storm and come down on the boat in long, oily swells. Then the night sailor calls on all of his instincts and sensitivities, searching the dark for a heading to which the boat rides with the least strain on her spars, rigging, gear, and people. All through such a dark night the sailor uneasily waits to see what the morning light will show.

But the darkness is not only a breeding place for unseen threats. Sometimes, the night ocean and sky provide a mysterious background from which flashes of beauty emerge and glow in Rembrandtesque highlighting. The sea is, at places, filled with countless tiny bodies of phosphorescent plankton whose luminescence is activated as the water is disturbed. As the boat sails through this, her wake spreads out behind in a long comet trail. At times, this phenomenon is encountered while in an area of swells and little wind. Then the impact of the boat, as it plunges from the crest of a swell, shoots a flashing sheet of light out from her hull and the boat seems momentarily suspended in an ethereal light. The quality of the light is to illuminate nothing. It silhouettes the boat like a figure in a shadow play. At rare times the plankton provide an opportunity to see a display of weaving patterns of light. It is when porpoises choose such a time to play under the bow of the boat. Then, under the pulsing glow of the bow wave, you can see the porpoises more brightly etched in silvery phosphorescence. The brightness from these creatures communicates the spirit of play to the watcher.

At times, the ink-black of night is relieved by the light of the stars. Then the spars and sails swing in measured arcs against a dark field picked out by diamond points, and the swing of the masthead and spreaders ticks off the bright giants: Betelgeuse, Vega, and Arcturus; or the even brighter planets: Venus, Saturn, Jupiter. When the moon rises, the spars and sails stand out starkly against the dark sky, or are silhouetted by the gleaming carpet runner laid down on the sea.

But the rarest pleasure of all is that, in this lonely immensity, you are not alone. Though the dark magnitude isolates you in your own sensations, you are conscious of your shipmates. They, too, are enveloped in their own mythos. Few words are spoken during night watches in order not to disturb those sleeping, but

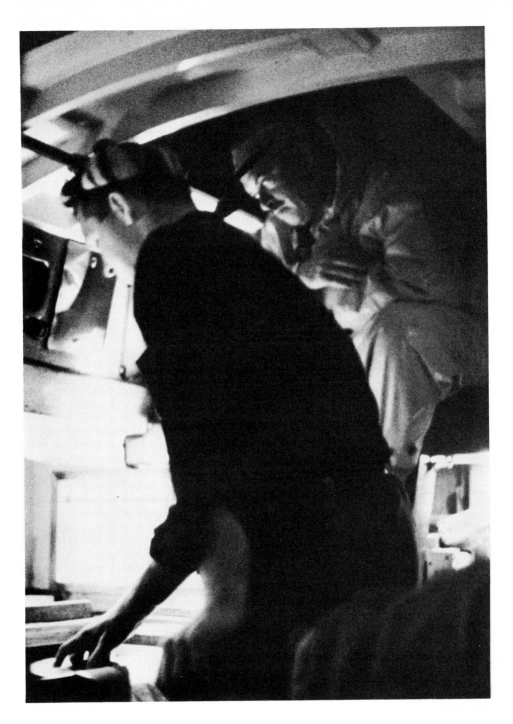

Nearing a landfall at night—the navigator and the captain

each man knows his job and you silently expect him to do it when the time comes. But, sitting in the darkness, you see them picked out in a variety of man-created light.

The center of the ship's life, the binnacle, etches the helmsman's face in red frontal chiaroscuro. Behind another single point light, the man patrolling the deck is sensed, but not seen, by the darting of his flashlight as it moves from the rigging in search of chafe to the sail in examination of its set. And below, a single burning oil lamp swings in its gimbals, casting a pendulum of soft-edged light and shadows as it moves up and back across the bulkheads and across the sleepers who rest secure in the feeling that those on deck will shield them from the surprises of the night.

Through the night, these varied hues of darkness melt, one into the other, until with the paling of the eastern sky and the first edging of the horizon, it is time to call the navigator to take his morning stars. And, as he brings the first star down to the horizon in the sextant, you jot the time at his crisp call of "Mark" which not only fixes your place on earth, but seems to put an end to the night and herald the coming of day.

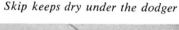

Skip keeps dry under the dodger

VI

THE GRAND BANKS

JULY 2—THE THIRD DAY

0100 Another day, and more of the same, a dreary continuation of dreary weather. We have rain. Cold, relentless, lacking any reasonable virtue. It neither waters crops, fills reservoirs, puts out forest fires, nor quiets a dust bowl. It is just a waste of water falling upon a waste of waters, an affliction to be borne with barely summoned stoicism.

0130 The rain has become intermittent.

0200 The rain is now very thin, drizzly and misty. Course 100°. Speed 6.4 knots.

0230 The wind is backing around, beginning to come more ahead. The barograph draws a straight line along the bottom of its dip. The changing direction of the wind and the pattern of rise and fall on the barograph indicate our altered position in relation to the center of the depression. Yesterday, the center began to move forward, but its forward movement is halted. It has run into another weather system which is blocking its progress. The center still remains in the north, but it is relatively stationary for, by the forward movement of the boat, we are overtaking it so that it makes the center of the depression draw aft. In addition, because of the increase in the weight of the wind, and its altered direction, I can only surmise that the center is sagging down upon us.

0430 The barograph is still steady and low. The wind keeps increasing. We have changed down to the smaller Number Three Genoa.

0600 All kinds of busy work this morning. The chronometers are wound. A water temperature is taken. It shows 52°. The air temperature is 54°. We are slowly working out of the Labrador Current. It is a cold, cold summer up in these parts.

0830 The wind is still freshening with fog and drizzle. Our course is 100°, speed is 8.5 knots. Any feeling of discomfort is erased by the exhilaration of our speed and by that extraordinary sense of purpose which the boat communicates as she drives ahead. I suppose that is why men love a particular boat. She may seem a dog to those who have not sailed in her. To them, she may be a less than successful arrangement of wood, metal, and fiber. But a boat is more than that. Far from being a mechanical contrivance of inorganic materials, a boat is invested with animism—she takes on a living character which communicates to those who sail in her. Each boat seems to contain a personality which manifests itself in the way she takes a sea. She may snap-roll back after being pressed down by a gust, or be soft in her movement of recovery. She may bang through the top of a sea or work smoothly over it. She may steer like a willful though speedy bitch on a run or a reach, leaving the helmsman with aching arms after a half-hour stint at the tiller or wheel, or she may be balanced and track like a proper lady, lacking the sense of danger and excitement of the speedy bitch but communicating the certainty that you will get there in one piece. But above all, her identity as a living creature, invested with personality, becomes apparent to the men who guide her in their separate watches as they weary and change. Untouched by the cyclically flagging strengths of her human masters and by the differing qualities of the hands that handle her, she plunges tirelessly on. Unchanged, unflagging, meeting each sea eagerly, she goes on hour after hour, day after day. At times, the sense of exhilaration and response on the part of the crew to the magnificent way she is behaving erupts into a simultaneous and spontaneous exchange of glowing opinions. Then the cockpit conversation seems to be that of men speaking of a magnificent creature. And, ridiculous at it may seem, I have—on more than one occasion while at the wheel and having become filled with an excess of joy in response to her sea-kindly movement—leant over and planted a kiss on her deck, as becomes a lover to his lass.

0900   The wind is still increasing and drawing still further ahead. We have struck the main. She moves well under Number Three Genoa and mizzen. That's the beauty of a yawl rig. You can balance the boat under any number of combinations. It also is an indication of the major difference between racing and cruising. Had we been racing, we would probably have put a close reef into the main, and carried it, thereby pressing the boat. We would do this in the hope of holding on to the last vestiges of the boat's speed potential. Sometimes you really don't gain the speed. Undoubtedly, the boat is carrying more sail and, theoretically, she should have a higher potential of speed. However, the very business of pressing down her hull slows her by reducing the effectiveness of her lateral resistance, and especially during the intervals when her waterways are boiling with the sea and you are dragging half the ocean with you. This all sounds reasonable, but you are never quite that sure and the thought that a competitor, somewhere out there over the horizon, is driving the hell out of his boat makes you do it, too. But we're not racing now and we seem to be going as fast as we should.

1000   The weather is getting noisy. There is a slight drop in the barograph. The center of the depression is getting closer and we must be somewhere near its leading edge.

1200   A lunch of hot soup, franks and beans—rough camp fare. It is filling, but not in the *haute gastronomie* tradition we struggle to maintain. It is lacking in the style to which we try to get accustomed when at sea. But then, this is no

The scullery—Bucky pearl-diving

weather for delicate repasts. The boat is quite active. As a matter of pride, a good sea cook in a small boat makes it a point to assemble as notable a meal as is possible while a boat is laboring in the sea. In part, it is a tasty symbol of his saltiness and indifference to the raucous elements (a virility symbol no doubt; who would ever believe that cooking could become identified with rugged masculinity?), and in part it is an assurance to the crew that all is normal and functioning. The hard-nosed sea cook will do this even though it is sometimes difficult to eat the meal he has prepared, either through a reluctant appetite or the bouncing nature of the banquet board.

Sea cooks take their work and art seriously. There is the story of the cook on a square rigger who contended with the elements in preparing a plum duff in his rolling, pitching galley. He served it to the fo'c'sle gang and stepped back, filled with the glow that comes from a selfless and successful attempt to bring pleasure to his fellow men. One unthinking miscreant, having taken a bite, pronounced it doughy. The cook turned silently on his heel, strode to his galley, and returned with a cleaver. Without breaking stride or his silence he came up to the unlucky *critique de bon goût* and clove him from crown to navel.

It was a most vigorous reaction and while I have never given in to my emotions to such a point, I have felt stirrings of the same feelings. On one occasion, I worked mightily to prepare a feast fit for my mates at a time when cooking was not easy. The weather had been bad and I felt we would all enjoy a taste of the good life. The meal was planned and balanced in the tradition according to the great Brillat-Savarin. The principal dish was *Poulet Estragon*—which, if I say so myself, turned out well, even though it was made with tinned chicken. The crew liked it, too. When I asked the younger set at the table what they would like to drink (quite prepared to offer one of the few bottles of wine left), they unhesitatingly said: "How about a chocolate milk?" All I could do was be grateful that they did not put catsup on my creation and give them the mixings. I refused to make the drink. Even the understanding from the others could not ease this affront to my gastronomic sensibilities.

We have taken off the Number Three Genoa and changed down to the even smaller Number Two jib topsail. Since we carried no main, the maneuver was accomplished by first setting the staysail. The comfort during the interval in which we carried the staysail felt so fine we were tempted to keep it that way. But the conscience of the racing man asserted itself and we went on to the jib top. She does not behave too badly. The wind speed is somewhere between 35 and 40 knots, wailing like Niobe looking for her young. We trust nobody up there or, for that matter, down there is looking for us. A nasty sea has made up, coming from ahead. The boat at the moment is not the most comfortable place I have been. It is alternately being hit by a sea forward of the beam or jumping off a crest. It is Hobson's choice as to which is the preferable spot—on the deck or in the rack.

1300   It is a decidedly unpleasant afternoon. The sky is pregnant with uninviting promise. It is filled with dark, lumpy striations on a gray field. The clouds are so low that the mast seems in the act of slashing at the feathery membrane which envelopes them, dumping torrents of water on deck. The surface of the sea is broken and tumbling. We cannot see the waves at any distance from the boat. Instead, we see them heave up suddenly and come hurtling at us. The tops are covered with cottony spittle from the broken water and the leeward side of the wave is streaked and spotted. FIGARO rides over most of the waves as she goes along. When the top of an unruly one hits her, she sloughs the water over the rail, through the freeing ports and down the scuppers. But she goes bravely on, at times actually shouldering the water aside; at others, just smashing through an obstructing wave top.

The sea is boarding frequently, churning down the leeward waterway as the top of a wave curls over the bow. A great deal of water comes at us from windward as spray, which is flung at us as the boat's hull is smacked by an oncoming sea.

We carry at least two inches of water on the cockpit deck at all times. The scuppers are kept busy and as the movement of the boat rolls the water from their gaping mouths, they make loud sucking sounds. No sooner is the cockpit near being drained than a fresh supply comes tumbling on the deck.

The angle of heel of the boat makes a V between the cockpit seat and our deep coaming. The V holds a constant triangle of water about six inches deep in its central axis; the small scuppers here are too small to keep ahead of the water. I am quite sure that much of it is finding its way down into the boat through the sail lockers. The truly waterproof sail locker hatch is still to be devised. On occasion, this puddle and the sitting end of a cockpit denizen make contact. Even through the so-called waterproof oilskins this contact is a chilling and unnerving experience.

Our weather cloth was blown out. (This is a length of heavy dacron sailcloth which is lashed to the railings, placed in position where it will break most of the wind and spray, thinly shielding the inhabitants of the cockpit.) It has been repaired and reset with urgency, as there is a considerable difference in the comfort quotient with it down. The deck gang huddles in moderate comfort under the dodger. The helmsman takes it during his stint.

Skipper, at the wheel, just got wet to the armpits. The top of a boarding sea broke over the side and over him. This kind of thing has been going on for a while and watch-captain Hoyt has abandoned his ship's duties for photography, waiting for Skip to really catch one—and catch it he did. A particularly big sea, breaking on our quarter wave, dumped most of its top into the cockpit and over Skip. He sat at the wheel in a roil of water. I don't think that student Skip enjoys the role of stake-out bait as much as schoolmaster Norry does his part of the deal, especially since Norry keeps out of the smother, dry under the dodger.

1400   The first brief glimpse of a blue patch in the sky! Way off on the horizon. The proverbial patch for a Dutchman's britches or, some will have it, for the Scotsman's kilt. We must be working toward the outer edge of the depression. We keep looking at the barograph for the secrets it will reveal.

Skip in the big sea

1430   The sun! In all its refulgent glory. Just a brief instant, but our spirits shoot up with the appearance of the great earth-warmer. The barograph joins our ascendant spirits by starting its own upward swing.

1500   The barograph takes a sharp upward turn. Crawford, who has been studying it, says the line looks like a coon dick. This is, to say the least, an extraordinary comparison; but then the coon dick is an extraordinary personal totem. It is a good-luck charm, new to all of us and I suppose that Crawford brought it on board to prove its powers under rigorous test conditions. Whether the coon dick is a general-purpose luck piece, or one that has mysterious properties directed toward a single objective as in the case of Haitian voodoo fetishes, is as yet unknown.

The coon dick, or raccoon's penis, is an esoteric sort of charm to carry. It was entirely unfamiliar to me, as I presume it must be to most metropolitans. What gives the penis of this nocturnal carnivore distinction over those of other fauna is the fact that, in the case of the raccoon, it is shaped like a fishhook, returning upward on itself, not unlike that of a largemouthed-bass hook. To the best of my knowledge, it is not armed with a barb; nor can I say from observation that it retains this shape in both dormant and erectile states. For all inquiring Darwinians, I must add that since I never saw one before, I do not have any idea how the forces of natural selection brought this design into being.

In any case, the naturalists who travel on the New Haven Railroad—4:58 out of New York to Darien, Connecticut—have, either out of envy or awe, invested this dismembered part of the raccoon-rampant with considerable mystic virtues. Whether it shares any of the virtues to be found in ground rhinoceros horn or tiger's milk, which appear in the older Chinese *materia medica* as an aid to virility, or whether as a good-luck piece it shares the powers inherent in a rabbit's paw, or whether it really only serves as an esoteric clan symbol for the gentlemen naturalists who ride the train, I cannot say. In any case, in its use it is a direct reflection of our affluent society. For, after the instrument is separated from its host, it is delivered to a famous Fifth Avenue jeweler where it is plated with eighteen-carat gold and thereafter worn as a watch charm. Since, as an object or symbol, it is unrecognizable to the world at large, it must give considerable satisfaction to the wearer who basks in the knowledge that he knows a secret the rest of the world does not.

1800   The wind lessens somewhat. We have reset the main on a course of 105° at 6 knots.

2300   Galloping along, a fine night so far. A promising close to what, on the whole, was an unattractive, wet day. It was tiring and unpleasant, but it was the sort of day that provides special memories for the future. The day was a dandy in retrospect, especially now that the worst seems to be over.

We have gone through a curious experience with the depression. I have raced across the Atlantic twice before, but never with a weather system. The nearest to such an event was during the '57 race to Spain. Then a low passed behind us from north to south and, after racing ahead in the south, changed direction and threw a loop around us. It crossed our bow, eventually going off into the northeast.

In the present case, we entered the trailing edge of this low on leaving St. John's and gradually have sailed through its bottom edge. We have traveled faster than the low most of the time and came out in front of it this afternoon. Luckily, it is a mild depression and its center has stayed north of us all of the time. Since the wind goes into a low in a counterclockwise pattern and since the center stayed north of us we had a more or less favorable slant to the breeze at all times.

Because of this, we are making good time. As a matter of fact, the navigator finally snatched a hasty shot of the sun in its brief appearance and got a sun line. Should the position be verified, it places us about 40 miles ahead of our D.R. (dead reckoning). If this is the case, it will demonstrate the speed picked up surging down the waves. In addition, it indicates the effect of a favorable current, for we are still in the Gulf Stream, however weakened its effectiveness in this longitude.

The navigator's evening star sights were less satisfactory, since the stars kept popping in and out of the overcast, scarcely giving time to bring them down to the vague and broken horizon. This is our navigator's first trans-Atlantic and his disappointment in failure to get a real cat's cradle of star positions is so great that Bucky has suggested that we turn on the masthead light so that Frank can bring this down to the horizon on his hambone and provide some certainty for him in an uncertain world.

I hope we are through with the low, though you never can tell. They have a way of turning back on you. And so, as this July 2 closes out, it finds the ship and ship's company fine. FIGARO is plunging on as undeviating in her round of duties as the inscription on the pediment of the New York General Post Office claims its postmen are in all kinds of weather.

JULY 3 — THE FOURTH DAY

0230 This day is ushered in with rain. Our course is 105° at a speed of 7.2 knots.

0300 A very heavy downpour. Cold and miserable. All thinking and longing is concentrated in the desire to get back into the bunk. For that matter, the bunk has become the Nirvana in which one can expect to find surcease from these trials of the flesh. In reality, it is a damp cocoon which, if offered ashore, would be considered a test of one's forebearance.

Of the six berths that FIGARO has, two are in the forward cabin. The main cabin has two regular, upper berths and two transom berths below. The transom

berths normally function as sofa benches, but can slide out to widen and convert them to a sleeping place. During a long voyage at sea, I avoid using the transom berths for sleeping. If they are used for that purpose all available free space in the boat is gone. Instead, in our practice, the opposite members of the port and starboard watch share the same bunk, and for that matter, the same bedding. The only nicety we offer in matters of personal taste is a private pillow.

It is interesting to note how each individual constructs his own kind of burrow out of the available materials, adapted to his own needs and wants. On rising, he makes up the bunk in a straightforward manner, ready for the new constructor to take over.

By keeping the sofas clear, we avoid the sense of being packed into a capsule, and the cabin affords reasonable habitability. It can be used by anyone off watch as a place to read and smoke, or do personal chores. It also provides place to repair sails and perform other feats of marlinspike seamanship. We can also set up the table for meals. But above all, it leaves open and accessible the drawers which hold each man's personal gear. Since these drawers (which have upholstered faces) are under the upper berth and form the back of the sofa, a sleeper would have to be wakened each time a man on deck wanted to get a sweater, cigarettes, or sunglasses. Great care is taken to give habitability support to men living together in physically trying circumstances. The same kind of care is expended in the original planning in order that mix-ups and misappropriations of personal gear by mischance can be avoided. As a trip gets longer and harder, personal reactions are set off by a quicker trigger. We try to avoid any focus for disagreement. To this end, each man's drawer space is sacrosanct to his own use, as is the cubicle for his toilet gear in the head. Towels and washcloths are coded, a different color for every man (although recently I have taken to using the new, disposable paper towels); toothbrushes are color-coded as well.

Through this process of sharing a berth, we live in "hot" bunks and, by a steady application of 98.6° body temperature, manage to keep the bedding damp-warm. Dampness is the curse of the sleeping man at sea. Despite extensive efforts in keeping the cabin heater going full blast (more as a drying than as a heating agent—without it we would be adrip), the bedding eventually becomes damp. I have tried many schemes to avoid this situation, but it is like Canute ordering back the tide. By hook or crook, salt water or just plain salt gets below. It comes down on boots, on foul-weather gear, sometimes wet, sometimes as a caked film. It gets on the floor and seats and from these points is tracked through the boat and eventually spreads in a microscopic layer over everything. Since salt is hygroscopic, it makes for dampness. But even this dampness is a desideratum as long as the berth is warm and provides shelter from the cold, wet, unfriendly world. In head-shrinker terms, I suppose the whole thing amounts to just one big yearning to crawl back into the womb.

0400   The wind is pooping. We set the Number One Genoa. Our course is 105°, the speed 6.0 knots.

A hazy sky and bad horizon—Frank trying for a sun sight, WTS taking time for him

0530   The wind has been steadily dropping. We have started the engine for propulsion and to charge batteries. We held off this operation until now in order that the watch below could wring the last full measure of sleep from their allotted time. But now, with breakfast about to begin, the iron mainsail is turned on. We had been reduced to 4.0 knots; the engine picks us up to 7.0 knots. We carry only 55 gallons of gasoline. The engine consumes about 1¼ gallons per hour. We therefore try to hoard our fuel and use it only when we must. For this reason, when cruising, we hold off the business of charging the batteries until it can coincide with the need for forward propulsion, that is if these can coincide.

The chronometers are wound. A splendid breakfast—poached eggs on toast with a side order of *frijoles refritos* (yesterday's leftover baked beans which a careful husbandman had put aside for some such occasion), coffee and cinnamon rolls to top off the repast. It is breakfast enough to take the fight out of any man.

1200   Intermittent rain until 1200. The wind has freshened again. We took in the Number One Genoa and set the Number Three. The wind is abeam. That old dayvil low must still be lurking around in the north. The barograph gives no hint of future action. It is steady.

I went below to prepare lunch. But the boat was jumping in a manner that made it difficult to keep pots on the stove without fastening them down. It looked as though lunch would be late, if at all. In an attempt to avoid such a calamity, or perhaps to avoid embarrassing their commander, the deck watch took down the mizzen. They all liked the effect so much that it was decided to keep it off. The course is 105°, speed 8.0 knots.

1500 (Entry by Navigator)   In view of the fact that we have been unable to take any sights, the following two positions are offered, arrived at by surmise and a ouija board.

   2 July   1200 D.R. Lat. 49° 51′ N Lon. 42° 26′ W
   3 July   1200 D.R. Lat. 50° 26′ N Lon. 38° 22′ W

We are northward on the great circle course. Our 1500 D.R. puts us 618 miles out of St. John's, or one-third of the way to Wolf Rock.

F. T. C., Navigator

1800   This day has gone to hell in a hand basket. The barograph has steadied, edging up on a very slight gradient. Hard rain and fog have been our lot. The wind is increasing again and worse luck coming ahead all the time.

Our course 105°, our speed 7.9 knots.

1930   The wind speed is about 18 to 20 knots, blowing from the southeast. We have a heavy sea. FIGARO is rearing and bucking as she drives on. It's pretty heavy going, probably hardest on those below who are tossed around in their bunks. Sleep is difficult to come by. I wonder why I don't put in bunk belts as in an airplane. It might hold a man to his bunk.

Hard rain. Hard wind. Heavy sea. A 3-H night. I have known more pleasant.

Our course 105°, 7.6 knots.

2359   Just to keep it July 3.

Steaming as before. It has been a day for the birds. It is not one we will treasure in our remembrance of things past. We thought we had it made when the barograph took its joyous upward leap and especially after we experienced that glorious patch of sunlight. But since then, the weather has deteriorated and this despite a constantly rising barometer.

As the ship's meteorological officer in charge of conjecture, I have tried to piece out the weather pattern without the aid of weather reports. There are several known facts and observed phenomena and it is upon these I base my assumptions:

A. There is a high somewhere ahead of us. We know this because it went through St. John's, going east, shortly before we left.

B. It must be moving slowly, or even moving backward into the low. I base this assumption on the fact that highs flow into lows and this low must have bumped into the high ahead. This seems possible because ordinarily a depression moving eastward at this time of the year travels about 600 miles a day.

C. We have been moving at a fairly good clip, making an average of about 180 miles a day and have been sailing through the low. This we know because of the changing direction of the wind. When we started the wind was southwest. Since winds flow into the center of a depression in a counterclockwise direction, it means that the center was north and slightly west of us. Gradually, the wind went into the south which means we were slowly bringing the center aft of the beam and to the north. Finally, when the wind started to come in from the southeast, it meant that the center was in the north-northwest.

Putting all of this together, it must mean that the high, having no better place to go, has slowed down in order to enjoy some reverse dalliance with the low, which has been stopped in its tracks by the effrontery.

Now for some advance conjecture. If this assumption is correct and the pattern continues, we will sail through the bottom edge of the low, gradually getting into the outer perimeter of the high. Since the wind comes out of a high in a clockwise fashion, we probably will experience head winds gradually diminishing and if we get anywhere near the dome of the high, the winds will disappear into a big nothing. We therefore must husband our fuel in order to power through the zone of the dome or, like the Ancient Mariner, we will be adrift in our own horse latitudes, albatross or not. I hope my assumptions are all wrong, but I have found in cases where the prognosis is bad, that that's the way it generally turns out.

THE GLORIOUS FOURTH OF JULY

THE FIFTH DAY

0600   It's the Glorious red, white, and blue FOURTH. Hooray, Hooray! The crew were aroused to consciousness of this star-spangled day by a blood-stirring rendition of the "Stars and Stripes Forever." Most of it I did on the harmonica, but a few parts demanding excessive dexterity were managed vocally.

Here we are, a miniscule extension of the United States of America, but stowed in the snug cabin is enough patriotic fervor and sentiment to bust the buttons off an "American Heritage" editor. FIGARO has been at sea on the GLORIOUS FOURTH before and it has become our custom to salute the Anniversary of Independence with the ceremonies and observances familiar to an earlier and less cynical time. On this occasion, it seems even more appropriate. Are we not off to beard the lobsterback in his nautical den? Despite the one-world ideal, it seems fitting and proper to maintain certain pleasant tribal rites. How else can we defend ourselves from becoming hopelessly impersonal, duplicating integers? Certainly if the vaunted English heritage of unruffled phlegm is admirable and requires that they form a square at the drop of a Zulu spear, or that they sit to a jungle dinner of boiled python and chips (having first changed to boiled shirt and black tie), then we, the spiritual descendants of the half-horse, half-alligators of the unrestrained frontier, can draw regenerate nourishment from preservation of our own boisterous heritage.

A noisy celebration is even more desirable at sea, for, along with the fact that we are fire-breathing, patriotic, red-blooded, one-hundred-percent Americans who never have forgiven poor mad George III for taxing us without representation and for his abominable Stamp Act, we are far from our families and the occasion becomes a ceremonial offering to other times—a sort of red, white, and blue Shintoism. In addition, it helps break up the repetitive cycles of the voyage, it is good for crew morale, and we like parties. The reasons are clear, the dinner is laid on for 1800, the day will be spent in a ferment of preparation.

The rain and leaden skies are still with us. Any joy we can summon must be called upon from our spiritual reserves; we are getting very little help from nature. The wind still lies in the southeast which makes for an up and down, lumpy ride. Our only consolation is that, according to our D.R. position, we have come 733 miles from St. John's, which is not bad for a boat which is cruising across. For four days we have made 183 miles a day, an average of 7.6 knots.

Breakfast this morning was a continuous experience. Bucky starting cooking at 0400, spurred by a complex of real and subliminal urgings. Undoubtedly, he was hungry. He also was concerned that on this disagreeable morning the other watch should have no valid reason for being late on deck. In addition, he was cold and uncomfortable and the galley is a warm, dry, honorable retreat from the cold, gray truth of the morning—that is, if one has the stomach for the duty. In any case, he overreached himself by his speed. No matter how he dragged out the preparations, breakfast was cooked long before he dared call the oncoming watch. Normally, you can expect the aroma of frying bacon and freshly brewed coffee to bring even a Rip van Winkle from his bed; but those in the bunks would have none of that. They knew that breakfast would still be there whenever; and, once out of the snuggling delights of the berth, you are immersed in harsh reality. In any case, we were faced with a cooked breakfast and no one to eat it. The crew on deck had been salivating for some time. They were chilled as well. It was easy to have compassion for the hasty porridge cook and so they ate ahead of their appointed time.

Bucky, now warm and fed, was beginning to make unpleasant sounds about the dreary business of cooking for an unappreciative set of laggards. When it's cold on deck, I can be as selfless as Bucky in taking over galley service and so I took over the duty. A second round of breakfast was started. By the time the new watch had fed their inner men, it was time for a snack and coffee for the previous watch who, after all, had eaten in the pre-dawn. In this way was a morning given to riotous prandial delights.

1100   A haze-covered sun briefly played peek-a-boo in the thick overhead. Its lower limb and horizon were defined just enough for Frank to snatch a sight. The single line of position indicates that we may be ahead of our D.R. An additional, if untrustworthy, verification is a shaky R.D.F. (radio direction finder) bearing on Ocean Weather Ship "C" (CHARLIE). I do not trust radio bearings of more than 50 miles. However, in view of the lack of other means, we gratefully assume that CHARLIE is holding position by loran within his proscribed 10-mile square and we have entered it so on our plotting sheet. Should this latter indication of our position prove out, our speed forward is even more impressive.

1500   Preparations for the party are under way. The splendid wife of the skipper, herself a peerless woman and ship chandler, has placed many "not to be opened until July 4" packages aboard. When opened, they were found—not unexpectedly—to be the usual paraphernalia of children's parties: streamer decorations in red, white, and blue; balloons; small American flags for the cabin and table decorations; favors; funny hats, and noisemakers. All these are instruments for an outrageously created nostalgia into which we unashamedly enter. In this fine company of men, the accouterments for a smoker or a bachelor dinner would be more in order, for the dinner conversation will undoubtedly go that way. But if this is the way it is to be, I suppose that in addition to her natural inborn delicacy is the knowledge that she has a young son on board and so, by the extension of the peace and sanctity of our home to this seagoing annex, she will do what she can to maintain his fresh outlook. She keeps forgetting that this one went to a progressive school.

Once the adult male inhibition is overcome, the eternal boy in every man swarms to the surface. Soon, the cabin is festooned with red, white, and blue crepe paper, balloons are inflated (some irrepressibly converted to overblown phallic symbols—just to keep reality in sight), flags are crossed and hung and a centerpiece created for the table that would be a credit to the Committee on Patriotic Decorations of the Daughters of the American Revolution. (Except for the unregenerate symbols.)

I have been caught up in the party spirit and have baked an apple pie for the occasion. Norris Hoyt, Ph.D., the official ship's photographer, while recording these proceedings on imperishable celluloid is rigging the ship with cameras, flash attachments, and other remote triggering devices, so that the revelry can be recorded with his own mug in the picture. A most amazing man, this Hoyt. He takes time from his intellectual pursuits to make photographs. His camera is stuck on the end of a broomstick or boathook, or hoisted, unaccompanied, to the masthead. All of these dodges produce unusual photographs. The amazing thing is not that they always come out, but that he absolutely expects them to.

We had planned a steak dinner for tonight. For those not in our situation this may sound like small punkins. Ashore—at a time of ever-increasing disposable income—steak dinners grow on trees, but for small-boat sailors at sea it is a highly appreciated rarity. To begin with, FIGARO has no mechanical refrigeration and the iceman cometh not. All of our food is of the tinned or dehydrated variety. In addition, space and weight are very important considerations when making choices of stores. It is our practice during the winter before a long voyage is undertaken to try the new varieties which are constantly appearing in the market. Our method is to feed it to our youngest son, Jocko, who has an unusual, if adventurous, discernment as a food taster. If he rejects it, we know it is unfit for human consumption. An unfortunate characteristic shared by most tinned and dehydrated foods is their lack of chewiness. After a steady diet of soft foods one begins to long for something that will bite back. Thus, the anticipation of steak.

But it is difficult to hold steak in our conditions. Here, my business affiliations come into play. I serve as a consultant to various institutions, one of these being the Supermarket Institute. At a convention luncheon, I had occasion to be seated at the head table next to the president of a large meat-packing concern. Instead of listening to the luncheon speaker, I indulged in a monologue of complaint about canned foods. The president let it be known that his company was involved with experiments to preserve large chunks of unmacerated meat. I unhesitatingly offered myself and crew as floating guinea pigs. The offer was accepted and the foods, on delivery, were stowed in the bilge against the day of their use. Unhappily, on being drawn from this larder and despite the unusual care taken in their preservation, the steaks were found to be inedible and so, to the accompaniment of lamentations, over the rail they went. But life goes on and a new menu has been prepared.

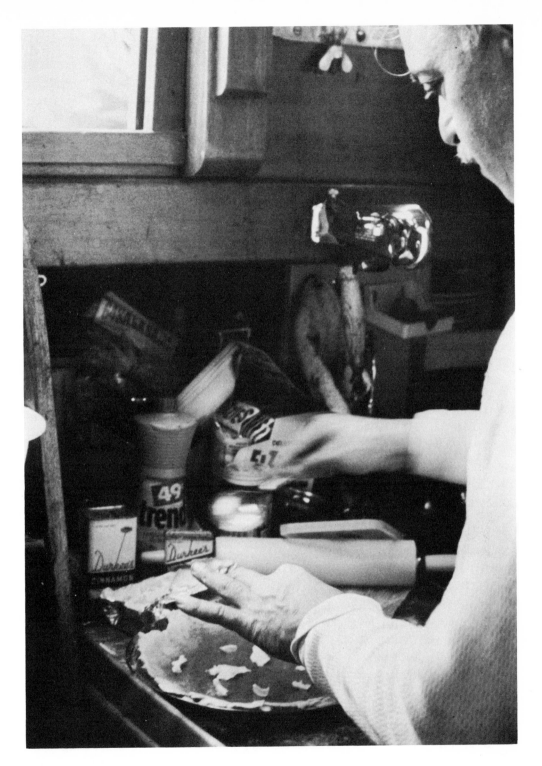

The pastry chef

For the Happy Hour	*Rhumb de* FIGARO
SMÖRGÅSBORD	Sardines à l'Huile, Harengs, Huitres Fumées, Langouste, Crevettes, Fromage Assortis
ENTRÉE	Bœuf Stroganoff
LÉGUMES	Pommes de Terre au Gratin Petits Pois
DESSERT	Tarte aux Pommes avec Fromage Cheddar
VIN	Lynch Bages 1955

COFFEE   COGNAC   ARMAGNAC   CIGARS

ENTERTAINMENT

All the foregoing may not sound very American, but then the French were our allies in those trying days instead of a trying third force. Remember De Grasse and Rochambeau?

However, our entertainment will be in the grand old Chatauqua tradition. Fourth of July orations will be offered by Daniel Webster Hoyt and Edward Everett Snaith. (The mouth that roared and the fastest gums in the east.) Old Glory has been gallantly flying from her staff all day in recognition of this final patriotic event, the convention of the North American Yacht Racing Union or some equally august body notwithstanding. This convention clearly states that an American yacht proceeding under sail and no power can display her ensign only from the leach of the aftermost sail. We thought that way out here no one would care, and anyway the spirit of successful rebellion is infectious.

2000   FIGARO's beautiful party manners counted in our celebrations. It was important that we all dine together. Therefore, the sails were trimmed so that the sweet witch FIGARO sailed herself for several hours with no man at the helm. On she went, climbing up the face of a green hill and down its backside, unwaveringly proceeding as though she were on a set of rails. We had turned our lives and welfare over to her without qualm or question and she responded like the lady she is.

What all this really means is that she is a beautifully balanced boat. Designed by Olin Stephens, of America's Cup defender fame, she clearly shows the hand of the master. Her builder, Joel Johnson, late of Black Rock, Connecticut, lived long enough to send a cablegram of congratulations and welcome to the crew of FIGARO after they had sailed to Gothenburg (his birthplace), winners of the Bermuda-Sweden Race. He died three days later. We have since felt that FIGARO is a magnificent memorial example of his craftsmanship.

To some, her witchery goes beyond the facts of her design and building. Knud Reimers, an old Swedish shipmate and a master yacht designer in his own right, has always held that a boat contains a soul which began with the tree in the forest and its relations to the wood people. Knud is a man knowledgeable in Nordic and Celtic sorcery and, after some mysterious communion, he announced that FIGARO was built of lucky wood. Now, how can you fight that? In any case, she is accorded an affection and faith rare to inanimate objects, and for that reason, without hesitation, she was left to sail herself. It was raining, anyway.

The dinner was an uproarious success. From the start of Happy Hour through the delicious meal and into the brandy, coffee, cigars and speeches, the unguarded abandon of the ship's company could hardly be squared with their situation. There we were in the cabin of a rather small yacht, sailing eastward in the middle of the Atlantic in the region of the low-powered steamer lanes, a southeast wind creating a lumpy sea. But in terms of lookout, we might as well have been in a private dining room ashore. There must be a providence that watches over patriots. The only mischance was the toppling of a wine bottle which went over in a roll of the sea. It unerringly singled out the captain, who emerged, bestained and sputtering like a baggy-eyed Bacchus. Norry, in recording the proceedings, set off so many flashes that we all will be suffering

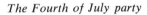

The Fourth of July party

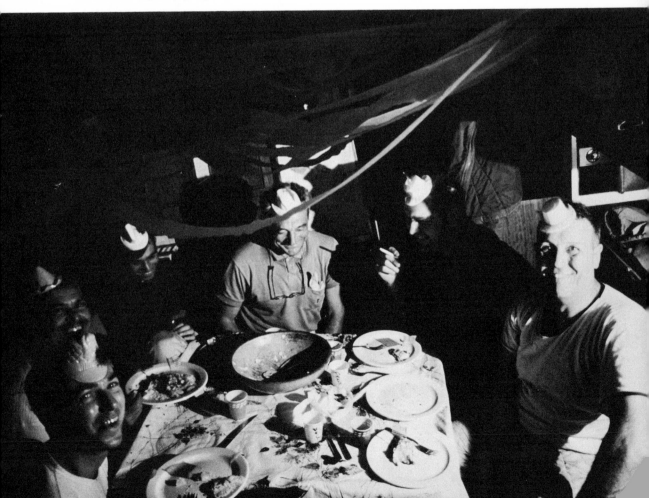

from night blindness. Halfway through dinner Skip discovered more decorations. The meal was halted until these could be hung.

The proper place to deliver a Fourth of July oration is from a flag-draped poop deck. But since we have no poop, and it was raining anyway, the oration was made while at table. I used the occasion to instill a fighting spirit in the crew. Since it is not given to every man to be terse and gifted as Nelson was, with his "England expects every man to do his duty," I chose rather to remind those who were about to race at Cowes of the massacre on Boston Common, of the destruction of the Danbury Arsenal, and for good measure threw in the 1812 burning of the White House. Despite the fact that most of the racing crew were absent and those present were comatose, the feeling persists that it was a clever move.

In all, it was a celebration worthy of the name and a fitting memorial to the thirteen original colonies and their GLORIOUS heritage. It was enjoyed so much that we are wracking our brains for another reason to celebrate. A reason is not readily apparent. Bastille Day and Orangeman's Day are too far off. There is a rumor that we are fast approaching the birthday of H.R.H. The Duke of Edinburgh, a distinguished yachtsman. If this is so, a dinner in his honor and *in absentia* will be held. The proper research is to begin when we can gather the energy.

2200   Rain and fog and what breeze there is on the nose and dying. Our chance for a fast passage is endangered. We must form a square.

The ship's company, bellies distended, eyes glazed, are as well and happy as their condition permits. Thus, ingloriously, does the GLORIOUS FOURTH OF JULY draw to a close.

2330   The wind has expired. The engine is on, the headsail down and the main strapped almost amidships. We are pushing our way through an oily sea, cleaving the fog down the middle. We are almost used to the idea of sailing in the middle of a visibly impenetrable curtain. At least we are relieved of some of the terrors of uncertainty which must have been the companions of earlier mariners. We are sailing in well-explored waters.

For that matter, the kind of weather from which we suffer has almost turned the clock back in one area, namely that of navigation. Because of the constant overcast which has severely limited our ability to get sights, we are heavily reliant on dead reckoning, just as in the case of the early sailors. We carry many of the modern navigational instruments on board. But if you cannot get a sight, then all of your knowledge of HO 214 or HO 249 (two U.S. Hydrographic Office systems of navigation) is for nought. The dependence upon dead reckoning instead of celestial bearings or the electronic marvel, the loran (which we do not have on board), heightens the feeling of kinship with old-time navigators. They found their way across the dark, mysterious and terrifying sea with primitive means. They sailed incredible distances with these means, but each time a voyage was successfully completed, the knowledge and understanding of the physical world was extended.

VII
NAVIGATION

At a time when man is planning a landing on the moon, his early struggles to find his way across the sea should seem like the antics of children as opposed to the struggles of giants. But even now when life is crowded with imagination —stirring technical discovery, when no natural secret seems impenetrable— we are moved to wonder at the intrepidity of the early voyagers and at the insights of the astronomers and mathematicians who gradually unfolded knowledge of our world. Certainly when we are shown close-up pictures of the moon, attained by a breathtaking co-ordination of most of the known physical sciences, we are thrilled. But we treat them as an exciting one day's wonder and quickly settle back, impatient for the next show.

In contrast to such scientific derring-do, the earlier explorations still hold a cherished place in our imaginations. It is because in them is compressed most of the history and romance of men and nations, a history of conquest and discovery and of scientific achievement. They come to us as events shaped by acts of courage and faith in the face of terror-ridden enigmas, acts which lift our hearts and make our spirits soar. This is the day of greediness for the new and the ability to get it. In the casual acceptance with which we greet almost daily miracles, modern men may be losing the sense of wonder at the magic of their own achievements.

The esteem accorded the early navigators springs in great part from the fact that the deeds were those of clearly defined individuals whose personal contributions not only were identified with them, but were accomplishments which lie within our understanding and comprehension. These marvels were not the product of whirring banks of electronic computers whose findings are incomprehensible to most men. The isolated heroes now are those who ride the space ships. Behind them are thousands of faceless men. But perhaps we are stirred most by the consciousness that the early discoveries emerged from the darkness of superstition and unknowing—that incredible achievements were made with tools and equipment of a limited range of use and on a sea which was thought to shelter jealous sea-gods and raging sea-monsters, and, most terrifyingly, was held by some to be finite with an unholy abyss at its edge. The conquest of such ancient enemies, the conquest of fear, is a victory in which we still share glory.

Today, we measure in decades, or less, the time from one imponderable accomplishment to the next. The edge of space having been penetrated, we confidently expect that its boundaries will shrink rapidly. The sea was slower in giving up its secrets. Navigation, the science which helped shrink the boundaries of the sea, was slow in developing. It has its roots in prehistory. It began with a primitive man afloat on a log in a flowing stream. His need was to go across the stream to a desired objective. His problem then, as it is today, was to calculate and allow for the drift of the current. From that primitive form of pilotage to the celestial and electronic navigation of today has taken 6000 to 8000 years—the recorded history of mankind.

We remember most of those who made the voyages, but as the art of navigation slowly took form, behind these courageous adventurers were astronomers and mathematicians whose brilliant insight and imaginative conjecture was developing information, methods and instruments of navigation. Many of these inventions still are in use. The compass is still the principal tool of the navigator. Its origins are in the dim past, but its use is identified with great men and events. It is said that Hannibal's pilot Pelorus used one in 203 B.C. when the conquering general sailed for Rome. (Pelorus, romantically, is the name given to the instrument with which modern pilots take bearings.)

With the decline of Rome and the darkening of Europe, scientific knowledge receded and the recorded existence of the compass dropped from sight. Its reintroduction into Europe is variously credited to Marco Polo, along with the rumored gift of spaghetti and gunpowder, or to the Moors who brought so many astronomical and mathematical concepts with them in their invasion of the European continent. It is known that those incredible voyagers, the Norsemen, were familiar with the compass in the eleventh century, and references in European writings continue from the twelfth century on.

The very card which forms the compass face carries with it the tracings of long history. It was derived from the wind rose of the ancients. The number of points of direction varied during the centuries. Homer gave names to the four winds—Boreas, Eurus, Notus, and Zephyrus—and thus, four points. Aristotle expanded these winds to twelve points, but the Tower of the Winds built in Athens in about 100 B.C. had eight sides. The Latin rose went back to twelve points, which became consistent on the compass in the Middle Ages. The compass, which started as a needle piercing a piece of straw afloat in a bowl of liquid, has evolved into the gyrocompass of today. Its principle has remained relatively unchanged.

As voyages grew bolder, men needed accurate means to standardize longer units of measurement. Modern units now are so commonplace that we almost believe them to have been here from the beginning. It is extraordinary to contemplate the fact that the United States did not accept the international standard for the nautical mile until 1954. Now we have stringent technical means to maintain units of measurement. As an instance, in the Pavillon de Breteuil at Sèvres is a platinum-iridium bar which is the standard length of the meter. But natural units were the standard for early man. The width of a finger or the *span* of his hand; the *cubit* (Biblical), from elbow to middle finger tip; and the self-explanatory *foot* and *pace*—all were such units. The *fathom,* a measurement of depth still used, was the distance of a man's outstretched arms. It is now set at six feet.

But there were no natural units for longer measurements. An early Greek attempt was the *stadium,* the length of the Olympic Stadium, about 600 feet. The Romans, great adapters, used this and created another, adapted to their hard-marching legions, the *mile.* It was derived from *mille,* or one thousand paces. These were probably double paces, or else the legions had an amazingly long stride. The distance of the Roman mile in United States feet is 4588.59.

This was a land mile, which had little relationship to the nautical mile. The latter bears a direct relationship to the circumference of the earth. As nautical charts were developed, it became customary to include a scale of miles. Slowly, as the concept of degrees of latitude came into being, each degree took on the value of sixty miles. The Roman mile was too short to accommodate itself to this necessity. When multiplied by sixty, the distance could not be made to match. Since none of the savants could agree on either an increase to the mile or an increase in the number of degrees, they settled for a land mile and a nautical mile as well, and so both came into use. The nautical mile, in a decimal relationship to the degrees of latitude, is finally 6076.10333 U.S. feet; the statute or land mile in the United States is 5280 U.S. feet.

As with measurements, so with charts. The early Mediterranean sailors used simple plane projections and sailing directions. There was no recognition of the shape of the earth. But as understanding of the world unfolded, cartographers and geographers began to represent this knowledge on charts. The first gnomic projection, using lines radiating from a sphere, is credited to the chief of the seven wise men of ancient Greece, Thales of Miletus, 640–546 B.C. As early as this the great Greek civilization had developed the concept of a spherical earth.

Even more dramatic is the fact that the earth was measured to near accuracy as early as the third century B.C. by Eratosthenes. He observed that at high noon on the occasion of the summer solstice, a certain well at Syene, on the Tropic of Cancer, was lighted throughout its depth as the sun swept across the meridian. In Alexandria, 500 miles to the north, the sun cast a shadow. Since, by Greek reasoning, this was due to the earth's curvature, he measured the length of the shadow against the vertical and determined the zenith distance to be about 7°.5 divided into 360° or 1/48 of the earth's circumference. The earth must therefore be 48 × 500, or 24,000 miles in circumference. Allowing for the probably imprecise nature of the measured distance from Syene to Alexandria, this is astoundingly close. The value established today is 24,900 miles.

The great astronomer, mathematician, geographer, and cartographer of the Roman civilization was Claudius Ptolemy. He left a great volume of work but little is known of him. All that is certain is that he observed in Alexandria during the reigns of Hadrian and Antoninus Pius between the years 127–141 or 151 A.D. Ptolemaic astronomy dominated European thinking until the revelations of Copernicus in the sixteenth century. In Ptolemy's immense volume of work was an error which affected the life and career of a great sailor thirteen hundred years later. Ptolemy did not employ Eratosthenes' value of the earth's size. Instead, he used that of Posidonius, whose miscalculation in 140 B.C. was 18,000 miles. This error was included in Ptolemy's book "Cosmographia," which was discovered and translated into Latin in 1409. The book became the basis for numerous geographical works. Tragically, this smaller distance was the basis for the error of the great discoverer Columbus, who died in the belief that he had discovered the short route to the East Indies.

But despite this miscalculation, Ptolemy's work was of enormous importance. He made the first conic projection of the world, and he forever established the convention that the north is the top of the world. Another convention which he established was the use of a prime meridian, though his is not the one used today. He used a reference point two degrees west of the Canary Islands. In 1493, Pope Alexander VI, faced with the need to separate the territories of two great Catholic powers, Spain and Portugal, ordered a line 0° in the Atlantic as the prime meridian. It was west of the Azores. In 1676, because of England's dominance of the sea, the prime meridian was moved to London, and at that time the convention of measuring 180° east and west of this line was established. It was not until 1884 that Greenwich, England, became the internationally accepted prime meridian.

The cartographer with the most lasting effect on our time was Gerhardus Mercator (which seems to be the latinized version of Gerhard Kremer—in those days the thought of an author using his own name in the vulgar tongue was probably as unthinkable as a movie star using his own name today). Mercator was a brilliant Flemish geographer. In 1569 he devised what became known as Mercator's projection, at a time when the known world has grown too large to be reasonably contained on flat charts by other forms of projection. His method is still used today.

Thus, by the time of the golden age of exploration, mariners were already equipped with instruments, charts, information, and theories when they set sail. When Magellan put out in 1519 he had many supports to his belief in a navigable pass to the Pacific. He had a world globe by Martin Behaim, another globe made in Nuremburg by Johannes Schöner, and a magnificent map of the world drawn by that gifted inquirer into the wonders around him, Leonardo da Vinci. In addition, he carried sailing directions, nautical tables, and instructions for the use of the cross staff (the first instrument that used the earth's horizon as datum in celestial measurement). Also, his equipment included an astrolabe, a wood and metal theodolite, wood and bronze quadrants, compasses, hourglasses to be used as timepieces, and a log to be towed astern to measure speed. There was still one great unsolved mystery—how to determine longitude accurately.

Because of the inability to determine longitude, mariners devised ingenious methods of sailing. One such, which also reduced distance, was great circle sailing. Verrazano, for whom the Narrows Bridge in New York has been named, sailed to America in 1524 using a great circle course. But the principal method in planning a voyage when longitude could not be determined was parallel or latitude sailing. In this, the ship was taken to the latitude of its destination and then traveled along this parallel to the port. A version of this kind of voyaging survives in a sailing direction in the form of an aphorism used by early Yankee skippers: "Take her south till the butter melts, then turn east."

But centuries earlier, in the Pacific, primitive people were making astounding voyages in frail craft. They used much the same method. The Polynesians, in their extraordinary voyages to Hawaii, would sail thousands of miles north until they arrived at the correct latitude and would then turn east to their destination. The instrument used to determine that latitude was the magic calabash—a hollow gourd filled with liquid to form a primitive theodolite and star mirror. The high priest navigator got his celestial fix by observation of a fixed star.

It was not until the middle of the eighteenth century that the first chronometers began to be used. With these, navigators could accurately determine their longitude and at last fix their precise position at sea. The dawn of modern navigation probably was ushered in by the three voyages of Captain James Cook, R.N., between 1768–1779. By the time of his second voyage, he had four chronometers on board. His voyages were made under the auspices and direction of the British Royal Society and were accomplished with great precision.

With this coming of age, navigation entered a classical period. Rapid advances were made, marked by new understanding of compass variation, prevailing winds, and the great ocean currents. Sailing directions, nautical and astronomical almanacs, tables for computation, and newly refined instruments were ready for the great age of sail—the short-lived, glorious day of the clipper. With the coming of power and electricity, navigation entered its own electronic age.

Electricity has brought a whole new array of implements to determine positions at sea. The navigator can tell the sea's depth when on uncertain soundings by an echo sounder. He can home on a radio beacon with the radio direction finder. Consolan is a radio system which emits directional dots and dashes. By counting these, the sailor finds a line of position on the consolan chart. This is crossed with another bearing to give him a fix. In loran, a computer-like system, he has a device which gives a precise fix in a single series of operations. The system is that of triangulating a measured time differential in microseconds, between the direct emission from a master station and the electronic reflection of that signal from a slave station. These are recorded on a cathode tube and the result is read out on the instrument. The read-out is transferred to the loran chart for a precise position. Soon the science of nautical navigation will join with that of the never-never world of space. Satellites adjusted to the speed of the earth's rotation are being contemplated. They will hold a position like a fixed beacon over a particular point of the earth. It will provide a visual and electronic assurance, in still another way, of the navigator's place on earth.

The yachtsman remains a classical navigator. While he may use one modest electronic device or another, expense and conditions permitting, at sea he depends basically upon celestial navigation. In most cases, the ocean-racing rules abet his enthusiasm by ruling out loran. But even if there were no rules, he could not escape his addiction to that lovely fossil—sailing. He is a hopeless romantic who treasures every reminder of the glorious days of sail. When he is at sea, he is in company with every great captain who sailed these waters. And in that time at sea he has the same thrill of experiencing the majestic order of the universe. It is a rewarding task for a navigator to stand on the pitching deck of a small boat when taking a sight. There is no stable platform here, no high bridge deck of a liner. His height of eye above the horizon is a mere eight feet, ofttimes less than that of a running sea. He must accurately bring the sun, moon, or star down to the horizon in the mirror of his sextant, and all the time struggle for balance so that he will not be pitched into the sea. Somewhere, perhaps near his ear, he should have another eye to watch for spray and spume which could fog his lens and mirrors. And while he patiently waits for the sun or star to pop out from behind an obscuring cloud, his timekeeper, together with the rest of the ship's company, is hushed and poised, waiting for the sharp call of "Mark." In a while, he is able to say to his waiting mates, "We have come two hundred and seven miles since yesterday."

Move over Columbus, Da Gama, Magellan—the world, for a moment, is as it was. A man still can feel a sense of individual accomplishment, the ability to unlock at least one little secret from the mysterious cosmos—his place.

VIII

MID-ATLANTIC

JULY 5—THE SIXTH DAY

0600 Our world is reduced to a dome of wet fog with a circular floor of gray-green sea about fifty yards in diameter. There is no wind and no visibility, only the sound of our exhaust and the susurrus of the bow wave. There is one promising sign of change—the barometer has started down. We may have gone through or past the dome of the high. Depending upon the size and shape of this high cell, we hope to pick up some wind in several hours.

We were awakened this morning by the aroma of Block Island turkey—codfish cakes—most artfully prepared by Hoyt, and served with a side order of potato pancakes. Coming on top of yesterday's heavy gourmandising, this is a considered assault on the alimentary system. We may be forced to concentrate so much on digestion as to leave us without energy enough to gripe about the weather.

0700 The barometer continues downward though it is still above the seasonal average for these latitudes, reading 30.32 as against a norm of 29.95. We still hope we are diverging with the high and into the prevailing southwesterly, that is, if such things still prevail in this disordered world. A slight ruffling of the water from a southerly direction stirs hope.

We have been sailing by braille for most of the voyage so far. With the exception of the hurried sun line, there have been no sights. A first! Across the Atlantic by braille! No one has done that yet. The deck log is rigorously maintained. At the end of each half-hourly wheel trick an entry of course and speed is made. As each helmsman is relieved he makes his entry. This record is the only source of information from which we develop our D.R. position. Spaces also are arranged in the deck log to receive other observations such as direction and weight of wind and sea, barometer readings, and other phenomena seen. From the composite of these we build a picture of where we are, what is happening to us, or perhaps what we think may happen.

For instance, yesterday a water temperature of 58° was recorded. This, coupled with frequent glimpses of bits of gulf weed, indicates that we are on the northern edge of the Gulf Stream and should, therefore, be receiving a favorable lift from the current. So far, no allowance for current has been put into our computations, although the North Atlantic pilot chart for this month tells us we are in the Gulf Stream. We believe our position to be considerably advanced over our D.R. and, in fact, yesterday's brief check shows this to be the case, but we will wait until we get a celestial fix to verify our position. Our precise latitude and longitude is unknown, but we have a reasonably good idea of where we are.

0800   A water temperature just taken shows a fall of 4° since yesterday. It makes one wonder if the Stream, this far into the Atlantic, has the same kind of meanders as we find in latitudes farther south. A meander is a wandering sub-current within the main current. It is a phenomenon one can see demonstrated in one's own bathtub. When adding hot water to a tub full of cooler water, the hotter liquid can be clearly seen entering the existing body of water. It has a clearly defined edge, a more viscous texture, and does not enter in a straight flow, but snakes into its host in looping coils. The great Gulf Stream, carrying its sun-heated water, acts in a similar manner. On occasion, giant sinuous loops of warmer water snake through the main current of cooler water.

This phenomenon is an important one to recognize when we race to Bermuda. The course to Bermuda from our start in Newport, Rhode Island, takes us through the Gulf Stream which is about 160 miles wide at the point where we cross. In this case, the change of direction cannot be seen as readily as it is in the bathtub, although I am told that it can be seen from an airplane. Instead, we take water temperature readings at hourly intervals. The range of temperature in Atlantic seaboard water in the latitudes of the race during June is in the middle sixties. As one approaches the northern slope of the Stream, the temperature goes up until it reads 70°, which indicates that the northern edge has been entered. From this edge, the temperature gradually ascends until it reaches 80° at the center. From here, it descends to 70 or 72°, which is the temperature of the Sargasso water, and remains so until Bermuda.

However, the temperature readings are not always an unbroken upward and downward curve. At times, there are reversals. Such a drop in temperature indicates a meander which can be either a backward or sideward flowing current. When this is discovered, the navigator tries to get a series of running fixes to gauge which direction and speed this sub-current is taking, for the rhumb line to Bermuda was adjusted for an average of eastward drift. This drift is made up of the average speed of the current over the time it takes to get through it, and naturally, anything which disrupts the average must change the rhumb line; for, if we should come out of the Stream farther east or west than is our plan, it implies increased distance to sail and consequently a longer time. The time differential between the competing boats is the deciding factor in winning, therefore a misjudged course could be a painful error. This ingrained consciousness of the nature of the Stream is what motivates conjecture as to the meaning in the 4° drop of water temperature. While it is relatively of small importance to us in the present circumstances, it might be more so if we were racing.

The air temperature is 58°. If it were not for the drizzly fog, the condition would be quite pleasant. Our course is 113° at 6.8 knots.

1130   We have sailed into a new time zone as we make our slow approach to the Greenwich meridian. The clocks must be moved ahead, but the action was delayed until now so that the lost hour could be shared equally by the two watches. Going eastward in the Atlantic by sailboat results in a series of time changes, as though we endlessly were going from standard to daylight time. We must do it five times, and no one wants to feel that he has been put upon in terms of his privileges or sleeping time.

Luncheon was served in the classiest floating delicatessen south of Iceland. Hot pastrami sandwiches! With pickles and, for local color and warmth, hot chicken soup. The pastrami is by courtesy of my meat-packer friend. In this case the meat, being pickled or marinated, has held up very well indeed. The cabin was redolent with the cooking. Odors play extraordinary tricks on one.

On occasion, I have walked down Fifth Avenue in New York and suddenly found myself thinking of Paris and wondering why. Listed among other secondary avocations is that of international girl-watching, and my first thought was that I must have caught a glimpse out of the corner of my eye of someone last seen on one of the inner boulevards or a Saint-Germain discothèque. Instead of such a glamorous triggering of the subconscious, I discover that someone ahead is smoking a *Gauloise Bleu*. It is not a girl in the back of my eye. I am breathing in the association. And so it is with the cabin of FIGARO. Suddenly it is invested with all of the highly seasoned *Gemütlichkeit* of a New York City delicatessen.

1200   A fair breeze at last. The sun was out long enough to assure us that it really is up there and for Frank to get another shot with his prayer wheel. The engine is off and the ship is, we hope, settled down to a peaceful afternoon.

1500   Rain and fog have returned and have become again the order of the day. The wind still holds, our course 110° at 6 knots.

1700   The wind is picking up a bit and is drawing aft slightly. Hot damn! Can this really be the southwester about to come in? We are being freed up, the sails are eased. The boat picks up speed and motion becomes more comfortable. We take the seas a little more on the beam and the lumpiness is gone. The mizzen staysail is set and the sounds of the racing man are heard once more. Nothing like a fair breeze to bring out the dormant sporting instinct. Our speed is 6.8 knots.

2030   Alas! Our high sporting fervor is damped, the hopes for a fast passage waning once again. The wind is falling off. The high we hoped to cross is crossing us up. We peer longingly at the barograph hoping to stare it down. If it would dip again it would indicate divergence from this no-wind system.

2100   The wind is off even more. We turn on the gasoline breeze—a motorboat again. Will there be no shred of pride left for the unhappy wind sailors? Course 118° at 6.0 knots, 900 R.P.M.

2200   The wind is extremely light and, piling outrage on insult, there is a slight sea running. We have taken down all sail. FIGARO was rolling in the sea and everything was slatting and banging. A condition such as this can raise more havoc than a strong wind. The constant jerk and snap is harmful to spars, sails and rigging. Sail slides snap, the mast track is wrenched from its moorings, and turnbuckles and tangs can crack and break. With all sail down we have tied off the rigging, the forward motion under power helps a bit. At least we are not rolling helplessly in one place Coleridge fashion.

The course is 110° at 5.5 knots.

The research committee, charged with the responsibility of developing adequate reasons for another party, reported earlier. They have come through with a few pallid suggestions. The line they seemed to be pushing was the astronomical fact that the moon is entering its last quarter. Perhaps because of the weather, or lack of wind, I found the reason noncompelling. After all, this sort of lunar change goes on all the time and it seems rather quixotic to create a festival recognition out of such insignificance. It would make more sense if we were a voyaging group of astrologers, or perhaps about to indulge in some exotic lunar mystery rite. But such ideas are far removed from our intention. Besides, someone forgot to invite the girls and anyway you would need a full moon and a goat.

In searching for ideas we stumbled on Bowditch. Beyond the great respect for this great systematizer of navigation was the fact that his "American Practical Navigation" was the only sort of standard reference on board. In essence, the accident turned out to be a version of the Renaissance game of *Sortes Vergilianae,* for an awesome parallel was uncovered. Separated by almost two centuries, the birthdays of the great Nathaniel and the captain turned out to be the same. I am overcome by this concatenation of days; the coincidence is strong, the omens are clear and must not be denied or the winds will not be fair for Hellas.

It was always in my mind to move the anniversary date of any event or personage if it fell anywhere near. It is a trick developed in benevolent parliamentary monarchies, where they will shift the celebration day of a reigning monarch's birth in order to insure good weather, a big turnout, and a happy electorate. But why be niggling in face of such an open sign? Since I am the magistrate of this community, I approached the task with the *force majeur* that I am expected to show, and announced that for the welfare of the ship's company tomorrow would be March 26.

Doctor Hoyt, being aroused by this extraordinary declaration, asked why the date could not be March 19 since that was his birthday. Feeling generous, I declared that the date would be shared. In addition, since March 26 is also the anniversary of the death of Ludwig van Beethoven, the passing of the great originator would be marked by appropriate rites.

OFFICIAL ENTRY

Be it known by the authority invested in me as Captain of the American Yawl Yacht FIGARO, feeling her way by braille toward England, I do solemnly declare and order the following:

1. Tomorrow, 6 July according to the Gregorian calendar, will from 0001 to 1200 become 19 March according to the Guilliaman calendar, and in this period the birthdate of Norris Hoyt, Ph.D., will be suitably recognized and celebrated.

2. That from 1200 until 2130, according to the aforesaid calendar, the day will be known as 26 March and the joint birthdays of Nathaniel Bowditch, navigator, and Captain William Snaith, mariner, will be together and separately celebrated and honored at a dinner for the entire ship's company.

3. That from 2130 the day, still recognized as 26 March, will be devoted to observances in memoriam of the death of Ludwig van Beethoven and will be solemnly marked by a rendition of the master's *Missa Solemnis* if it be heaven's grace that anyone can.

4. At 2200 the date will be returned to Pope Gregory and 6 July and shall pass into its own history.

2300   The crew continue hale and, considering the unpleasant weather, in remarkably good spirits. In the pressure chamber of a small cabin, set thus on the great ocean, we see one another not only nakedly and in truth, but constantly. These must be sterling men. Their foibles are not oppressive, rather marked by a respect for one another and the clear emergence of their personalities.

Norris Hoyt has used all of his eleven cameras indefatigably and repetitively and given us the benefit of his scholarly opinion on a vast array of matters. Having been a PT boat commander, as well as being a Republican, he has standards of comparison for most things.

Skip, who, in self-acknowledgment of his youth and lack of political experience, abstains from political debate, fills his days instead with constant trips to the larder. There, he erects and consumes astounding edifices of bread and cheese or of peanut butter and jelly sandwiches. He seems to be truly hungry and does not at all give the impression of being a compulsive eater. At the very least, he is not being furtive. Anything he eats is eaten in the open, in the full glare of daylight except, naturally, his midnight snacks.

Frank, who, on the surface, projects a quality of equanimity and openness, continues to dig up and consume cases upon cases of beer, to the chagrin of the captain, who feels his authority flouted and betrayed. At the outset of the voyage, even in the planning stage, I let it be known that since FIGARO would be heavily burdened, no malt beverages would be carried. Now, faced with such a flagrant contravention, I can only describe myself as nonplused. Frank continues to be gentle and obliging and salutes the captain's good health with each can.

Bucky continues as the tireless ship's husband and bosun's mate. He is, however, in league with Frank at putting one square in the captain's eye. He disclaims any knowledge of how the beer came aboard and, after one is dug up, gives assurance that it is the last—until the final can—then, miraculously, remembers where another malt treasure might be buried.

As for me, I am grateful that the crew has seen fit to adorn the overhead of my berth with a ravishing picture of a magazine playgirl in an exotic state of undress. However, there must be more to their action than meets the eye.

JULY 6—THE SEVENTH DAY

*To Be Called 19 March, Thereafter To Be Called 26 March
And Finally Return to 6 July*

0600   The starboard watch wakened Hoyt with a serenade to start his unexpected birthday. The singers had warmed to their work by first setting the spinnaker and mizzen staysail. At last, the god-damned engine is silent. Norry takes to a serenade like a señorita without a duenna. He started beaming even before he was fully awake and when, in a birthday gesture, he was served coffee in bed, he wondered why his wife never thought of the idea.

The boat is relatively upright and comfortable, but the day is drizzly as usual.

Our digestive systems must be monuments to American boyhood and home cooking—the things we eat! Bucky prepared a Grand Banks omelet for breakfast—Portuguese *linguica* and sautéed onions encased in scrambled eggs. Served with this dish were croissants which had been on the boat since it left the United States. (These packaged breads have an extraordinarily long shelf life.) We eat it all with relish.

0700   The chief blind mouse, our navigator, declares that we have come 1055 miles as of the hour. Yesterday's run, 167 miles.

0900   Our position by D.R.: Longitude 26° 05′ W. Latitude 51° 15′ N.

1130   Hoyt, playing his birthday role to the hilt and enjoying it, has ordered a particular luncheon. Chow mein, rice, and Earl Grey tea. As the capstone to this modest celebration, a special birthday cake was constructed—pound cake cut in the pattern of a Y and lavishly covered with chocolate sauce. We had no candles, but some of the July Fourth flags were found and used to decorate the top. To make his cup of bliss run over, he joined the FIGARO glee society in the singing of Yale songs. Norry is an unrepentant Yale man. Carried away by nostalgia, he was on the point of giving his own many versions of Stover Hoyt at Yale. The captain, by exercising a nimble ploy, was able to cut him off at the pass by declaring at . . .

1200   . . . "By order of the Captain, 26 March and a new day begins!"

1500   Frank has succeeded once again in capturing both the sun and the horizon in his magic looking glass at the same time. This gives us only a latitude, but we will settle for small blessings. The results of his work show us to be considerably north of our D.R. On the other hand, if we have underestimated our speed forward by not allowing enough for a favorable current, or by underreading the Kenyon speedometer, then we could be much farther ahead. This is eminently possible, since the angle of the sun line converges with our course.

The sun is appearing with greater frequency and the air is warmer. We have begun to peel some of our outer layers. I am down to long johns and no foulweather gear for the first time since St. John's. The effect of being freed of these constricting garments is quite heady. I expect at any moment to see someone gambol around the decks like cloven-footed Pan (still in rubber boots).

1530   Glorious, blue, blue skies seen ahead on the horizon.

1545   The chief blind mouse finally has worked up a fix from the assorted bag of sights he has been able to snatch from time to time. The fix places us on the same longitude as the D.R. did. It appears that we have been keeping an accurate estimate of our forward speed. However, it does put us forty miles to the north. We have either been set up or our steering is not as sharp as we thought. Some honest-to-goodness sights would be welcome. We shall wait to see what the next episode of these Perils of Pauline will show.

Norry, having no better place to go, went to the masthead in order to take photographs from aloft. The ship was wearing all of her light stuff and should make a pretty picture. As long as he was going aloft, he was asked to change the masthead light bulb which had snuffed during the night. For that matter, so had the stern and starboard running lights. This must be more than coincidence. It is difficult to believe, but then, as Shakespeare put it, "There are more things in heaven and earth than are dreamt of in your philosophy." I can only assume there is a plot, and certainly collusion, amongst inanimate objects. They are forever in league, crouched down behind doors, ready to spring upon men on signal. There is no other way to account for three quite disconnected lights to go out on a given evening.

To ask our doctor in humane letters to be nimble with tools while concerned with a camera was a mistake. He changed the bulb all right, but managed to lose one of the machine screws that hold the glass shield down, leaving the light slightly open to the weather. "But it's really not too bad," said Norry, "I got some beautiful shots."

An extraordinary and wonderful shipmate, this Norry. The sun at last has induced him to shed a few of his layers. He subscribes to the theory that many light layers make for better insulation against the cold than is given by heavy clothing; except that heavy and light are inexact values. It appears to me that a few of his light layers could, in another context, be considered heavy. Most of those he uses look as though they have been borrowed from a road company production of "The Beggar's Opera." When the true Norry emerges from this assorted bundle of Care packages or Salvation Army dross, he is fifteen inches less in circumference and, clearly, the sterling leader and educator his yearbook at Yale announces him to be. But his attachment to these garments is understandable. He has sailed across the Atlantic eight times (he has made three more passages since the voyage recorded in this log), and each article of clothing must by now be endowed with some particular memory. Like the Crusader who is attached to a dented helmet which has saved him from a Saracen sword.

Hoyt's wit and conversation are stimulating. In sustaining amusing banter, he has few equals, although the length of his periods has become proverbial, as has his classroom voice. As a matter of fact, in the choosing of the watches, one fellow, who had sailed with both Norry and me before, asked to be put in his watch. With a straight face I suggested that he might get tired of those stories all

Norry hears the clash of palm fronds

across the Atlantic. He said he would take his chances, it was difficult to sleep in the other watch. I put him in Norry's watch, but I never believed him. I know he looked forward to those wonderful storytelling hours in the cockpit.

Last night at 0200, during the change of the watch, Norry and I exchanged some unresolved thoughts about Ezra Pound, T. S. Eliot, and James Joyce. Our conversation had grown rather animated when some insomniac Philistine invited us to hold it for Hyde Park. We never were able to assign properly weighted values to style, originality, and erudition. However, the long chat did keep me off the deck and down in the warmth for three-quarters of an hour and did him out of the same amount of sleep. Naturally, I showed no mercy in the morning. He got up with everyone else.

1730   Alas, the blue horizon has turned out to be a sunny hole in the cloud cover. We are back under the overcast. It is remarkable, the degree to which sunshine can lift one's spirit and, conversely, dampen it when it goes. To add to our dispiritedness, the wind is dropping. Our speed is down to 4 knots on a course of 125°.

The cloudy sky has put a blight on the enthusiasm which had been building for tonight's repast. However, the wheels of ritual once started churn relentlessly on. And so, after a brief ceremony in the form of a toast honoring Nathaniel, son of Habbakuk and Mary Bowditch, the assembled ship's company devoted themselves to the principal business of the evening. They witnessed a moving, if somewhat extended, ceremony in recognition of the qualities of the ship's commander. The ship's laureate, Hoyt, Ph.D. in humane letters, unabashedly declaimed some unending stanzas composed between photography.

The crew have been sworn to an oath never to reveal the scabrous contents. Overwhelmed with the power and force of the sentiments, they sat to dinner.

2020   We have sighted our first ship! What is she doing out here, so far north? Is she lost? It is a Swedish freighter bound west, one mile to port. Her crew lines the rail—in awe, we assume.

2130   Oh, the horror! Catastrophe!
THE HEAD HAS BROKEN DOWN!!!
Worn and abused through outrageous overuse by the crew, those swilling, inordinate consumers of beer, our head has given up its ghost.

Everyone, naturally, is stricken with psychological gripes. Anticipations of dreary periods hung over the rail, with one's bottom bared to the toothy gale, or alternately being forced to use a bucket with protruding bits of metal at the handle. These horrifying images come crowding in. Vision after vision of undelight parades before the inner eye.

There is nothing to do until daylight, so the watch off duty turns over for a last snooze. But the watch on duty has time to ruminate over the threat to regularity. Modern advertising makes us aware of such dangers.

FIGARO, within whom this colonic drama is taking place, moves steadily across the face of the sea, unruffled by the gastric disturbances that are threatening.

JULY 7—THE EIGHTH DAY

0400   It is time for dawn stars, and a gracious providence has opened a heavenly hole, a deep indigo vault soaring above the overcast. The moon and a few isolated stars are exposed. Frank is able to cross Jupiter with the lower limb of Luna, a neat trick in anyone's mythology. Having played pander to this celestial covering, he dove back into the sack. The sights will be worked out later when he is on watch.

It is not yet time for the starboard watch to go on deck, since they came off a scant two hours ago. The flurry of sight-taking woke me in the after cabin and induced a brief visit on deck for a look around. Below again, in the sack, you can sense the quickening of the boat as the wind slowly picks up. The bag (spinnaker) is beginning to pull. The southwest wind is filling in. Perhaps this is the long awaited prevailing breeze which will blow us to England. In the bunk you can hear and feel the increased tempo as the displaced water rushing by is pushed downward and alongside the hull. You sense the power by a combination of sound and a subtle thrumming vibration as the boat thrusts through the water. One lies dozing in the bunk, mildly conscious of being lulled as the chill of the deck visit gradually dissipates in the snuggery of the berth. Soon, overcome by the warmth, the sound of the water, and the occasional creak of a sheet block, all waking senses are blotted out in a final snooze.

0600   Breakfast this morning is monumental. While there are no sautéed kidneys, or a roast joint to hack from, it is nonetheless a veritable hunt breakfast. It was Norry's turn to play chef and since he could not decide between certain of his favorites, he finally threw together a varied offering of delights—sausage, scrambled eggs, creamed finnan haddie on toast, and hot coffee. I don't know why, but a breakfast of such scale inevitably makes me think of Mr. Pickwick. It is a long time since I read the adventures of that venerable gentleman, and I must confess that a few of his adventures threaten to run together in my mind with those of Surtees' John Jorrocks. But it is curious that despite the hoard of new fictional characters thrust upon you every day, there are none who come to mind so readily and are such a delight to know and whom you can so identify with simple pleasures.

Out on deck after breakfast, stuffed and happy. The Upmann is drawing nicely and all is well with the world. Long ago, I established a rule for the care and treatment of cigar smoking. To my taste, it is heinous to smoke a good cigar out in the wind. It burns too hot and too fast, and the aroma, which is half its pleasure, is dispersed in the breeze. Therefore, by mutual understanding, cigar smokers on deck duty are permitted to finish their cheroots under the dodger, relatively undisturbed but still on call if needed. It is true that some of our smokers can bend this understanding to the point of impatience on the part of their watch mates. Bobby Symonette (a cherished companion on former transAtlantic crossings and on many ocean races) can make even the most modest cigar last an hour, and I notice of late his Monte Cristos are growing longer and

Passage routine above decks—Frank washing up, WTS keeping the log, Bucky steering

longer. The custom does, however, give me an opportunity to sit quietly for a moment and savor the morning as well as the cigar.

I have been looking over that boast chart, otherwise called the deck log, and find that for the last four hours the boat has been sailing a course of 120° at an average of 5 knots and the speed is on the increase.

The deck log is a most important record. It is a primary, if rudimentary means of navigation, since through this record of course and speed, the boat's dead reckoning position is established. I once made a voyage from Annapolis, Maryland, to Charlotte Amalie in the Virgin Islands by dead reckoning alone because of the mechanical failure of all other means. The dead reckoning also is a basic input into the calculation of celestial fixes. For all of these reasons, the deck log should be scrupulously honest and, to all intents and purposes, so it is. Why, then, call it a boast sheet? Well, human nature being what it is, the log infallibly goes the way of all flesh. To begin with, there is an unavoidable, if subtle, competition which exists between helmsman and helmsman and watch and watch. When given a course to steer, the helmsman makes it a point of pride to hold the boat along the required course as closely and as speedily as possible. But it is impossible to steer a boat in an unswerving, arrowlike flight. It does not move in what we presume to be the relatively constant environment of the space ship. Instead, because of its response to wave action and fluctuating winds, and the tendency to charge up or down due to the changing balance, a boat's course is made up of swings to left and right of the desired course, some longer lasting than others. It is the helmsman's duty to assess the average of a steering period. The new atomic submarines have inertial guidance systems which record all such divergence and arrive at a precise answer. But a human helmsman must use his judgment and subconsciously he will favor an estimate of course and speed which makes him look good.

There is no conscious desire to cheat. After all, that would be ridiculous since there is no escape from the reality of position. You cannot will yourself somewhere else. Those days disappeared with the Arabian Nights. Unfortunately, the navigator is dependent on the deck log for part of his background of information in arriving at a fix. It shakes him up when his computations and the D.R. are at great variance, and he spends several harried hours trying to work out the differences.

0700   Our run for seven full days has been 1173 miles. It leaves 680 miles to Wolf Rock, a lighthouse landfall in the western sea approaches to Britain. We have been making an average of 167 miles a day. Yesterday was a gasser, a bust day. I am grateful that we are not racing. You would think that on the great big ocean what happens to one boat in a race happens to others as well, but such is not the case. Unless there is a very large and dominant weather system prevailing, the weather at sea is a complex of many smaller local conditions. There can be isolated squalls and showers in one part, while miles away clear skies are the order of the day. So it happens that one boat can be relatively becalmed while yonder, over the horizon, another can be enjoying a rail down breeze. The soothsayers of the rules committee would have it that since this weather travels, the conditions average out, but too often unhappy experience has proved the contrary. For this reason, I am grateful that we are not racing. I'd have split a gut wondering how fast Dick Nye in CARINA or Hank du Pont in CYANE was going.

0800   And on the subject of the lower intestinal tract, the crew have been assuming test positions on the stern pulpit to see how it will be done when it must be done. As is their wont, there are complaints about the coldness of the metal of which the pulpit is made and about the unfortunate placement of a stern chock. Surely, is the unspoken comment, it must be clear, even to an idiot, that anyone designing a boat should take the possibility of a breakdown, and the ensuing horrible necessity, into consideration.

While in truth I share the dismay of the crew, I cannot help but think how our manners and mores have been influenced by technical progress. The invention of the inside toilet has not only exerted a powerful influence upon our standards of sanitation, but upon our code of behavior as well. The unhappy circumstance which now upsets us was once a normal condition on land and sea. Indeed, the very name "head" is a contraction of "knightshead," which was a grating that overhung the sea in the bow or head of the boat. Here, in the eyes of the ship, in the days when knighthood was in flower, was a place reserved for the gentleborn sword and mace wielders to attend certain bodily wants while exchanging knightly viewpoints. But this aspect of obeisance to rank was not the customary order of the day, for even in the midst of a feudal and tyrannical society certain elements of democratization and leveling persisted. Not the least of these was communal toilet facilities. It is difficult to retain arbitrarily imposed social conventions of rank when one is being just another human animal.

But we are spared the perils of democratization. We have been so involved in the sorry contemplation of this affront to our privacy that we had momentarily forgotten that our vessel is very well founded. She has another head, hidden from view and memory. She was built to provide facilities for a paid hand in the fo'c'sle, including a head. She never carried such a man, and the space above it has been usurped for the storage and generally is crammed chock-a-block with racing sails. Out of sight, out of mind. But we remembered, we remembered.

Bucky manfully clears an operating arena around the precious utility. By reassignment of berths, the port forward berth is cleared for sail stowage. Skip, who has been displaced from his nest, moves aft to share the use of my berth, since we are on opposite watches. Until now, I had been enjoying the loneliness of command by keeping the berth to myself. One more surrender of a perquisite of rank. The leveling process begun by the toilet strikes again.

A cozy nest is built around the throne. It is padded like a space capsule, the most comfortable head ever seen. It is lined with sail bags from sole to overhead. Bucky reports the arena ready for action. And action it sees. After a while, the pent-up rage of nature is assuaged and the ship's company returns to the contemplation of loftier things.

0900   The sky is breaking clear again. It presents a very dramatic picture. In the foreground the bright sun creates a sparkling sea which is seen against the last vestige of the overcast that still hangs over the horizon. There ensues a flurry of picture taking by our own Mathew Brady, who uses all eleven cameras several times. To make matters even more inspiring, the wind continues to increase. We are on a course of 115° at a speed of 6.5 knots.

Frank gets a morning sun line. The indicated longitude falls across the embrace of Jupiter and Luna and confirms our position. Frank positively glows with pleasure. At last, he has an opportunity to exercise his newly acquired skills as a navigator. We have sailed together for donkey's years, but this is his first trip in the role of navigator. He recently has taken up the study of that art and science and he now faces a real test of his knowledge. For this reason he frets when there are no sights to be had, and he crows when things work out to confirm his divinations. I took the chance of signing him on such a long voyage as navigator because Frank is a no-nonsense sort of fellow who will not take on a job unless he feels he can do it. Besides, he needs the practice in navigation and I in checking navigators.

He obviously has prepared for this voyage in a most thoroughgoing manner. No matter what sort of abstruse information pertaining to our navigational problems one asks for, he has it extracted and filed under a suitable heading in what he calls his "cookbook." He has a passion for precision and detail, a most laudable quality in navigators. His only weakness now is the inability to snatch a sight of a now-you-see-it-now-you-don't star. Some long-practiced navigators seem to perform this as though they were making wing shots, but Frank will get it too. All it takes is practice.

His very size communicates reassurance. To see his bulk stretched across a chart table, his backside jammed against one bulkhead and his head braced against another, makes him appear a Gibraltar of men. He is locked in and immovable, like the Baltimore Colts' defense line. So he looks braced below. But on deck, his quiet bulk at the wheel as he stares off at the horizon is more reminiscent of those Landseer engravings we had in the dining room of our house when I was a boy—perhaps one of the noble stags or even one of those great guardian dogs, big and impassive. Whatever he may seem to be, the embodiment of a sentry rock, a defensive left guard, stag or mastiff, he is a great guy to have aboard.

1200   The day continues to be beautiful, a rarity on this trip. We wallow in it. Shirts are coming off as we peel to the bare skin. There is lots of back scratching; we were so long encased in long johns. Our course 115°, the speed a sprightly 7.5 knots.

1400   Steaming as before. Course 115° and now our speed is up to 8.4 knots. The wind stays in the southwest, but the sky is beginning to cloud over once again. What gives? The barometer remains high, a most unusual high.

The crew is happy, but there is a noticeable squirming and an increase in shifting from one haunch to another on the part of the sitters. "Teakitis," a cockpit affliction, is back again. Unupholstered teak is the bane of the long-sitting man. One wonders how Bernie Baruch managed that park bench for all those years.

1700 Happy Hour once more. We fraternize again, but in stronger symbols of friendship—martinis. The desire for a sip from the cup that overwhelms has been sneaking up. A vagrant thought was aired to the effect that it might be nice to have one—not a suggestion, mind you, just an opinion. The response was clamorous, at least from the older members of the crew. The authority that a warm martini can assume is remarkable. Not that we are partial to them warm. We have no ice. The water temperature is 56°, the coldest thing around; we try to cool them there.

I make an attempt to contact Ocean Station Ship JULIETTE in order to find what surprises the weatherman holds in store. The younger crew members also want to find out if JULIETTE has any ice cream (although it is certain that they would not expect us to go out of our way in order to get them a couple of ice cream cones). It's just sublimated rancor over our martinis. There is no success for either cause.

1800 As a last social note, we had stew for dinner and then out on deck to recover. It's rough to have to sack out after a heavy meal, although we do it

The break of the watch during a Fastnet Race—Bucky, Mike Blake, Cleody, Bobby Symonette, WTS

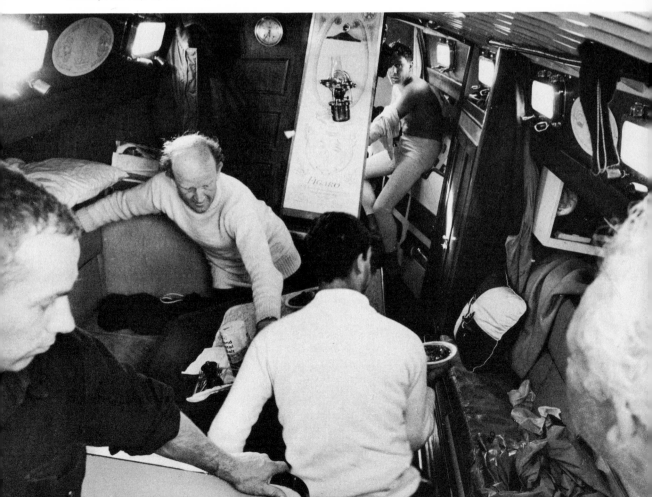

most of the time. However, in this case, the starboard watch should be in good sleeping form by 2200. Course 115° at 8.0 knots.

2200   The night's dews, darks, and damps oppress us once more. A misty drizzle has set in just in time to greet the port watch. Hot cocoa or tea all around; an exchange of pleasantries, and the ship quiets down once more to the routine of steer and snore and the restless prowling of the deck in search of any chafe which could be eroding our running rigging.

The passage routine has stabilized, there is no impatience, no boredom. The days go by rapidly, which in itself is strange, for normally a repeated routine brings with it a measure of boredom. This is not our case. The boat rushes along in the night, a cushion of gray foam under her forefoot. She alternately lifts and settles as the moderate seas pass under her. She sets a tireless purpose. We are not quite as tireless, but are certainly filled with purpose. We are trying to get across as quickly as we can and we are helped along by the quips, pranks, and meals, making it a most pleasurable passage thus far.

IX

PASSAGE ROUTINE

The first few hours after putting out to sea are not noticeably strange or different for the small-boat sailor. He goes about his tasks in very much the same manner and mood as when he left the dockside. Certainly, he is conscious that he has committed himself to a relatively frail vessel in which to go out on a great and sometimes violent immensity. No matter how hardened or casual he may be, he cannot avoid the sensation growing out of that fact. But in the first few hours, as a rule, no out-of-the-ordinary physical changes take place to make the break with the immediate past. If it were not for the movement of the boat and of the sea, his work would be an extension of what he had been doing just a short while ago. His hours of work and of sleep are still a continuation of shoreside living.

The first change is a subtle one. The watches are chosen and he is told by the skipper to get some sleep at 1:00 P.M. Hell, he hasn't done that since kindergarten! (Unless, of course, he is a veteran of other passages.) So he starts out by not being able to sleep when he should. It is a rather quiet and insignificant way into a complete upset of his normal habits acquired over the years. Every pattern of sleep, work, and relaxation is subjected to change. His hours are different. He is subjected to the wind and sea's whim. He must perform difficult physical tasks when cold, hungry, or even ill. His nervous system is strained when the boat is pushed beyond comfortable limits and under these conditions he is not rested or slept out. It sometimes takes days to get settled in. On shorter races one never does.

On a long voyage the settling in sneaks up on you. The ease and spell of the passage routine takes over. The strangeness goes. You sleep and eat well. The odd hours seem normal. You take time to look at the sky and the sea. There is, in this tumbling waste around you, a certain order and beauty and you are part of it. Preparation for a threat of violence from the sea is faced as a job of work, a little more disagreeable than you would like, but you know that this, too, will pass. Your tipsy world is accepted as a natural state of things. You accommodate yourself to it as you do to the boat's constant movement.

Ordinarily, one would place this sort of accommodation into the same order of experience as those indulged by college boys when they pile twenty-six men into a telephone booth, or stand under a shower for twenty-two hours. Who needs it? But the hardship or endurance is not the central factor of the experience. It isn't the hardship which brings the inner harmony to this part of the passage, although extreme physical reactions do heighten sensation; the secret lies rather in the fact that you are concentrated on one thing—moving the boat along the desired course as rapidly and safely as possible. There are few instances in men's lives when they are so utterly concentrated over so long a period on a single purpose. It becomes the central purpose of every waking moment and is made possible by the fact that you are cut off from every other kind of problem, interest, or diversion. Importantly, it is not an individual experience. It is the common incentive for every man on the boat. There may be disagreement as to the best way to accomplish the goal, but none as to purpose.

And so there you are, part of a consonant group, one-directed as men rarely are. You are isolated on your bounding wooden island under the bowl of the sky which limits the circle of the sea around you. For a time, at least, the rest of the world can go hang—unless, of course, you are racing. Then you widen your interest to include those you want to beat. This stage of a passage is a vigorous sort of Nirvana, a muscular way to reach the peace and concentration said to be the goal of certain Oriental religions.

X

A BREWER'S DRAY

JULY 8—THE NINTH DAY

0200   The wind is shifting aft, now blowing right up our exhaust. In order to keep FIGARO footing, we head up slightly on the port jibe. When we run dead down wind it slows us down. Our course is 120° at 8 knots. The sky is overcast and there is a heavy mist, giving an eerie flavor to the night. We expect any moment to hear the hound of the Baskervilles.

The navigator suggests that we should make every effort within reason, short of stopping the boat, to keep her on the planned trajectory. Ever since we discovered ourselves north of the great circle we have put corrective southing into our course, but he still has visions of landing in Reykjavik or Fayal, thereby nipping his reputation as a navigator in the bud. Nuts to him! We have our own problems. We remind him that the navigator's job is to tell us where we are, not where to go. After all, each department must maintain its own prerogatives—if they don't, who will?

0400   Once again, frustrated in efforts to get dawn stars. Only Jupiter is out and he is playing peek-a-boo in the clouds. This is a hell of a way to navigate. Sights have been few and far between. Only one sequence to give us a running fix, one crossing of Jupiter and the moon, the rest has been a rag bag. We have no thought but that we will hit our landfall on the nose. There are too many new aids for navigation to miss our target for the want of sights. Yesterday, for instance, we got an extremely long-range consol bearing on Bushmills in Ireland. The bearing locked with our D.R., so that sights or no, we are on target. We got the long-range signal by hooking the radio-telephone antennae to the Zenith portable.

Our course 112°, speed 7.8 knots, barometer steady.

0500   The accident to the head has altered the ship's routine, but has not yet stripped us of the veneer of custom and manners. Ordinarily, using one head instead of another would not be of importance. In this case the exchange makes for a marked difference, because before leaving we took all the doors off the boat, with the exception of the one which closed off the regular head. Despite our desire to lighten the boat for racing, we held on to that one door in order to maintain some proprieties. Now our ship has been turned into an open-plan suite with exposed plumbing.

We cannot quite regress to the mores of the seventeenth century when an intimate bodily function was performed in plain view of one's companion in conversation. It is still a shock when reading memoirs of the Restoration to encounter incidents of great ladies relieving themselves in the presence of swains, or that in the courts of Louis XIV and Louis XV, the same kind of relief in public view was enjoyed. We cannot make that transfer to older custom with any degree of aplomb. Ours is no private closet in the Court of the Sun King. When our mariners go to their sail-bag-lined closet, it is more like a Hong Kong slum, all rags and bodies.

Privacy, once experienced, is hard to surrender. We now go when permitted rather than when we will. It is the problem once described so feelingly by King Edward VII, who, when instructing a prince in kingship, told him to sit down whenever he could and to relieve himself at every opportunity that presented itself. Our method is to abandon the below decks at the break of the watch to him who must go, thus turning the entire boat into a private closet. The time allotted is quickened. There is a sense of pressure and haste. Gone is the opportunity for protracted rumination. This is no place for a Leopold Bloom in his jakes, no place for the stream of consciousness recall of Dublin days and nights, no wondering if Molly really is taking music lessons or remembering how delicious the kidneys tasted. There is only the sense of an unspoken comment: Get on with it, mate, I want to sleep.

Course 128°, speed 7.6 knots. Barometer steady (despite open plumbing).

0700   Miles made good since departure St. John's, 1361.

1030   The wind veers slightly; it is now on our quarter. The spinnaker pole is squared and the old Raymond chute is pulling like a mule. We are able to go back to a course of 112° at 7 knots.

The sun peeps out from time to time. Norry at the wheel hears the wild clash of palm fronds and dons his Yale Class of '36 boater. It is a sporty straw, replete with blue band and large class letters emblazoned in white. He has been moved to honor the return of summer.

1100   It is now 12 noon G.M.T., our D.R. position 50–56 N latitude and 17.45 W longitude.

1130   The clocks are moved ahead an hour on the half hour and luncheon is served.

1315   Frank gets a latitude sight which, when crossed with our advanced morning sun line, puts us some 3 miles west and 1 mile north of D.R. That's close enough.

1500   The wind is playing tricks, working around to the WNW. We are forced to jibe. The course 118°, speed 7.8 knots, barometer level.

1800   I have made lasagna for dinner. The method of its preparation, from canned ingredients, is to build up imaginative layers between sandwich levels of pasta—meatballs, cheese, tomatoes, onions—flavored with garlic and oregano to taste. The non-consistency of the recipe affords a surprise-party atmosphere to the meal. It is impossible to recognize what you are eating until you have bitten into it.

Skip, who shows special affection for a certain few garments, rolled out of his sack looking more and more like an agent for Jack Kerouac. Skip is the beat generation's representative on board. He is determined that when he sets foot in England he will be sporting a beard. But nature seems to be plotting against him. The scraggly growth, along with his baggy long johns, marks him a product of a liberated prep school. On the other hand, there is a curious parallel between the clothes worn by the progressive-school boy and those sported by our high-Episcopal schoolmaster mate. There must be a unifying principle to be developed from this, but for the moment it escapes me.

Skip, despite his scraggly whiskers, has stood up to the trip very well and I am pleased. In the early part of the trip, when we were going through the low, he was quite obviously fighting for stomach stability. But during his private anguish he clung manfully to his bunk which was pitching and tossing like a bronco with a burr under the saddle, served all of the wheel tricks and other duties without demurring or faltering. He even made trips to the larder, between qualms, for cheese and bread and for peanut butter sandwiches, life's great staples for Skip. He even shows preference for these over the *haute cuisine* offered on board. This is a source of deep disappointment to the ship's head chef, his father. He washes his chaws of sandwiches with a concoction made from a lemon-flavored instant powder. Until now, his struggle for stomach stability, coupled with the load he places on his digestive system by his choice of diet, has kept him somewhat subdued. Now, with better weather, and his sea legs gathered, Skip has opened up a bit and seen fit from time to time to give us the benefit of his point of view. It is a fresh view of the world, expressed half in a cant redolent of the jazz scene. He has a sly wit and a wry judgment of many of the men and institutions which we, his elders, accept on their face value. I see that I have something to reckon with in the not too distant future.

2100 The wind has shifted around again, coming in from straight aft. We should jibe, but why hurry, we are cruising. Why make all that fuss now? How much better when everyone can join in the fun.

Course 12°, speed 6.3 knots, barometer steady.

2200 The day nears its end as it began, drizzly with heavy, hanging clouds overhead. God's in his heaven, Poseidon's below, and we're for England.

By the way, England is leading Australia in the Test Matches. We hang around the radio expectantly while a BBC voice reports it to us. We cheer each over and run. It would be even more interesting if we knew what they were saying. That's all, chaps.

JULY 9—THE TENTH DAY

0400   The dawn struggles out from under a dense cloud cover. If it were not for the fact that at sea one becomes long suffering (what is there left to be), I could get pretty tired of this kind of morning. If it has any virtue, it only can be to protect us from hostile aircraft and from sunburn. Poor Frank has no chance to practice. There is nothing more soul-satisfying for a navigator than to get star sights at dawn or twilight, have them work out into a tight cat's cradle, and then diffidently pick up a very sharp 4H pencil, put it into the middle of the mircro snatch and say, "We are here." But not much chance for that so far. We will probably carry this weather right into Cowes.

0600   Awakened to the smell of corned-beef hash cooking. It overrides other rare odors. We are swarmy in our many layers of clothing, each man locked into his own particular fragrance. This morning, for instance, I thought I smelled a horse. When I turned to look, there was nobody around but me.

0630   We have jibed again and squared for Bishop's Rock. Jibing yesterday ruined another potential title for Norry's account of the voyage. His first choice was, "To England by Braille." This was spoiled when Frank got a sight. His second choice was, "Starboard Tack to England." Then we jibed.

0800   I AM SHAKEN TO THE CORE. I have been put upon. When Norry turned this lovely yacht into a common carrier, what with his eleven cameras, cases upon cases of film, and his Tom Swift Electronic Portable Dark-room, I looked upon it as a foible of a shipmate. I let it pass. But now, together with the Clan Buchanan, Tiny Tim the Landseer Stag, and James the Lesser, known as Bucky (they both wear Buchanan headgear), he has turned this once-proud racing yacht into a *Brewer's Dray.*

For days, the Lesser Buchanan has been furtively drawing cases of beer out of secret hiding places; from the sail lockers, from the bilges and from the lazarette. (It would be no surprise to learn that the hard lump under my mattress, which I presumed to be a spare set of mainsail battens, was yet another case of beer.) Now, brazenly, he dives down in my full sight and comes up with still another case, assuring me as he had done each time that it is the last one. When I think of the gear and goodies that I hesitated to bring, nay, even sent by expensive air freight, because I believed the boat would be too deeply burdened, I am moved to indignation so keen that I am reluctant to drink the stuff. Being a realist, I swallow my chagrin and still another mouthful of beer.

The shock of discovery that I had been put upon is at the heart of my reaction to the unfolding scandal of the beer, more so than any thoughts about the probity and loyalty of the crew. After all, it was a prank and successfully pulled off. The trouble is that it was on me. Perhaps I take the burdens and perquisites of command, to say nothing of ownership, too much to heart. In any case, I am mollified by the assurance that this was not a planned stunt, it just turned out that way. It seems that while in Halifax the crew were invited by a distinguished

Haligonian yachtsman and brewer to visit his brewery. Having expressed so much admiration for his plant and product, they found, on returning to FIGARO, eighteen cases of beer stacked in the cockpit. They were faced with affronting either their recent host by rejecting his generous gift, or my orders—so guess what? In my constant search to find the brighter side of any given set of circumstances, I convince myself that beer is at best an ephemeral cargo. The boat is less burdened every day. Drink up boys! We'll soon be back in racing trim.

Tiny Tim Buchanan drinks beer with the regularity of a time signal from W.W.V.; his sequence is one tube every forty-six minutes. The man is a veritable distillation mechanism, turning brewer's gold into waste by reverse alchemy. We, the new-day Pascals, can no longer consider man as a thinking reed. He is a drinking reed, an unfeeling pipeline from the beer can to the waiting sea.

It is only of late that I have become aware of the unholy union between the Buchanans. It started with the fact that they both wear the tam of the Clan Buchanan. Their partnership is proof of the theories concerning uniforms. Clearly, the value of a uniform exceeds the rudimentary purpose of recognizing one's friends or enemies. It has the power to unite diverse personalities toward a common purpose which may be foreign to either when alone. In this case, the uniform is only a tam—a small thing it is true, but such a violent piece of headgear that awareness of it is inescapable. The pattern for the tartan must have been chosen by a color-blind chief who indulged a part-time passion for action painting and must have been picked in a fit of blind rage during a black night of fog and mystery. Its colors, so help me, are lemon yellow, purplish blue, black, vermilion, and white. The Buchanans must certainly have been brave men. They hid from nobody.

The tams were introduced and left on board by the brave Celt and Swedish Highlander, Knud Reimers, during last year's race to Marstrand in Sweden. The headpieces have been known to light up the ship with their fluorescence, even on the darkest nights.

0900　　Tiny Tim, the navigating Buchanan, announces that as of 0800 D.R. we have made good 1515 miles for a daily average of 168 miles.
　　Course 106°. Speed 6.0 knots. Barometer steady.

0930　　The sun breaks through and the navigator gets a sun sight, assisted by James the Lesser, who takes time from the chronometer. The sight puts us back of our D.R. some 5 miles—a ridiculous waste of time, truly.

Skip, after considerable pressure, explains his reluctance to shave. By some peculiar amalgam of reasoning, he feels that imprisoned in his beard are all of the adverse magics to be found in Samson's hair, Pandora's box, and the bag of the winds. Once freed, this collection of furies would rage against us. Being hardy mariners, we are willing to brave the consequences in order to have the pleasure of seeing his face once more. He is moved, and is considering it.

1200　　The watch is relieved as a haggis is piped or threatens to be piped around. Chili, beans, chopped onions on rice—what digestions!!

1300   Frank, frustrated once more in an attempt to take a noon sight, has suggested to Skip that perhaps his shaving would clear the skies.

1305   Our navigator has been planted on deck, patiently playing hide-and-seek with the sun. From below, we can hear him call, "Stand-by"; followed by, "Mark." He must have finally snatched a latitude sight.

1310   A most interesting ten minutes; flotsam at sea is always interesting: the watch on deck spotted a nearby unidentified object. A long discussion, followed, naturally, by the choosing of sides. Group A calls it a mooring buoy; the alternate group, far more dashing, names it a floating mine. No one could reasonably explain the presence of a mooring buoy at longitude 13° 7′ W and latitude 50° 28′ 8″ N, far from a gas dock, or what a mooring buoy would be doing with all those barnacle-encrusted protuberances. The weight of opinion swings to a mine. It is more exciting that way.

1325   The age of miracles! Yuri Gagarin may really have made it.

SKIPPER IS SHAVING!

1630   A lovely, lazy afternoon. Tiny Tim was right. Skipper's fears were groundless. Soon after he shaved, the sky cleared and the sun in all friendly glory shone. Norry is down to one layer of clothing and two cameras. Jack steers with one hand and hides gaping yawns with the other. Inspired by Skip, a rash of spruce-up-and-feel-better has broken out. The captain brushed his teeth, so did the navigator, who said that everything he ate of late tasted like mentholated cigarettes.

The wind is aft and very light.

1900   The vessel is settled down for the first of the three night watches. We had a splendid Happy Hour. Sunshine, rum, pineapple juice, lime juice. Skip had a warm, foaming beer. We sang along with BBC on an exceedingly light Light Programme. Dinner was excellent—Chicken Cacciatore—relished by all hands.

In the midst of Happy Hour we jibed to the starboard tack. A smart racing maneuver, the pole is dipped, snapped to the alternate guy, and trimmed into position in one flowing movement, sheer poetry in action. We congratulate ourselves and have a freshener. Course 110°. Speed 6.01 knots.

1930   Could Skip be right about the fury pent up in his beard? The sky is clouding over again. Very heavy cloud formations appear in the west. Ordinarily, this is a sign of miserable weather for the next day. It seems hardly likely, since the barometer continues to stay high and fairly steady. The line shows a slight downward slant, but at a very minimal angle of decline. Perhaps it will only be a rain shower. *Quién sabe?*

2100   It is raining and very little else. Course 110°. Speed 6.2 knots.

2130   The wind has gone into the WNW and is light. We have put up the light chute and jibed once more. I hate to use this chute. It is gossamer—.75

How we look to the masthead man

ounces—and tears with an unkindly look. I try to save it for racing. But conditions being what they are, what will you?

Course 110°. Speed 4.8 knots.

2300   Wind going back into the SW, even lighter. This is like racing in Long Island Sound, except there is a scend to the sea that, coupled with the light air, makes us fight to keep the bag full and drawing. We must work hard to subdue its oscillation in the roll—to keep it from snagging, from hourglassing around the head stay and net, and from undue chafe. We cannot belay the sheet, it takes constant tending; a helluva way to cruise the Atlantic.

Course 92°. Speed 4.0 knots.

With the exception of having to sail on our toes, the night ends like most others—drizzle and unloveliness. The ship's company is hale, although I occasionally hear a sniffle. Small wonder; we have been rained upon steadily. I feel webs growing between my toes inside the boots. Despite this, the crew is in fine fettle. As for me, I nurse a bruised spirit. I have almost grown to dislike beer.

JULY 10—THE ELEVENTH DAY

0400   We greet a gray-fingered dawn while sitting in a drizzle. Again, a dispiriting promise for the day. The barometer, which looked as though it was stuck, is showing a slight fall. The reading, however, is still above the seasonal average—30.24. Course 90°. Speed 6.0 knots.

0500   We see one of the first outriders of the shore existence, a trawler, two miles to port.

0600   Bucky noisily rattling pots in his diner, The Sailors' Rest.

In one of its periodic roll-overs, the old Raymond chute snagged between the spinnaker pole lift and the net. How defies explanation. We got it down, set the old Hood spinnaker in its place, and then jibed. Old spinnakers make cruising a little more relaxed. We always watch a new one like a hawk.

A slight casualty during the jibe. We lost one of the blocks on the main boom foreguy tackle. Someone forgot to tie a figure-eight knot in the end of the line and it ran out through the block. Tying this kind of knot is such an elementary and almost automatic precaution that the failure to do so in this case is a little disturbing. We may be letting down too much; getting too casual. The sea punishes careless sailors.

The tear in the Raymond chute is repaired and it is stowed in its bag. Course 110°. Speed 6.5 knots.

0730   The drizzle had changed to rain. It has just stopped.

0800   Distance made good as of now—1648 miles. Yesterday's run, a puny 133 miles for an average of 165 miles a day.

1200   A trying drizzle once more and the wind dropping.
   Course 115° at 5.6 knots.

1230   A very wan sun peers through the muck overhead, enough for the navigator to get a sight. The wind continues to sag.

1245   We hear a BBC shipping forecast. The British Isles have a most vexing pattern of weather. Two great permanent systems vie for influence of the weather over the Islands. One is the Arctic air mass, which sends cold, wet depressions down from the direction of Iceland; and the other is the warmer high, roughly centered over the Azores which moves up and down the western coast of Africa and Europe. When the Azores' high advances north and east enough to hook over the peninsula at Brest and spreads over northwestern Europe, then the lows are held to the north. When the Azores' high retreats, then the opposite happens. The lows descend like wolves upon the sheepfold. It is therefore possible to have several different kinds of weather within a relatively small geographical area. An anti-cyclone in one place and cyclonic weather in another.

Britain and the sea are not only inseparable names in history, but they are linked now as they have always been by geography and economic necessity. She is a maritime nation with a busy intra-coastal trade and a large fishery industry and, therefore, a good weather service. The weather service has devised an explicit method for communicating weather news to mariners in British waters. The waters around the United Kingdom and Eire have been divided into squares of areas on a chart. In British fashion, these carry romantic names such as Fastnet, Biscay, Finisterre, German Bight, Rockall, etc. The weather reporter on the shipping service gives weather forecasts, present wind speeds, barometer readings, and sea conditions for each area. From these, the mariner constructs a weather chart. As each chart succeeds the past one, the speed, direction, and nature of the weather system become apparent. This record, added to the fairly accurate reporting of the weather, gives mariners a solid basis for decisions. We are in Fastnet and in an anti-cyclone. He said it, we didn't, but he promises more wind later.

With the expectancy of wind later, we turn the engine on. The spinnaker comes down. We cannot carry it with the power on. Our speed was down to 3 knots. The speed picks up to 5.8 knots and our batteries are getting a recharge. I guess power is here to stay.

1330   Land must be just around the corner; we see our second trawler.
   Course 110°. Speed 5.6 knots.

1400   There is an immutable law of the sea: as soon as you take sail off, you get a breeze.
   Course 110°. Speed 6.1 knots.

1430   Engine is off. The batteries fairly well up, and the spinnaker is reset. Course 110°. Speed 6.6 knots.

1500   A spanking breeze for a change. Our speed picks up to 6.9 knots. Frank gets an R.D.F. bearing on Mizen Head. A consol bearing on Bushmills indicates that it, too, is coming into a reliable sector. Ireland lies squarely in the north.

Bucky looks reverent; it's the sacred soil. His people are from County Cork and he is a wonderful distillation of many beautiful Irish characteristics that are shaded from view by the more popular legendary tales of American-Irish politicians and cops and such bully boys. He is a wholesome, direct, and religious young man. He went to a Benedictine prep school, a Dominican college, has Jesuits for relatives, and looks on Ireland as the birthplace of poetry and beauty. His intellectual guide in most things is St. Thomas Aquinas. His simple, straightforward rectitude is formidable and unexpected in these unchivalrous times, although he is not above joining in a prank such as the beer scandal.

1600   I thought that once having discovered the great beer swindle and expressed my indignation, I would be over it. But the Buchanans rub my nose in it and it rankles. I am constantly reminded of how I have been had. The Lesser Buchanan, upon signal from that beer-swilling Saxon, the Greater Buchanan, has gone down into the port sail locker and, after digging around under some spare running gear, come up with two more cases of beer. Wet and broken, the cardboard case spilled cans all over the cockpit floor. I can only presume that despite the extraordinary rate of consumption, the conspirators must be secure in the knowledge of ample supplies, and I can only mutter under my beery breath.

1730   Just heard another BBC shipping forecast; we are promised gales tomorrow. Albion holds out a traditional greeting. This is the third landfall for me on Britain, and each time we had a gale. The frequency of gales makes English yachtsmen into a hardened lot. While gales may not be exactly their dish of tea, nevertheless they occur often enough so that not only a type of boat but an attitude among yachtsmen has been the result.

Curiously differing characteristics in boats and attitudes are developed in other parts of the world as a direct reflection of sailing conditions. We, on the leeward side of the Atlantic, do most of our sailing in shallow waters with traditionally lighter winds. Our boats tend to be of shallower draught and therefore a little beamier in order to gain stability and with more comparable sail area to maintain speed in lighter airs. Our gales being less frequent, when one comes along our yachtsmen are prone to ride it out in anchorage, waiting for it to pass. The English boats are generally sharper and deeper with much less sail area. And the English yachtsman, having made his plans and come from London to go sailing, does so; even though he cannot count on a string of good days. He puts a deep reef in his main, puts on a spitfire jib, and goes out in anything up to a half gale. Not all of them do, naturally, but it is a heart-catching sight to see a small boat, snugged down to a couple of handkerchiefs of sail, stick her nose bravely out into a boisterous sea and slowly bob out of sight as she makes her way to some other yachting haven.

Our own wind has drawn ahead slightly, enough to make us change from the spinnaker to the Number One Genoa.

Happy Hour was a pleasant period of story-swapping. The captain fairly wallowed in reminiscences of his student days in Paris, telling so feelingly of the gay Bohemian existence that, to a casual listener, he might be indistinguishable from Henri Murger.

2200   Wind force 5. Cloudy, but no rain. The watch changes with no significant incidents. Course 113°. Speed 6.8 knots.

2330   We have just heard another cheerless forecast from the BBC. Gale warnings are posted in Fastnet and Sole. We are in Fastnet with force 8 winds prophesied. A force 8 wind on the Beaufort scale is roughly 34 to 40 knots, or 40 to 46 miles per hour.

The weather to come is described as a rapidly moving Atlantic depression of 985 millibars. Our own barograph is drawing a steady downward slope, now at 30″.

The Scilly Isles lie about 70 miles to the east. We are moving toward them on a course of 113° at a speed of 6.8 knots. The wind is in the southwest and about at force 5. Despite the threatening talk, the heavens are peaceful and calm. Jupiter and Saturn shine brightly on our starboard beam.

2400   We are all hale and well rested—ready for whatever tomorrow brings. The sea is an honorable adversary. We have all at one time or another been to sea in a gale, but the fact that they advertise themselves so far in advance gives one time to think about what it will be like. Anticipation, as a rule, is worse than the reality—or so we hope.

THE BEAUFORT SCALE

FIGARO is entering British waters and when in Britain, we do as the Britons do; and they are different. For instance, there the speed of the wind at sea is given in terms of the Beaufort scale. For everyone else, miles per hour is clear enough, but our English cousins have given us another one of their mysterious measuring symbols (12 and 36 as multipliers for inches—12 pence to the shilling, 14 pounds to the stone). In the Beaufort scale it is a series of forces from 1 to 12. Admiral Beaufort devised it in 1806, and if he went to the trouble to organize it, then by Jove, they are going to use it. It does have a virtue. Without measuring instruments it is impossible to give the wind speed absolute quantitative values. Hardly anyone is that good an observer and estimator. Each force of the Beaufort scale indicates a range of miles per hour in a single designation. The scale and its description follows:

Wind Force	Sailor's Description	Speed MPH	Speed in Knots	Estimate on Land	Estimate at Sea	Height of Waves
0	Calm	– 1	– 1	Smoke rises vertically.	Calm sea, like mirror.	0
1	Light air	1– 3	1– 3	Smoke drifts.	Ripples.	0–1 ft.
2	Light breeze	4– 7	4– 6	Feel wind on face, leaves rustle.	Small wavelets, low starry crests, no break.	Slight 1–3
3	Gentle breeze	8–12	7–10	Leaves in constant motion, small flag lifts.	Large wavelets. Scattered whitecaps.	Moderate 3–5
4	Moderate breeze	13–18	11–16	Raises dust and loose paper.	Waves take longer, form frequent whitecaps. Some spray.	Rough 5
5	Fresh breeze	19–24	17–21	Small trees begin to sway.	Large waves begin to form many whitecaps.	5
6	Strong breeze	25–31	22–27	Large branches sway. Umbrellas turn inside out.	Large waves, extensive whitecaps everywhere.	8
7	Moderate gale	32–38	28–34	Large trees in motion. Hard to walk against.	Sea heaps up and foam blows in streaks in direction of wind.	Very rough 8–12
8	Fresh gale	39–46	34–40	Twigs break off.	High waves, edges of crests break into spin-drift streaks.	8–12
9	Strong gale	47–54	41–47	Chimney pots and slates fly.	High waves. Dense streaks of foam-spume.	12–20
10	Whole gale	55–63	48–55	Trees and buildings damaged.	Very high waves. Sea becomes white and rolling.	20–40
11	Storm	64–72	56–64	Widespread damage.	Mountainous waves. Small boats lost to view for long periods.	40–45
12	Hurricane	72+	65+	Holy Mackerel.	Air filled with foam. Sea completely white. Visibility almost impossible. Phenomenal waves. Holy Mackerel.	45 feet & over

JULY 11—THE TWELFTH DAY

0200   The glass slowly falls. The night sky is dappled with broken clouds. The wind from the SSW blows at force 5, a moderate sea is beginning to build. In spite of the Sword of Damocles that the weatherman has hung over us, it is thrilling sailing and sitting at the wheel is an exhilarating experience. What a change from the recent past. Our barometer has a reading of 29.96, slightly under that of the barograph, which reads 30.05. Every time the barograph stylus is cleaned and re-inked it probably gets bent a little, thereby making it inaccurate for a precise reading. The stylus can be adjusted, but what we want from the barograph is a continuous record of experience, so we don't bother. The steepness of a slope is indication of the shape and speed of a depression or a high. Since we have both instruments, we are well protected.

Course 113°, speed 6.8 knots.

0330   The wind continues from the same direction at the same speed. It is always hard to believe on such a pleasant and peaceful night that a blow can be making up. The glass continues its slide.

0445   Round Island R.D.F. signal in the Scillys has been in range for a while. It bears 128°. We have altered course to 125°.

0600   Dawn blooms. We have been impatient to see what it will uncover. We see a clear sky spotted with broken clouds. It carries no visible threat. Perhaps the gale will pass us by, although the glass continues its slide.

We stoke up for anything to come. Our breakfast fuel is pancakes with maple syrup, bacon and coffee. I am reminded of a similar breakfast and Francis Chichester's reaction to it. Francis is a soft-spoken Englishman who performs difficult feats in a most diffident manner. Early in his life he flew a Gypsy Moth solo from England to Australia. Since then, he has done many adventurous things, including a singlehanded race across the Atlantic, which he won. During a particularly miserable Fastnet Race when Francis was navigator on FIGARO, we turned the Rock during a lull. The wind went down to 35 or 40 m.p.h. between gales. We tried a hot breakfast, our first in days. Because we were in the boisterous Irish Sea, we thought French toast and maple syrup would be easiest to manage. Francis looked on us as a strange lot, "eating fried bread and treacle."

0700   In spite of everything the BBC tells us, it is hard to convince ourselves that anything is brewing. It is a beautiful morning—bright sun, blue skies between the broken clouds, and the *glass has leveled out.*

0740   LAND HO!

Bucky was at the wheel, everyone else with his nose buried in a book. Looking up briefly, to prove my continued interest in the welfare of the ship, I suggested that he might soon see a lighthouse, sort of making light conversation.

"No," says he, "I can't see a lighthouse, but land frigging ho!"

He had had the land in sight for the last ten minutes and had restrained the

Near the end of the passage, and a gale is on its way

news so that when turning over the wheel, instead of telling the next helmsman the course, he could casually say, "Steer for that island." It's all a matter of personal style, very important at times.

0800 Everyone on deck for a look at these outlying inhabited rocks, a beer in every hand and pounding Frank on the back for a job well done. He had fewer sights than we normally take in the first two days of a Bermuda Race.

0930 Round Island abeam. We see a bleak and rocky land, some cultivated patches are visible on this beautiful morning—a storm-girt group of rocks reminiscent to us of the Isles of Shoals off New Hampshire.

1000 The BBC interrupts a music program to announce gale warnings in Fastnet, Sole, Finisterre, and Biscay. The affected area is widening. They must mean it, and with some urgency to interrupt a program. The English reverence for form seems to extend even to reluctance to interrupt a composition by Eric Coates. It is still a beautiful morning—the sun is bright, the heavens, for the moment, show a few scattered clouds, the sea sparkles with a million diamond points of light, and the barometer is steady after its fall.

The clocks will be advanced to British Summer Time to put us in step with life on land. An early luncheon with cocktails, a little warm, but tasty—Manhattans, in honor of the girls we left behind us and to celebrate our landfall. I make a chicken curry, a good one if I am forced to say so myself. Everyone else must have been rendered speechless.

1100 A small squall passes over us. An advance agent? But the sun returns and we eat lunch.

I have prepared some alternative plans if the gale should come. We will shape our course to Falmouth and continue to listen to the shipping forecasts, as well as making our own observations. If conditions become too severe, we go into Falmouth. It is not far away and it is one of the few harbors for which we have charts aboard. If the gale is not severe, we will hold on for Cowes or some prior port. We can enter these on sailing directions.

The wind increases and we change the Number One Genoa for the Number Two jib topsail, carried over the working staysail. All other sails remain as they were. Our speed of 7.0 knots holds.

Instinct must have guided us in taking off the Number One Genoa at that particular moment, for as it was coming down, the luff wire parted near the head. We would have had to send a man to the masthead to retrieve the halyard; in addition, the Genoa might have flogged itself badly in this weight of wind.

1115 We sighted a cruising ketch ahead, the first sailing yacht we have seen since leaving home. She has just borne off, probably having heard the same foreboding broadcasts. She seems to be heading up for Penzance Bay, although she doesn't look a pirate or a pilot.

1130 Wolf Rock light is abeam. Our course is for the Lizard, 105° at 7.3 knots.

1347 The shipping forecast stresses gale warnings. The Atlantic depression has been split in two. One section is heading down over Finisterre, the other to go over Rockall. We probably will feel the influence of the depression to the north with southeast winds at force 8. If this catches us out, the English Channel will be an unpleasant place. A force 8 wind against the Channel tide, and the tide inevitably turns, creates a remarkably uncomfortable sea. We will stick with plan number two and make for Falmouth around the corner from the Lizard.

1430 The Lizard is in clear sight. We are sailing a course of 110° at 7.2 knots. I trust we are not getting blasé. *Sang-froid* is all well and good, but they still threaten to throw a gale at us. The watch below indicates its tension by sleeping soundly and the watch on deck, with the exception of the helmsman, reads on and on. The book club is hard at work. They want to finish books that were started. Once land life begins there may be less opportunity.

1700   Abeam of Lizard Head. The Lloyd's signal station makes signs with a blinker. After some mild perturbations on the part of signals officer Hoyt, he deduces that we are being asked to identify ourselves. He gets out the signal book, the half-mile ray light—we have no signal lamp on board!—and an exciting paperback, "The Guns of Navarone," to use as a shutter. Either the lack of speed of our transmission, the inaccuracy of our sending, or the absence of power of our half-mile ray makes us difficult to read. Figurative steam is seen coming from the station, a flurry of signals. I hope they don't get petulant or mistake us for smugglers or an invading force. Consternation abounds. I go below and after some weary repetitions succeed in raising the signal station on the radio telephone. They do not recognize us as the boat with whom they are holding such frustrating blinker dialogue. They ask us to give our position. We declare ourselves to be the boat directly under their nose. Why didn't we reply to his signal? I say our Aldis lamp has broken down. This saves our status and gives him a reasonable explanation. We are identified for all the world to know, and carry on toward Falmouth.

A suggestion is made that we hold on for Cowes. The reasoning given is that if we were at sea in a gale we would have no choice but to carry on, so why not here? But the captain and Bucky have been in the Channel during gales, once in a force 10 blow. They found out what it is like and don't care if they are never reminded again. With that dreadful suggestion taken care of, we decide to have a drink. And with martinis in hand we make our way toward the harbor.

Land Ho!

LATER

Into Falmouth, a snug and deep harbor. We were hailed by a launch in Her Britannic Majesty's Customs Service, directed to an anchorage, and boarded by two exceedingly pleasant gentlemen. They were extremely helpful, making sure that we would give them answers least embarrassing to us. An awkward moment arose when they asked for our engine number. In a lifetime of answering questions I have never before been asked for my engine number. I did not know where to find it. "It should be right on top of the engine," said one of Her Majesty's servants, and with that he borrowed a flashlight to have a look. None was visible. An embarrassing stalemate—they had a line on the form that cried out to be filled.

Bucky, who is not Irish and a relative of Jesuits for nought, explained that when an engine is maintained as well as ours and painted as often, the number is soon obscured, but that he would find it. He promptly dove into the engine compartment and shortly called out a most convincing series of numbers. These having been recorded as fact, the rites and ceremonies of arrival were completed. Her Majesty's Customs Service settled back to sample some American beer, which they found too tame, and cigarettes, which were more to their taste.

Our splendid relations with the Government of Great Britain were further improved when some time later the Customs launch took all but Bucky and Skip ashore, landing us at the public pier. H.M.S. MONGOOSE is a fine yacht club launch.

We were hardly ashore and stretching our legs when Frank stopped. He seemed to come to a quivering point. You could almost visualize one leg curled up under him. We followed his nose and read a sign saying, "Star and Garter." Frank said he wanted to do some research, he must find out if they took American money. They did. After a complicated series of instructions in what really amounts to a foreign tongue (we don't speak Cornish), we got a passable martini with which to salute the Tight Little, Right Little Island.

Down the middle of the street to a gate in a wall with a steep stairway going down behind it. We managed this safely and now find ourselves in the precincts of the Royal Cornwall Yacht Club. It is a former manor house of stone, steep-gabled and many-chimneyed. Very handsome in a most English way. We find our way into the bar, are instantly stood a round, and settle back to warm ourselves in fine hospitality.

Skip and Bucky joined us for dinner at the Yacht Club. The cooking was not as good as ours, but they prepared it, not us, and did the wash-up too. Then back to the boat for unbroken Z's. No more four-hour watches.

2330   The gale socked in, and the wind out of the southeast. Had we held up Channel we would be in for a miserable night of smash and bang. Cowardice has its own rewards, although in some areas it goes by the name of prudence. We are snug and comfortable. FIGARO is riding well to a 35-pound Danforth anchor. It is a little light for my own taste, but the 100-pound yachtsman anchor is buried under a mountain of gear. We don't use anchors at sea.

The hand on the boat behind is standing anchor watch. We ask if we can let out a little more scope in order to flatten the angle of the rode line. He gives his okay. Our transom swings by his bow by a whisker as we gyrate in the wind.

The decision to come into Falmouth was well made. We save wear and tear on our gear as well as ourselves. After so long at sea we are unaccustomed to a long, unbroken sleep, and from time to time one member of the crew or another wakens, hears the wind, and goes topside to see if all is well. We are sailors, safe in the heart of a sailor's England, the home of many of Elizabeth I's great captains. The noise of the wind as it sweeps down from the moors is comforting. It reminds us that we are safe. Out in the Channel each gust would have held its own threat.

XI

LANDFALLS AND ARRIVALS

A landfall on a foreign shore is the ending of one kind of time and the promise of another kind to come.

Up until the first spirit-catching sight of land, there is only a single-minded concentration on the business of getting there. Now, suddenly, we are aware that the adventure so long planned and anticipated is about to end. We are assailed by mixed emotions. The sense of excitement, which may have been lulled by the routine of the passage, is now reinvigorated. For now that the voyage is near its end, an unspoken feeling pervades, a desire to bring the passage to a close with dash and élan, fitting for such an adventure and for such a company. At the same time, mixed with this desire to get there is a sadness and a wish to prolong the enterprise. Soon it will be finished and there is reluctance to give it up.

Despite this undercurrent feeling of reluctance, the ship is sailed with greater sharpness and attention to details. No matter how long the sail has been or how tired we are, the first sight of land calls for greater energy. Sails are trimmed to save seconds where minutes, even hours, may have been thrown away during the passage itself. And from time to time, in this hand-busy period, one peers at the land, watching it unfold its form. Like a stage curtain opening ever so slowly, it is revealed as it rises from under the curve of the earth.

Each landfall is a separate experience, made so by the sailing and the place to which we have come. Sometimes a landfall is made at night. Then beauty extends in time. A landfall on Havana, during friendlier times, was such an unfolding drama. It is normally approached through sharp, triangular seas kicked up by the southeasterly wind against an east-flowing current. We are first made aware of Havana by a glowing aurora on the black horizon of the early night sky. It is the light of the city reflected from the underside of the heavens. After a time, the glow becomes more defined. Suddenly, at its bottom edge, like beautiful jewels set on a dark velvet background, we see an emerald-and-ruby cluster.

The jewels move higher on the horizon as we come nearer, then under it a string of pearls rises suddenly from the sea and dips as quickly from view, only to rise again as our shortening distance lifts it clear of the rolling seas. And then, as we are in the midst of making the approach to Morro Castle, we see that the beautiful emerald-and-ruby gem is a Texaco sign on a towering structure high over the city, and the string of pearls is the lights on the Malecon. But we don't feel cheated by this mundane transformation, for by now we are caught up in the finish of the race.

The wind generally drops in the shadow of Morro Castle, and with the easterly set of the current it can be a hard spot to get through. But you have to go through at that spot because that's where the finish line is. The boat quiets down as though any conversation, excited until now, would impede progress. FIGARO is nursed through, we finish and sail into Havana harbor. After the salt-clear freshness of the open sea, the hot smell of the harbor rises and hits you in the face. It is a jasmine garden in a garbage pit, but the Cubans greet you with fireworks and guitars. At least they used to. (Once we were greeted with 50-mm. machine-gun bullets.) The International Yacht Club, where you tie up, is a big, noisy bar.

That's one kind of arrival. Others stretch the nerves for a longer period. There may be a coral bar to skirt. Water breaks on the one hand, on the other jagged, high rocks loom. A sea may be rolling through the cut. The navigator stands by the helmsman, calling off the bearings, checking them off the chart as one succeeds another. The crew look elsewhere.

At times a landfall is made while still far out at sea. Puerto Rico is a volcanic island with a high dramatic silhouette. Approaching from the NW against a dawn sky, the distant mountains are a deep violet color and blend with the high columns of clouds which hover over them. The effect from a boat is that of a romantic painting—a lofty landscape painted in vibrant color rising from a pale sea.

Coming up New York harbor at dawn is to see a contemporary fairyland illustration. The tops of the huge glass towers are etched in sharply contrasting horizontal sunlight, while their bases disappear into the dawn haze which still clouds the quiet city.

Sometimes a landfall is made by day on low-lying land. You see Bermuda first as a gathering of clouds on the horizon. The sky is clear azure blue all around the inverted bowl, except for this one point of the compass. According to the navigator, under those clouds should be Bermuda. It looks like a bunch of clouds and nothing else to us. We cannot go for it. First we must skirt the off-lying shoals which are being approached at an oblique angle. We can only turn in to the land when Kitchen Shoals' buoy has been rounded. But we find the land is not really under the clouds. It is sunny and bright and fun. The clouds wait offshore to bring rain while you are asleep.

An arrival after a landfall brings an active mixture of feelings, of elation and of tension; then, suddenly, it is over. The hook is down. The boat, which has been alive with constant motion, suddenly is still, lifeless, placid. The ship is partially cleaned up—we cannot face a thorough housecleaning yet. We run out of things to do. Regular duties have come to an abrupt end. Our regular time sequences no longer hold. A bunch of Pavlov's dogs on a treadmill which has suddenly stopped running. New schedules and occupations are made, adapted to land. We have talked so much about our passage while we were on it that now there doesn't seem much left to say.

If there are family or friends ashore, we look forward to seeing them. When it is a new foreign shore, we look toward exploring it. But, for the moment, there is nothing to do but to have the ritual drink, congratulate the ship and ourselves for this successful conclusion, and begin to accustom ourselves to the idea of living ashore.

An Old World port—Falmouth, from which many of Elizabeth I's great captains sailed

XII

IN THE CHANNEL

JULY 12—THE THIRTEENTH DAY

0200   The wind howls like an avenging fury. The water is covered with flecks of foam. We are holding fast, although it is hard to see how. The wind is stronger now than at any time tonight. We make numerous trips to the deck, the wind whipping and snatching at our clothes. A little while ago we got out the 100-pound yachtsman anchor and set it. We see to the parceling on the anchor rodes and tuck in the flogging flaps of the sail bags which are piled on deck. Time is also spent peering ahead in the harbor to see how our neighbors are riding. If they break loose and drift down on us, we will be in trouble. So far, everyone is secure. The cabin heater radiates comfort after a tour of the deck.

0500   The wind has slackened—the worst is past. I have been standing an anchor watch. For the last two hours I could hear the wind change its rhythm. The wind blows with a pulsing action. As a gale comes in there is a contrasting rhythm of wind speed, sharp gusts punctuate the constant speed of the wind. As the gale heightens in force, the period of the gusts lengthens until, at the peak of the storm, the lulls are hardly discernible. As the height of the blow passes, the pulsing returns with the lulls becoming longer until the gusts become occasional, rather than regular. Now the slack periods are becoming extended. The back of the gale has been broken. I sack out.

0900   Intermittent bright sunlight and a slackening wind; however, it is still strong. The smoke from chimneys ashore is whipped away. The clouds scud across the sky. It looks promising; perhaps we will sail this afternoon. The met office, through the BBC, announces the gale warnings now have been posted in the east. They are now in the Dover, Tyne, Humber area. We came through unscathed and we are impatient to leave and complete the passage.

1257   We hear the shipping forecast. Someone is screwed up; maybe it is us. It can be interpreted any way you want to take it. We are told that there is another low behind this one, but no one seems to know how far. I feel optimistic about the lead time we have over this second low and propose that we leave at 1400. Frank and Jack take their leave, they are going to London and on to business. We have a farewell drink and begin preparations for departure. The

104

anchors are singled up, the Danforth taken in. The dinghy comes aboard. Somehow or other, we lost an oar during the night, probably blown right out of the boat. They were not tucked under the seats.

1430   We take off, the wind in the southwest at force 5. The ensign is dipped in return to salutes. Visiting yachtsmen are up on deck waving farewells. Everything is stowed and lashed for sea.

1500   We make our departure from St. Anthony's Point. The course is .097. The main and Number Three are set wing and wing, the Genoa is out to the end of the spinnaker pole taking us along at 7 knots.

The watches will be two-man—the captain and Bucky, Norry and Skip.

1800   The weather report sounds a little better. The gales have gone on east. For a while, according to BBC, it sounded as though a second one was hard behind. To verify this bleak outlook, our barograph took a sharp turn downward. However, we hold to our resolution. We will go on to Cowes rather than Plymouth or Dartmouth, our alternate ports.

Course .097. Speed 7 knots.

1840   Famed Eddystone Light abeam—no keeper, no compliant mermaids are visible. We are making good an average of 8 knots. Our dinner is ham-

Fastnet Rock

burgers, goosed up with any condiment which comes to mind. Our digestions still hold as monuments to reasonable boyhoods.

2200   The wind is piping up from 5 to force 6 and flawing from southwest to west. The sea is building up. We must outrace the blow, which apparently is coming.

In spite of these hidden threats, outwardly it is a fine night. We are making good time and all seems well.

JULY 13—THE FOURTEENTH DAY

0200   The sky is brilliant with stars for the first time since leaving St. John's, as the last of the clouds blow over us. The wind comes fresh from the northwest. We intentionally jibe but with a shocking wham, and break two battens in the main. We could have used an extra man on the main sheet. The wind force up to 6–7. Our course .087 at 8 knots.

0400   Portland Bill and the Shambles showing clear. We are 8 miles off the Bill, but even out this far the adverse tide makes for slow forward progress. The tides run very strongly here. In a race we once took the whole six hours to get past the Bill, being swept back on every tack.

0600   The tide turns favorable and we start making good time. The course is .085 at 8.0 knots, the wind force is 7. We had been carrying our full main and the Number Three Genoa wung out on the spinnaker pole. Now we have taken off the Genoa and are under the main alone.

0930   FIGARO enters Needles Channel. The spiny, chalk rocks on the starboard hand, from which the Channel gets its name, are being smashed at by seas and smothered in spray. A bright sun shines through intermittent rain squalls. We go from zoom to gloom in a twinkling. Because of the adverse directions of wind and tide, the mouth of Needles Channel is boiling, the water covered with foamlike soapsuds. We whip through.

1000   Finally into smooth water behind Hurst Castle. We are now scudding along under full main and nothing else. The smooth water, after all of that roll and go, is great. We burst into song.

1100   The wind is even stronger. We wear around to go on the other jibe. No use knocking the hell out of our mainsail, spars, or rigging any more than we can help. Close in shore, near the Squadron Castle, we can see yachts maneuvering for the start of the Cowes-Dinard race. We are entered in the race and for a brief, vain, glorious moment, talk of continuing on. But common sense returns. We have beaten the gale into Cowes, that's victory enough for this time.

We cross the starting line anyway, in front of the Squadron Castle, display our colors and receive loud hails from Gerald Potter and Johnny Coote, who are off for Dinard on the Royal Ocean Racing Club boat, GRIFFIN. Up the river we go to one of the sheltered trots, feeling sorry for the poor chaps who are off to Dinard. They are going to take a beating. (We learned later that a man was washed overboard from RAMROD and not recovered. At least three sinkings of yachts, with some deaths, were reported in three different places in the Channel due to this gale. The second low didn't catch us until we reached Cowes, for which we were properly grateful.)

Ashore to the Prospect to pick up mail. The Prospect is the house belonging to the Honorable Max Aitken (now Sir Max). It was once the sail loft for Ratsey and Lapthorn, whose sailmaking history goes back to sails for Nelson's fleet. Max has converted this into a charming apartment and a nautical museum, with dormitory accommodations for visiting yachting friends. The Honorable Max is coming down this afternoon, but we are to use his house as headquarters. To the Island Sailoring Club for lunch with the apostle, Alan Paul, the secretary of the R.O.R.C. He is about to leave for Dinard by ferry to preside at the finish. We watch boats that have abandoned the race straggle back. The racers are catching hell. It didn't seem so bad to us, but then it was not blowing as hard and besides, we were going with it. Those poor guys are beating into it. In addition, we have been out at sea for two weeks and consequently are a little hardened, but most of these fellows are fresh from the office. What a way to enjoy!

And so, in the happy prospect of the Prospect, we end our passage from St. John's to Cowes. There are few places devoted to yachting which have so much charm and tradition, and few friends such as Max, Uffa Fox, and Bobby Lowein with whom one can dine and be permitted to talk of the wonders so recently passed and of days and events to come.

RACING

TRANS-ATLANTIC 1963

Brenton Reef, Newport, Rhode Island, U.S.A.

to Eddystone Light, Plymouth, England

Running back from the Rock—Commander Michael Blake, R.N., and WTS

XIII

CRUISING AND RACING

If sailing across the ocean is the ultimate in cruising, then racing across is the distilled essence of the sport. While both adventures share the same theater of action, in many ways the experience is wholly different. The change is certainly not due to a difference in the behavior of the wind and sea. Man's puny changes of intention have little meaning to the more important business of the universe, to the cycle of threatening storm and frustrating calm which go on whether he's there or not. It is rather the yachtsman's attitude which undergoes sea change. It is the prod of competition which makes the difference.

During a race, every incident is magnified, each reaction heightened. The lack of wind is an agonizing experience, not to be borne philosophically. The engine, which can help a cruising man power through an area of calm, is now just another lump of iron since it cannot be used for propulsion. In a calm the boat just sits inert and lifeless while the crew is drained of energy and enthusiasm. When the wind and sea kick up, the boat is pushed to the limit of its structural capabilities. Chances are taken which would not be considered when cruising. Decisions to carry on in a threatening set of circumstances are made as a matter of course. There is nothing like skirting the edge of danger to make the glands put out.

It is a many-leveled competition which makes for the sea change. There is the direct contest with another boat, but there is also an abstract competition with time and distance. Abstract, because it takes place when you are alone. There is no one around, and so there is nothing to measure against. You want to go faster, but faster than what? The result is that you sail under a dominating and nagging idea—the thought that no matter how well you are moving, you ought to be doing better. Once the fleet scatters over the sea, there is no longer anyone with whom to match boat speed or ability to point. You work against an unknown potential.

Theoretically, it should not be difficult to reach an optimum speed. The job is to work at sail trim and sailing angle until the maximum attainable is shown on the speedometer (if you trust it). But it is not as simple as that. As an instance, when the wind, which has been ahead, tends to shift aft to a point where it is just possible to carry the spinnaker, the choice, as a rule, is to carry the bag. However, if this favorable shift is accompanied by a sizable running sea and gusty winds, the decision to go from reacher to spinnaker is not so clear. For, with the latter sail, and under these conditions, the boat hangs on the verge of taking charge in an uninvited roundup. The result is strenuous steering which affects the constant speed of the boat. When carrying the bag, the maximums shown on the steam gauge may exceed those shown when carrying the reacher; the speed with the latter sail is relatively constant. But the speed while carrying the spinnaker fluctuates. When fighting off a threatened roundup, considerable rudder pressure is applied, with a consequent drop in speed. This may lower the average, but the true average is not easy to estimate, for the high points of recorded speed have a euphoric effect. The low points on the gauge are beneath notice; one's objectivity disappears. It is only in the presence of competition that it is possible to find non-deniable proof.

Once, during a Bermuda Race, I raced alongside of FIGARO's near sister ship, WHITE MIST, under such conditions. We were both carrying spinnakers on a beam reach. WHITE MIST's main spar was fourteen inches higher than FIGARO's and because of her larger spinnaker, or because of the skills of her master, Blunt White, I usually had trouble with her in that kind of going. On FIGARO, as a gamble, we shifted to the Yankee jib topsail over a Genoa staysail and, to the amazement of all, slowly pulled ahead. It was one of the few times I could ever prove a thing I have felt to be the case and, unfortunately, still wonder about. (Conditions are never quite the same.) In a race, when sailing alone, the rule of thumb says carry the spinnaker whenever you can and you do it even though you wonder if the other sail wouldn't be better, to say nothing of easing the threat of broaching.

Racing down wind when a strong wind is blowing requires even more complicated decisions. For, at this sailing angle, a change from the spinnaker without question means a drop in speed through the water. If you take the gamble and carry on and the boat broaches, you run the chance of considerable damage. There is a deceptive sense of ease on board when running off. The spinnaker can be carried in high wind speeds, because the speed of the boat running off reduces the apparent speed of the wind, and because at that angle of attack of the wind the boat can be sailed relatively upright. This situation changes in a twinkling if the boat takes charge, or goes into an involuntary or "Chinese" jibe, for then she puts herself broadside to the wind. When this happens in a heavy wind and sea, she is brutally knocked down and you face the potential of being swamped, in addition to possible damage to the boat, spars, sails, and gear. The decision to shift from spinnaker to wung-out Genoa is made only after long soul-searching analysis of sea and wind conditions and the quality of the helmsmanship. What makes the choice even more difficult is that it is hard for a racing man to assume that when they say danger, they really mean him. So, during a race, the decision generally favors carrying the spinnaker. Damn the adrenals—full speed ahead!

These are racing decisions. In cruising, the thought never even enters one's head. Without question, you shorten down for comfort and safety and, surprisingly, this shortening of sail is accompanied by only a slight drop in speed. Time and time again, racers have reported that on having lowered the main in order to reef or make repairs, and while carrying on under the Genoa alone, there was no significant drop in speed. They held on in this way until the worst of the blow was over and did themselves little harm in the standings. But it is not the sort of decision you make beforehand; you may get backed into it after the fact. Theoretically, the choice of taking off the main as against carrying a reefed main should hurt ultimate speed and therefore can not be a pre-planned tactic.

This is a sampling of the decisions as to the sails to be carried. Naturally, the more sails there are, the more questions. But there are enough other kinds of decisions to make, which can crowd out the quiet contemplation of a sunset. There is always the one about the most effective course to steer. I have simplified this problem to a small degree by giving up the sport of wind hunting. I have absolutely abandoned the idea of trying to make sense out of radio weather reports when well offshore. To my mind, wind hunting at sea is a most useless enterprise. The speed of a sailboat is too slow to do anything about major weather systems, other than going on the tack away from hurricane-scale depressions. Favorable wind hunting is okay for airplanes doing 650 miles an hour. The smaller didos within the major system seem to be as much of a mystery to the weatherman as they are to you. This is the case out on the ocean. It is not always true when sailing near the land. Changes near a land mass are smaller and the met man has more reference points to work with. Important advantages can be gained in these near-in waters by proper information and interpretation. On the ocean, I have settled for my own weather observations from where I am, and do the best with what I have. It has somewhat reduced the business of course changes, at least in the hopeless business of looking for a breeze.

But in the matter of course, there are also straightforward tactical decisions to make.

Boat speed can be increased by freeing the boat a bit when sailing hard on the wind, or going up a little higher on the wind when running dead off. The natural question is how much divergence is valuable in the total strategy? Traverse tables are one scientific answer, but in a shifty wind, needing quicker responses, traverse tables are a cumbrous device. I use a rule of thumb on FIGARO to help eliminate some of the questioning. For any 5° divergence from course, we must get an 8 percent increase in speed or else hold her on. Speed and distance are the only considerations. The comfort quotient, so important in cruising, gets short shrift in a race.

As a matter of fact, the slogan on board FIGARO in the 1960 Swedish Race was, "Sail her to the point of discomfort." When I unburdened myself of this instruction at the start, I probably had the romantic notion that every captain is entitled to at least one deathless phrase before or during a major event. This was the best idea I could come up with, but it was turned against me one miserable afternoon. I was trying to sleep on my off-watch while FIGARO was working her way, head on, in an uncomforting sea. I was being bounced off the bunk board with regularity and all of the time my ears and imagination were assailed with creaks and groans from the boat as she slammed into one wave top after

Next page: Keeping cool in the Needles Channel during the Fastnet Race—Ed Raymond at the wheel, with Mike Blake, our navigator
London *Daily Express*

another. In my half-sleep I was hallucinated with visions of shipwreck. Having held my counsel to the point where continued silence would be dereliction of duty, I called out to the watch on deck and suggested that they be a little more understanding of the ship and her needs in such an unfriendly environment. The unfeeling response from the port watch captain, Bobby Symonette, was a polite inquiry, "Are you uncomfortable, Captain?" My automatic rejoinder was cut short by the assurance that he was only fulfilling my fondest dream of "sailing to the point of discomfort."

I have given a very brief indication of tactical differences in cruising and racing which make for a change in attitude. There are many more.

But even more basic is the make-up of the crew and what is expected from it. The essential difference between a desirable racing crewman as against the kind of companion with whom you like to cruise is the degree of skill he has. For cruising company one looks for a good companion with reasonable skills as a seaman and helmsman. Most important is the ability to live in a tight community which contains various shadings of personality, all living in rather constricted space. In cruising, indifferent helmsmanship is not a serious mark against a man if his company is enjoyable. In racing one is more forebearing in the matter of personality, but less so in the case of indifferent skills, one of which is helmsmanship.

On a long race, every man expects to get a chance at the wheel. It is too much to ask a man to go to sea for a long period and not give him a chance to steer. For that matter, you won't get many men if they can't share that fun. It is only the twelves and other afternoon racers that can get away with the kind of galley-slave treatment where a man is told to pull on a certain string on orders and is at no time permitted to come aft of the midship point. While most yachtsmen are convinced they are able helmsmen, some are more able than others. All my crews are told before the start of a race that the watch captain has orders to replace any man at the wheel who is not doing as well as he, the watch captain, believes it can be done. No matter how clear the understanding of the purpose, when this removal takes place, feelings are ruffled. If for no other reason than to reduce such inimical morale factors, you look for excellent helmsmen.

In addition to the ability to steer, and even more desirable, are men with great skills in sail handling. You want men who are strong and nimble and have sure and quick hands. Sail changes, tacks, and jibes must go in split-second timing with no foul-ups. This generally means younger men who may not have as much experience on the ocean and consequently tend to be more daring and impulsive, thereby creating a fine problem in relationship with the older, more seasoned men on board. A good crew is made up of this kind of balance of skill and experience.

Another factor for change in a man's attitude when on a long ocean race is the degree to which he must adapt to the ship. "Other ships, other long splices" is an old sailing aphorism. It means that on each ship there is a particular way of doing things. While in cruising there is room for personal idiosyncrasies and ways of doing a job, on a racing boat the crew is asked to conform to the ship's way. It is unavoidable in order to insure smooth performance. This degree of acceptance of teamwork, the utter concentration during every waking moment on getting the boat there *fastest with the mostest,* welds the crew into a single community. The extraordinary dedication to a single purpose shared with the other members of the community, almost to the exclusion of other goals, provides the participants with a rare human experience. In a sporting marriage of the will and the idea, you belong to something, it belongs to you. It is the opposite of existential nothingness.

We win the Admiral's Cup

XIV

BEFORE THE RACE

In the summer of 1963, FIGARO was entered in a race to England. Once there, she was to represent the United States as a member of the Admiral's Cup team in defense of the premier English ocean-racing trophy. After her cruise to England in 1961, she had joined the team which won it. The team then was FIGARO-CYANE-WINDROSE. This year it was to be FIGARO-DYNA-WINDROSE. One out-of-the-ordinary sidelight: FIGARO had been sold, but her delivery date was held up until the fall and her return to the U.S. At that time, she would again be subjected to survey and if she passed the examination, the sale would be consumated. It was, therefore, her last campaign under the old management, who already had a leg in a new boat, now being built back home.

But first, there was the trans-Atlantic race under the joint direction of the New York Yacht Club and the Royal Ocean Racing Club. A good-sized fleet had been assembled, fourteen yachts, among which were some of the most ardent campaigners in the U.S. The yachts were divided into three classes. There would be an over-all prize and individual class prizes. Handicapping a race at sea is a chancy business. Since the boats sail at such vastly different speeds, they can be sailing in quite different kinds of weather systems, having little relationship one to the other. Nevertheless, some basis for handicapping must be provided and the C.C.A.* does the best it can.

The entry list and the allowances were as follows:

Class	Boat	Owner	Days	Hours	Minutes	Seconds
A	BOLERO	Sally Ames Langmuir	3	19	6	37
	CORSARO	Italian Navy entry	4	10	57	16
	DYNA	Clayton Ewing	5	5	47	36
	ONDINE	Sumner "Huey" Long	5	8	05	33
B	BACCARAT	George Coumontaros	5	21	49	25
	CARINA	Dick Nye, Jr.	5	21	49	25
	FIGARO	Bill Snaith	6	09	06	45
	WINDROSE	Jake Isbrandtsen	6	14	22	45
	CYANE	Hank du Pont	6	14	49	58
C	SITZMARK	Dr. W. Neumann	7	6	28	52
	KATAMA	Fred Adams	7	17	36	11
	EN RAPPORT	Robert Sheppard	7	50	42	55
	CHINA BIRD	Horace Beck	7	33	38	00
	GUINEVERE	George Moffett	8	00	15	14

* Cruising Club of America.

118

Sailing on board FIGARO in good health and in reasonable spirits:

William Snaith	Captain	Owner and pays all bills
Elliott "Buz" Knowlton	Port Watch Captain (Standby Navigator)	Publisher
Michael W. Richey	Navigator	Executive Secretary, Institute of Navigation, The Royal Geographical Society
Jon Rohde	Leading Seaman & Boatswain	Student
William MacLeod Snaith	Leading Seaman	Student
Shepperd Snaith	Leading Seaman	Student
Frederick Hibberd	Leading Seaman	Flyer
Conn Findlay	Leading Seaman	Oarsman and Sailor, Olympic Gold Medal Holder

The fleet is ready to race

Jon Rohde and Cleody

Skip Snaith

Cleody Snaith

Buz Knowlton

The fleet was assembled in Newport and busy with a flurry of preparations. A great deal of the winter had been spent in planning and preparation, but that seems to make little difference. The last two days before the start of such a race witness a spate of preparations so intense that it would seem as though all preparations had been held off until this time under the gun. On FIGARO, most of the work was restrained to final stowage and the entry of the location of all gear and comestibles into our master inventory list. Every locker and space, including the spaces between the floors in the bilge, is given a code number and description. As each article is stowed, we enter it in an appropriate place on the list. In this way we not only know exactly what we have on board and where it is kept, but have a running inventory as well; for, as things are used, they are checked off the list. Secondary lists are maintained for food, for medicaments, for navigational equipment and "bosun" stores. Along with this are menus, recipes, and instructions for use. The idea is that, if the person charged with a specific responsibility cannot function, an alternate will be able to carry on with the lists and instructions for use.

The night before the race was to start, a captains' meeting was held at which final instructions were given, and questions which arise at every such occasion were again aired. The first instruction was the establishment of Point Able, a point on the chart at a given latitude and longitude; we would not be permitted to go north of this point until we had passed it, then we were on our own. The purpose of a Point Able is to insure the fact that we would be kept clear of the ice fields coming down with the Labrador current. If such a point were not established, then in all likelihood some yachts might sail far north in order to sail the shortest great circle course and in search of the traditionally heavier winds below the Arctic Circle, and would take their chances with the ice. The prudent racer, who was moved to more concern with the safety of his crew and yacht would be at a disadvantage unless, of course, the north-going adventurer should be sunk. The committee, in a search for equalization, therefore sets a Point Able just before the race. Its location is determined from the latest ice-field reports.

As a suggestion of further equalization, "Huey" Long proposed that all yachts be enjoined to sail around Nantucket Lightship rather than be allowed to elect a shorter course by sailing through Vineyard Sound and Pollock Rip Channel. But the other liberated souls, already chafing at restrictions, shouted him down and the committee officially rejected the idea.

An additional point raised and discussed with some heat and acerbity by Fred Adams: Would the committee permit the use of a masthead light? Dooley Roosevelt, Race Committee chairman, already apprised of this movement, read some correspondence with a Coast Guard official. Unquestionably, most yacht owners would feel safer with a high, all-points light which could be seen by an oncoming or overtaking vessel rather than with only a pair of red and green bicycle lamps some five feet off the water and a white stern light at the same height. These lights lack power, brilliance, and height and are further complicated by the fact that they are often hidden by a sea or behind a sail. Since a

Freddy Hibberd

Mike Richey

Conn Findlay

WTS, the Skipper

sailing yacht is more apt to be the runnee than the runner-down, the question is close to an owner's heart. The Coast Guard official, standing behind the law, explained that the rule of the road frowns upon an all-points masthead light, therefore the committee refuses to make a decision. The floor is temporarily surrendered to Alf Loomis, who calls for a vote to see if all contestants will abstain from a protest if another yacht were to use its masthead light. Since he could not get a unanimous vote, the matter was left to the skipper's option, if an emergency should arise. Fred Adams averred that if he cannot see which way the night fly is leading, he will deem it an emergency.

One further proposal from the Senator from ONDINE: namely, that we exchange positions by radio as they do in the Trans-Pacific Race. This, too, was voted down. We on the East Coast seem to be more ornery and anti-social. Those skippers who wish to can make a private pact. I, personally, don't like it. I like the isolation at sea. That's part of the reason that I go. In addition, I like the suspense of a long race with despair or hope running high up until the end instead of bleeding a little each day as we watch our morale erode. That's what happens when the daily positions of our competition make them all into Charlie Barrs (a great professional racing skipper of a bygone era). Conversely, you can be lulled into a false sense of security when the opposition gives a position behind their actual place. In any case, I wouldn't believe the lying bastards. In the 1960 race to Sweden, during an optional exchange of positions, a boat gave a position some forty miles astern of FIGARO and while the skipper's voice was coming out of the speaker we could see the top of his spinnaker clearly framed in our companionway. The sail was just a few miles astern. So much for legalism and the exchange of sportsmen's information.

On the morning of the race, I wakened early to fog and drizzle, a rather cheerless aspect for an auspicious day. After breakfast there was a general leave-taking of our families, who had to rush to the Navy Yard in order to board a U.S. Navy Y.F. at 0930. It was to take them to the starting line. When it is time for us to go, we have some trouble getting the engine started which, in itself, is an uncomfortable augury, but it finally catches and we head out into the fog for the starting line.

Once at the line, we join the other yachts jockeying around in search of their families, like so many fledglings in search of the nest. We finally find ours. They naturally missed the Navy boat, but did get on the N.Y.Y.C. committee boat, Hank du Pont's motor sailer, NOR'EASTER. Freddy's family come by on their yacht, CAPRICE. Having found those dear to us, we can turn our attention to other important matters such as making brave talk with other contestants, and try to unsettle the confidence of our adversaries. It appears that we have as little effect on them as they do on us, but at least it is a diverting way to fill in the time until the prep gun. It has just gone off—from now on things get serious.

XV

THE FIRST TWO DAYS

SUNDAY, JUNE 30

1200   The start! Everyone is jammed up at the line as though this was to be an afternoon romp around the buoys. I never will understand it. What you want at the start of a long passage race is your wind clear and the opportunity to decide your own strategy. What you don't want is to be pinned by a couple of boats, with one sitting on your wind or threatening to, and the other holding you up on course so that you can't get out of the box.

And yet, every time one of these races starts, there we are playing the same old game, a crush at the line, fighting for stupid seconds when we probably will be throwing away time by the handful during the long period of the race. What is worse is that we sometimes get carried along by the boat's position in the over-all pattern, delaying the time when we should exercise a predetermined strategy. Sometimes a skipper is even loath to break out of the pattern because it will put him in a hated rival's wake. It's too much for pride to swallow. In the shorter, overnight races, I have even known the occasion when a boat has been committed to a plan counter to the original one because of failure to take its medicine at the outset.

However, we make a creditable start—at least there are no noteworthy foul-ups. The wind is light, but we are close reaching and seemingly out of trouble. WINDROSE is under us to leeward. CORSARO is to windward, but aft. If she holds her present course she may come down on our wind. She is big and we can't hold her off. For the moment, we'll do nothing, but hold our course; let's see what they do. Out of the corner of the eye we see Hank du Pont's CYANE just pinch by the Brenton Tower. Hank was pretty early making for the line and had to cut this one tight. It's hard to see the rest of the fleet. The light southerly is bringing a pretty thick fog with it.

1400   We are the leeward boat of those we still can see in this fog. Near us are WINDROSE, CARINA and CORSARO. The time is approaching when we must choose whether to go through Vineyard Sound into Nantucket Sound, then into Cross Rip and on through Pollock Rip Channel, as against going east around Nantucket Light. We still have a couple of hours until we must absolutely commit ourselves. Certainly the group we are sailing with gives every indication of going the inside way. That's the reason we all are holding up to the north. If you get the breaks, it means an advantage. If not, well, you have almost three weeks of sailing to try to make it up. Anyway, the race should go to the brave. It is an enticing choice to make, not only because it is a more direct course to our ultimate objective, but if the wind holds the tides will be favorable most of the way; they run fast. The difference between winning and losing an around-the-buoys race is the accumulation of minutes and seconds. Unfortunately, it is as true for a race across the Atlantic. I lost second place in the 3000-mile race to Spain by 2¼ minutes. I lost that one in the Bay of Biscay. The few minutes that could be saved here might be the difference for those who are counted in at the finish.

1430 The fog lifts and we see nearly all of the boats. They are spread out, but still in sight. We are the most leeward which, as a matter of fact, bothers us. Our planned course should have put us south of where we are. Those near us obviously are using the same strategy we are: namely, to be in position to delay the decision to make the turn up Vineyard Sound, or to continue on around Nantucket Lightship. About half the fleet already have committed themselves. They are unwilling to take a chance on the tricky shoals and tides in this in-and-out wind and now-you-see-it-now-you-don't visibility. They are going for Nantucket Lightship. The danger of the course we are contemplating is that you can be becalmed in adverse tides inside and there are not too many options of course to choose, once committed. Outside, you have room for maneuver.

Later. The wind picks up a bit. We change the light 5-ounce Genoa for the 8-ounce, which is the same size. It's not that we are burdened, we are riding comfortably enough, but there is no use stretching our light Genoa out of shape. It's a good sail and we will need it when the going is really light. In this misty fog we keep finding ourselves too far north and as we go (unplanned) between the land and the Texas tower which has replaced the Buzzards Bay Lightship, the heavy fog really socks in.

There are mutterings about the compass being out of true. The steering pedestal was rebuilt this spring and after the compass was remounted, it was swung. There were no glaring compass deviations recorded. When I joined the boat in Newport, the boys said they thought they had detected a compass error. Since most of the steering was on visible points ahead, and since I had just had the whole installation checked, I didn't pay too much attention, especially when Mike and the boys took the boat out on Friday and ran some lines without finding anything wrong. But now, in the fog, we keep turning up north of where we think we ought to be.

We are on the lookout, or perhaps in the fog I ought to say hearout, for the bell on Sow and Pigs, a rocky reef jutting out from the land with thin water on top. It should be well to port. Suddenly, while standing at the wheel, I hear it. *It's to starboard!* And up to weather at that. We are almost on top of the rocks. I yank the bow over on the other tack, ready or not, and backwind the jib which really spins the boat's head. We get ourselves squared away and after five minutes of sailing on the new tack, flop back to our original course, right at the bell. To say we are shaken is putting it mildly. Our voyage could have ended disastrously in a wreck, right then and there. The five minutes we lost is bad enough, but here we are, just setting out to cross the Atlantic and there is something just as wrong as hell with the boat, the compass, or with us. We couldn't have been set up so consistently by a current. Even if we were, every other boat would have been there too, and our steering can't be that bad. Something is fouling us up.

1615   We have made the decision. It will be Vineyard Sound. For ten minutes I sweated it out as we were running out the time to the point where we must make the turn. Everyone kept looking to me as though I were the oracle at Delphi. They were waiting for the word one way or another and I didn't have any more basis for a decision than they did. This was a decision I had to make. I talked out the options loudly and clearly, hoping for guidance. Nothing to the point was forthcoming, nor did I expect it, but I did get the sense indirectly from the navigator and watch captain that they favored such a course. We squared off for Vineyard Sound, committing ourselves to the inside passage, hoping that it would work out and, naturally, hoping that we were the only ones. However, if this heavy fog holds out, it may be foolhardy.

1700   I am sweating it out again. The wind is dying and we are squared off to it on the course we must hold in order to clear middle ground. This is our worst point of sail in light winds. What if the wind is holding on the outside of the Sound? It seemed to drop as soon as we came inside. If this is the case, then we are taking a bad hosing. Even if they found the same weight of wind, the outside course still would give a faster sailing angle to boats going that way. If we are going to turn around, we had better do it soon. I suppose I keep delaying that decision in the hope that the wind will pick up, or because of the fact that we will soon be committed too deeply to turn back. It's a bad time for captains.

The tide is under us with a vengeance, but we are not using it well because of the sailing angle (AND THE MARKS KEEP SHOWING UP ALL WRONG!). Something is decidedly on the fritz.

1730   Breakers ho! For chrisake! Land right ahead! It's enough to give a man the yellow stain. In the fog, a creamy white mass showed up where the horizon ought to be. It came up suddenly and we were damn near in it when we made it out to be a slight sea breaking on low-lying bluffs. We turn the boat on its heels and sail a line up the beach, diverging slightly with it while identification is made. These waters are Buz's happy hunting ground. Between him and the navigator, they identify the land as Nashawena Island. Again, we are either steering or being set to the left.

As we came closer to the land, the fog became thinner. That's what enabled us to see the beach. Also there was enough wan sunlight for the sun to throw a shadow of the quarter lubber line across the compass card. Mike hurriedly took a reading and worked out a sun bearing for that time of day. Thank God we have the executive secretary of the Institute for Navigation (Royal Geographical Society) along as navigator. He is quick and sure. He comes up on

Clearing a pennant for the helmsman

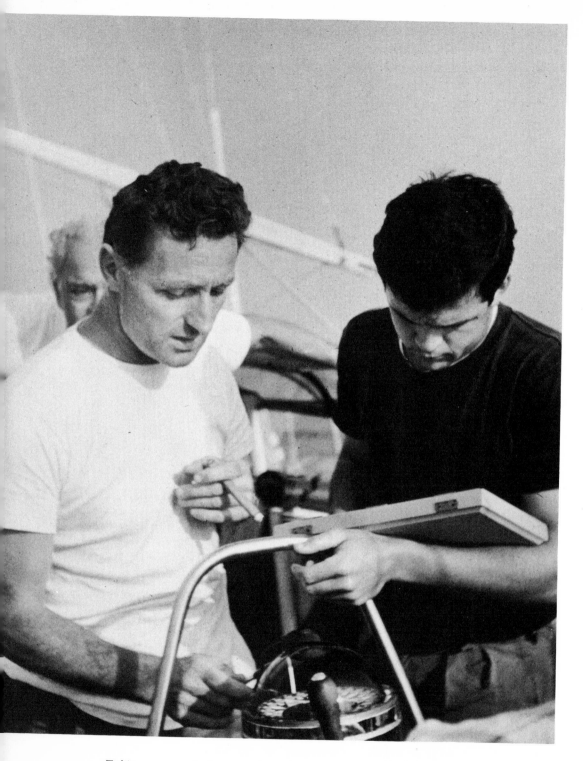

Taking a sun shadow on the compass to discover compass error: the shadow of the lubber line falls across the compass face, the time is taken, and the result worked out against the position in the nautical almanac—Mike Richey, navigator; Jon Rohde, timetaker

deck after running out his figures. The prognosis is bad. He takes another check. Meanwhile, we are sailing by guess and by God. His first computation is verified. Our compass has an 8° error to the left on an easterly heading. What a monstrous fuck-up.

1830   We are sailing along as though we knew what the hell we were doing, in one of the trickiest bits of water anywhere in the neighborhood. Night is coming on. The fog is still dense away from the shore. There is very little wind and we have an untrustworthy compass. You couldn't ask any more from Columbus. What a crowded time we have had, and what's ahead? How the hell did we get into this?

We are steering a new course with 8° of correction cranked in.

1900   The fog is lifting, although the breeze still is light. And there's the competition! We see them up ahead on the starboard hand. Visible are DYNA, CORSARO, CARINA and WINDROSE, in that order. They are hard under Martha's Vineyard and, hell and high water, a little aft of the beam is the smaller KATAMA. She must have been going like the hammers to be up here. Dimly, way back aft, we can see two more spinnakers. We didn't come in here alone. More than half of the fleet had the same idea.

Obviously, while we were steering a course, thinking to keep clear of middle ground, as dictated by our wacky compass, we were squared off on a dead run. Our competition was not only enjoying a better sailing angle but we were sailing away from the course. They therefore worked out a lead. We have our work cut out for us. However, the Great Equalizer is at it; now we have a better angle and are catching up. We will be in their wake, but we hope not too far behind.

Later.   We go past Hedge Fence Shoal soon after WINDROSE. The stern lights of the leading yachts are disappearing into more fog ahead in Nantucket Sound.

2000   It is a dark night with fog and there are rocks all around. It makes for nervous sailing, especially because of the compass. We don't know what caused the error or whether it will be a constant factor. This is no water in which to go staggering about in the dark. We hear the horn on Cross Rip Lightship. It is right over the bow. Our factor of correction seems to be right.

We sail right up to the lightship under the spinnaker. It makes for an eerie experience. The ship is dimly seen as the occulting light, shrouded in mist, casts blinking shadows of her spars on the particles of mist filling the air. Its horn, hoarse and penetrating, keeps sounding relentlessly. She is laying to the tide. It is against us.

Our steering from now on must be super-accurate, there can be no goofing off. Our next turning mark is a bell off Halfmoon Shoal. Everyone is quiet. You can almost feel your ears pointing forward. Finally, we hear it over the bow. So far so good. We sail up to it and hear it distinctly. We do not see it. The next mark is the hooter off Handkerchief Shoal, and it's the same deal—hear, no see.

Stone Horse Light is where it ought to be. Again we don't see the light. We must make our turn for Pollack Rip Channel before reaching Stone Horse, and we don't want to allow even the tiniest margin for error, so we sail right up to the quick flash at the beginning of the channel. It is so thick we can barely see the light.

Now we are squared away for Pollock Rip Channel down the succession of buoys. This has been a day of tension and tautly drawn nerves. It is not over yet, but our confidence in the compass with its correction factor is returning. One never realizes the dependence placed on a taken-for-granted instrument like the compass until something goes haywire. While we don't feel all relaxed, warm, and comfy, we begin to believe we have this part of it made. Tomorrow, in daylight, serious work on finding the cause for the compass error will be undertaken.

The gods must be holding something good in store for us. They certainly have put us to a series of trials at the very outset to make us prove our mettle. There may be many more trials in store, but we are grateful that it has turned out this well so far. In all of this, the crew was calm and alert. I am proud of them. Many rueful jokes were made during the day, but for the life of me, I can't remember one.

MONDAY, JULY 1

0230   We are south of Pollock Rip Lightship and at last safely on our way out to sea. At least we have sea room and are not threatened on our left hand and right by shoals and reefs. It is a comforting feeling to know that if any errors develop now, we won't wind up on rocks. We lucked out. It was a tight bit of going, but the wind held so that we could make it past the shoals and we found out about the compass early in the day.

Here in the dark of a new morning I still look for kindly omens. I am never as hagridden with the idea of omens and signs as when at sea. It must be that the saline content of the blood holds atavistic memories which are stirred and quickened when near the great mother of us all, the sea. But there can be no doubt that yesterday a kindly eye was on this sparrow. We could have bricked up at any time, starting with the Sow and Pigs and on to any of the nasty clumps in the tricky water which lies between the Vineyard and Nantucket on one side and the Elizabeth Islands and Cape Cod on the other. For that matter, our voyage could have ended on Nashawena. But the fog lightened and we saw it in time and there was enough brief sun for us to get a fix on the compass shadow. Truly, someone on board is wearing a garland of garlic, or whatever it takes to ward off the evil.

I cannot conceive how the compass went out. It seemed right as rain all of this spring and now, suddenly, it begins to bug us. I can hardly wait for daylight so that we can get at it.

I'm for the rack now, feeling a lot better than I have for the last twelve hours. May flights of angels and a fair breeze attend us.

0530   Breakfast sounds and smells. Ocean routine is setting in. The ship's business goes on as usual. We are on our way, even if we are not absolutely certain where we are going. The wind is in the southwest. Visibility is under one-half mile. Trawlers are working around us. We can hear their engines and horns. We toot our mournful horn back at them. Our horn is no heldentenor or basso profundo. It sounds more like a sick cow. It annoys us more than it warns approaching vessels.

Another piece of gear is on the fritz—the barograph. In changing the graph paper and cleaning and re-inking the stylus, we opened the nib of the pen. The result on paper, after the instrument has run for several hours, looks like an encephalograph taken in a booby hatch after the inmates have broken into a hashish locker. We are working on it, but it still doesn't look good.

0630   The great detection has begun. With morning light we are going to find out what is bugging the compass or bust. At first, all metallic objects are moved from the sail lockers on either side of the binnacle to see if they are having any effect. But since they all prove to be non-magnetic, there is no change. We then clear out every piece of gear from the sail lockers and the lazarette and pile it on the deck midships. If a picture were to be taken now, we would look more like a Chinese junk than a sleek ocean racer. We think for a moment that we have found the culprit—a mound of brownies in foil containers stowed under the bridge deck—but this, too, is a false alarm. The same kind of emptying-out process goes on in the galley and navigation area. We shift the position of the radios, but nothing makes any difference. With all of this effort, it is still for nought. The compass remains as obdurate as before. The best guess so far is that one of the compensating magnets which was affixed to the bulkhead in the cockpit area was torn off. In our search we cannot find a newly bared place on the wood which would indicate a recently dislodged object. For that matter, we cannot find any compensating magnets at all. No luck whatsoever. We are nonplused. How can you fix anything when you can't find out what's wrong?

0700   A reading from the barometer (as distinguished from the barograph) shows 30.05. It is going up slightly, which generally portends no wind. Mike and I have agreed on a course to Point Able. Able is the position C or Charlie located on the pilot chart. We will not sail immediately for it, but head slightly south at first in order to avoid going over the top of Georges Bank. Both Mike and I have had disappointing experiences there. The Labrador Current sweeps across the top of the Bank. It is not only very cold, but runs adverse as well. I rarely have found wind there and with the present indications from the barometer, we think it is not the place to be.

The Hood spinnaker is up. All of the go-fast is on and the speed is about 5 knots. We are doing a lot of experimenting with the centerboard, moving it up and down, leveling it at varying heights. Even at this late date, I have never been able to decide absolutely where it carried best for each separate condition. Theoretically, it makes a difference, since it radically affects balance and wetted surface, but we do not have instruments on board which are sensitive enough to record the difference. We usually settle for a centerboard position based on feel or by gauging performance against another boat. But there is no other boat, we are alone.

1000   The wind is getting lighter and our speed has dropped. It has gone down to 4 knots.

1200   Our assumed position is 41° 35′ N 68° 34′ W. The sun is clearly visible but our horizon is limited, thwarting sight-taking. We sail in a narrow, charmed circle of bright haze.

Luncheon and a concert. Our music comes from an ingenious tape recorder, made by Phillips of Holland and which produces great sounds while running on flashlight batteries. I don't know whether breasts at sea are more savage than elsewhere, but at times music is very welcome. For a while I had a battery-operated turntable to play records. It worked well when tied up in a marina, but any movement at sea halted the turntable. The tape recorder is the answer. It plays at any angle of heel.

My son Jocko put in many unselfish hours recording a series of tapes from our home record collection. We have concertos, shorter concert pieces, symphonies, and the complete "St. Matthew Passion" and the "B-Minor Mass." We also have a large collection of fine jazz, and that's what we are listening to right now. To name them all on this long-play tape: we hear Mose Allison, John Coltrane, Miles Davis, M.J.Q., Thelonious, Chico Hamilton, Ray Charles, Charlie Byrd, and, naturally, scads of notable sidemen, a veritable Newport Jazz Festival.

1230   We see sparm! Great whales, by God! "Stand ready to lower."

1430   The wind is going flat and shifty and our speed, unhappily, is down to 2 knots.

Conn Findlay, our shipmate from California, is still wearing shorts and a short-sleeved sweater; he is barefooted. The rest of us are swaddled in sweaters, foul-weather gear, and boots. He is different. As a gold-medal winner, hoping to compete again in '64, he is in perpetual training. Always disappearing up forward to do isometrics (regularly breaks the nylon line he stretches against), he eats sparsely and carefully. I am now beginning to think he drinks freon to control his body temperature.

1600   Our position carried forward is 41° 35′ N 68° 18′ W. We have made little progress. The position was established by consolan and sun lines.

1800   Our speed is down to a discouraging 1 knot—just barely maintaining steerageway. It is my unhappy and unquestioning belief that while some boats may be broken down by the absence of wind, there is always someone who is sailing on a private zephyr. At least it always seems to work that way. In any given number of instances we have finished after heartbreaking periods of being becalmed only to find some beaming winner who assures us that he never stopped going at all. Someone may be winning this race right now.

1930   The wind speed has improved slightly. Our speed is up to 2.5 knots.

Happy Hour turned out to be a jolly affair; mostly because dinner was late, therefore the diverting period was extended. Cleody and I prepared the dinner of roast beef and scalloped potatoes (the latter were the offenders, they took forever), salad, pears, cheese, coffee and cigars. The weather being fine, some of us ate topside while the traditionalists ate below.

2000   We are still moving along. The sleeping tonight is a little better. The tensions of last night's passage no longer haunt us. Another pass is made at fixing the barograph. It still looks lousy.

2300   The ship is quiet and settled for the long night watches. Our speed is better, 6 knots, but the wind is beginning to puff, indicating that it will lessen. You are always conscious of the sound and feel of the wind at sea, but during a race you respond as though you had special antennae.

XVI

THE THIRD AND FOURTH DAYS

TUESDAY, JULY 2

0030   The unhappiest, most soul-trying condition for racing and men—we sit in a flat-assed calm. Speed 0–1 knot. Barograph 30.00.

0200   Shades of "Captains Courageous"—a trawler crosses our bow. We hear his engines, but cannot see him in this deep fog. Manuel is looking for his leetle feesh. We are somewhere in the area of the Texas tower on Georges Bank. It is supposed to be floodlit, but we doubt if we will see it.

0300   A most wearing series of sail changes in this pale, pale air with its constantly veering wind directions. We shift from the light Genoa to our blue top .75-ounce spinnaker, back to the light Genoa, and finally to the gossamer balloon ghoster. Sailing in this kind of wind is extremely trying, not only because of the physical expenditure of energy in the hoisting, lowering, setting, and re-setting, but in the dodges and care taken in trying to keep whatever sail is up drawing and effective. The settings rarely work for any period of time. In addition to the frustrations while fighting one sail, comes the nagging thought that perhaps some other combination would be doing a better job. When you assess the distance gained by all of this jackass labor, you are led to wonder if it would not serve just as well to go below, sleep or play cards, and be ready to take advantage of the wind when it returns. But the conscience of a racing man cannot permit such an idea to percolate. Besides, yards gained, in whatever increments, eventually accumulate into something important.

We are shrouded in heavy fog and it is miserably cold. Our rowing blue is still barefoot on the deck. He still wears shorts, but has made one concession to the lowered temperature—he has donned a light shirt under his short-sleeved sweater. He regales us with stories of the really hard men who sail on San Francisco Bay who wear nothing but shorts and T-shirts even in the coldest weather. Just to hear him talk makes my blood run cold.

0430   Our speed is not only down, it is nonexistent. But in spite of our suspension of animation, life goes on in the invisibility around us. We hear whales snorting and blowing. From the sound of the activity, we presume this to be the season when the females are in heat and males in rut. Perhaps lady whales need this kind of darkness to mask their size and give the illusion of daintiness.

Skipper gives his own imitation of a lonesome female whale. I once heard a demonstration of the mournful call of a lady moose and soon thereafter saw a bull, and so I take no chances—he may be right. I wrestle him to the deck. We do not want to invite the fate of the PEQUOD. All we need now to make this journey all of a piece is the frustrated charge of a horny bull whale.

0600   The wind is back, bringing with it even heavier fog. We will settle for the lack of visibility if we can move in it. Our speed is up to 5 knots and is slowly rising.

Breakfast today—hot oatmeal, hot cakes, and bangers (an anglicism for sausages, maybe because of the way they pop open). It is apparent no one will starve. In fact, everyone is in fine fettle except Jon, who has been stricken with trans-Atlantic constipation. He wears a worried look. He is going to study medicine and lives very close to his subject. I assure him that the one sure cure for his ailment is to keep eating.

0900   Our speed improves and so do our spirits. The gauge reads 6.1 knots.

1030   *Eureka, it is found!* We have located the cause of the trouble with the compass. When my binnacle was replaced, a new kind of chassis for the compass was installed, unbeknownst to me. It looked almost the same and I therefore assumed it was the same kind. This one, however, had the compensating magnets in the binnacle chassis below the compass itself, rather than having the magnets at a distance and installed in the cockpit as separated elements. Ostensibly, once the magnets placed under the compass have been checked out, they are made fast. We found, however, that the set screws which should do this job were loose and something had shifted. We fasten the magnets in their present position so that whatever error is now in the mechanism will remain constant.

1130   The compass has now been adjusted by new azimuths taken. Naturally it holds true only for this heading. When we can, and if we can, it must be adjusted to other compass headings. For the moment, we are sailing east and the indications are that we will be able to hold that course. If, however, we are forced to go on the wind and tack, and especially when on soundings, we will need to know and be assured of our direction on other headings.

It is almost as though the compass were the king log in the jam that affected all malfunctions. The moment this was taken care of other functions improved. Freddy went below last night and disappeared from view for almost two hours—to fix the barograph, he said. Since it was damned cold on deck, I, in my role of righteous captain, accused him of malingering. But to do the boy justice, the barograph is working.

And Rohde's plumbing functions once more. He received hearty congratulations from the crew and is seen to smile again.

1200   Our noon position is 41° 51′ N 66° 40′ W. We have made 89 miles, a distressing early performance for a race. We can only hope no one had anything better to work with.

1315 Mike shakes me up. I found him engrossed in Mixter's book on navigation which is part of the ship's library. This is no time to find that our director of the Institute of Navigation is taking a brush-up course. Perhaps he is just going to do a much delayed book review.

1500 The wind is slowly moving aft. It is blowing at about 12 knots. For the last hour we have been doing better than 7 knots on a course of 110°. This is the direction from which the prevailing winds come—maybe we will move regularly from now on.

1600 The wind is building up. The fog—which was patchy, never disappearing, sometimes getting thicker and thinning out as we moved along—is now thick again. The wind is far enough aft so that we have replaced the Genoa with the spinnaker and we have finally put on the hatch covers, just in case it blows. It would have been better seamanship to put them on at the start, but this reduces the ventilation of the boat, and since our start was in muggy weather, we delayed until now. Not that there is any urgency to do it now; it is done to satisfy our conscientious approach to good seamanship. The barograph has fallen, but holds a steady line. We are prepared.

1630 Mike, still haunted by our compass failure, holds our second compass in his hands above the binnacle. The second compass reads 5° higher on this bearing than our binnacle.

1700 A fine Happy Hour, at least for those who had a whiskey and water. Mike is still assailed by acute compass depression. I assured him that wherever we are going now, we are going at our fastest sailing angle; he can tell us where we are sometime in the future. He refuses to be consoled. I refuse to let his truths get through to me. We go merrily on.

A dinner of Chicken Cacciatore and rice is served by our barefooted shipmate. It is getting colder in this outer edge of the Labrador Current and interest runs high as to whether Conn will put on pants and shoes. Night will surely tell.

1900 Fog all around us. We are still logging 7 knots at 110°

1945 We have suddenly entered warmer water and the fog disappears. FIGARO must have been skirting the lower reaches of the Labrador Current where it meets the limits of the Gulf Stream. We therefore assume that we have entered the favorable current and alter our course for Charlie, the Point Able. We have adhered to our strategy and are sailing an open-angled dog-leg course to Charlie. A slight additional amount of distance has been added by that course as against the most direct great circle course. We did it in order to avoid much of the adverse Labrador Current and with the hope of picking up the favorable drift of the Gulf Stream sooner. If all this happens, it will more than overcome the disadvantage of added distance. To help our frame of mind, the sailing angles up to now have been favorable, at least when the wind blew.

2015 Our D.R. position is 41° 37′ N 65° 28′ W, pretty near where we had predetermined our shift off course.

2300   The course is 100°, the speed 5.9 knots.

2400   This has been an in-and-out sort of day. We had no wind in the early morning, but as the day wore along, it built up into a fair sailing breeze. Now it gives promise of weakening again. We wonder if the competition suffered the same tribulations as we did. It is reasonable to assume that since this is the early stage of the race the fleet would not have had time to spread out and therefore the larger boats cannot be far enough away to have sailed into another weather pattern. There is always the chance of small, local differences. In the most unsportsmanlike manner, we hope they have suffered with us, perhaps even more.

The crew is in fair spirits. Morale (if not morals) is high. Stories are directed toward locker-room subjects in direct relationship to the square of the distance measured from shore, multiplied by the number of days at sea.

As the ship's chief medical officer, I must record several minor ailments and complaints. Skip complains of a sore throat. I have induced him to gargle with salt water and a fantastic water display results.

Buz has loaded sinuses and a severe headache. I give him an occasional Chlortrimeton, which seems to help.

The sun went down as a great red ball. It should be good weather tomorrow. Red sky at night, sailor's delight.

WEDNESDAY, JULY 3

0030   An inauspicious beginning for the new day. The wind is in the southeast, ahead and very light. Our spinnaker comes off and is replaced by the light Genoa. The speed hovers around 3 knots.

0200   The wind has picked up speed and our spirits. Things are a little more sprightly. The spirits have a curve in direct proportion to boat speed. We are moving along at 5.4 knots on a course of 100°.

0300   The wind has now increased to the point where we have taken off the light Genoa and put up the heavier Number One in its place. There is no obvious reason for this wind shift into the southeast. The immediate indicator, the barometer, stays high and steady. But we know that wind shifts do not come about without reason, not when the wind speed accelerates at this rate. Something is going on, high or low, local or part of a larger pattern. But we'll find out. It's a secret not to be kept from us. Whatever is coming will soon show its hand.

We are in the middle of a spectacular show of watery phosphorescence. The boat leaves a milky-white luminescent wake which fades slowly behind us. We are a water-borne shooting star, accompanied by a fiery comet tail. When the boat plunges in the sea, a white sheet of light flashes out from her as though someone had snapped on a submarine electric light attached to her underside.

Since this is a recurrent and an extraordinarily dramatic phenomenon of nature, which must have first flashed in the sea long before recorded time, I wonder that ancient sailors gave it no name. We know now that it is caused by vast numbers of sea creatures in whose bodies luciferin and oxygen react when they are triggered by some physical stimulus. As a secret of marine biology, this phenomenon was not unlocked for ancients any more than the causes for the atmospheric fluorescence which at times plays around masts and shrouds. Yet they called the atmospheric fluorescence St. Elmo's fire, ascribing it to a spectral heavenly fire, but found no name for this watery fire. If no deserving saint or martyr could be found in the martyrology to earn the right to have this burning water named for him, certainly somewhere in Poseidon's realm was a demigod with sufficient power and saliency.

But all of us are not equally awed by the mysterious phenomenon of nature. One man among us, moved by a natural force of his own and exercising the privileges and liberties of a freeman, unburdened by fear of witches, warlocks, or of giving offense to angry demons, makes his own water over the quarter. His mark is inscribed on the dark face of the water in disappearing luminescent ink. It is far more ephemeral than that sort of writing in the snow.

0430   FIGARO, unmoved by natural spectacles and human responses, sails on at a speed of 6.5 knots on a course of 100°.

The low angle of the morning sun gives Mike another opportunity to check an azimuth against the compass deviation. He finds a deviation of 5°, a difference of 3° to the error we have been cranking in. Since a deviation of 3° would amount to a divergence of one mile from the desired course after twenty miles of sailing (and we have thousands to go), he is, of course, absolutely correct in keeping after this problem. It is an unfortunate and unnecessary problem for us to be faced with, but it is with us and we cannot brush it aside. The course is altered to 93°. We will continue our checks. To keep the record straight, our deck log is a complicated affair. Sample:

Time	True Course	Varia-tion	Devia-tion	Course Ordered	Course Steered	Course by 2nd Compass	Speed	Remarks
0400	078°	20°W	05°E	100°	100°	098°	6.6K	BALLS!

0700   The barometer is going down slowly, now at 30.15. The fog returns and our speed drops from 6.8 to 5.5 knots.

0800   The wind is remarkably unsteady. It does not settle down in either speed or direction. It keeps us guessing as to what is in store and we are unhappy when the speed drops. It has us on the go, changing sails to keep up with its vagaries. Right now, the wind is farther aft and much lighter. We change sails once more, putting up the light, blue-top spinnaker and changing to light sheets. Our speed has dropped to 3.8 knots. At the moment, this does not have the earmarks of a fast passage.

0930   The wind freshened again and with it another sail change. We baby the blue-top at all times. It tears with a hard look, so we take it off and replace it with the 1.2-ounce Hood spinnaker. Our speed is now up to 6.0 knots.

1000   The course is as before, 093°. The neverguesser gets himself a sun line and a consolan fix.

1130   Things are getting better. Our speed is up to 7.5 knots as the wind holds its direction and continues to increase. Strains on the gear show up. We replace the rope spinnaker guy with a wire guy. Ordinarily at sea, we rig this from the moment we put up the spinnaker, but because of the unsteady quality of the wind and the constant sail changes, we simplified things for ourselves by working with rope throughout. It is now time to get on all of the go-fast.

While clearing up the deck, coiling down running gear in use, and stowing the light stuff we no longer need, the mast is checked to see if all the halyards are running clear, just to make sure that all will be in working order if we should need anything in a hurry. It appears as though there is a foul-up of the jib halyard and the leeward spinnaker halyard. In the normal order of things it is best to insist that the jib and spinnaker halyards be cleared after each new sail setting, as they have an unnerving habit of crossing at the masthead after a sail change. However, since this has been an up spinnaker, down Genoa, down spinnaker, up Genoa kind of morning in relatively light airs, the boys up forward have delayed checking and straightening things out in their urgency to get things drawing properly. Often a twist can be seen at a glance. On FIGARO, this is a little harder to spot since she carries places for three spinnaker halyards. It adds gear at the top which must be isolated and identified visually.

She was designed primarily for deep-ocean racing, and running and reaching for long periods are important aspects of that kind of racing. She is rigged with a centerline spinnaker block for a rope and wire halyard, though it is our custom to carry a rope halyard in this block. We use this rig for inshore and passage racing. At sea we unreeve this halyard and replace it with a light messenger line ready to send up anything we might need. Our spinnakers at sea are carried on windward and leeward wire halyards. The blocks are arranged on a V'd crane at the masthead in order that the spinnaker halyard will always have a clear lead, never tangling with or sawing across the head stay. Inshore, these blocks are rove with messengers or the blocks are removed. Offshore, we send up wire halyards with rope tails. The way it works is like this: the spinnaker is hoisted on both halyards; the leeward one, however, carries the strain. When jibing, the strain is taken on the opposite halyard and the first one is eased. It may sound complicated, but it pays off in preserving gear, especially when you consider that on the ocean you can be running dead off for a couple of weeks as they do in the Trans-Pacific Race. It pays off, that is, if you are not careless, and we may have been guilty. If they are crossed, we may be getting chafe. It should come down and we ought to start the set over again, but that's the trouble with racing, you take chances. After all, how long is this wind going to last?

Creaming along

1200   Noon fix is 41° 50′ N 62° 40′ W. 176 miles made good in the day's run. That's a lot better than we seemed to be doing. Course 086°, speed 7.3 knots.

1400   Spinnaker is down and the Genoa is up. Another sail change, and damn it to hell, this is the sort of trip where all you have to do is imagine some sort of trouble and presto, there it is. It looked like the halyards were crossed and that we might expect chafe, and in taking down the spinnaker halyard, sure as shooting, it was cut. The wire had several strands gone about a foot above the snap shackle. We re-splice it a little above the cut and still have enough wire for a few turns around the barrel of the winch. Meanwhile, we rove a spare rope and wire halyard. Luckily, on examination, the jib halyard escaped damage. It's more than we deserve for our carelessness, but all contributions are gratefully accepted.

1500   After much discussion, counting on fingers and toes, and calling on a mathematics major for a certified audit, the ship's clocks were advanced one hour. The problem, as always, hangs on the belief that one watch is being favored over another by faulty arithmetic, Machiavellian planning, or downright stupidity. The only point on which there is agreement is that some accommodation should be made to the existence of a prime meridian and time zones, but since the meridian itself is in England, why take it so seriously here? After all, tomorrow is the Fourth—why the hell did we revolt if not to throw off the impositions of a distant empire? Withal, when the dust is settled, an agreement suitable to most is reached.

1700   This is a voyage for first-class passengers. Sailing has come a far piece since the days of bucko mates, bloodied buntlines, and the taste of the cat. Now we sail with all of the appurtenances of culture, refinement and other civilized adorments for the spirit. We have just heard the "Passion according to St. Matthew" by Johann Sebastian Bach from the tape player. It should have a profound and uplifting effect on the crew and can be considered in lieu of Wednesday evensong. Not that we ever hold such a service, but I am sure we would sail faster if we did. The effect on some members of the crew is stupefying. You would think they had just slept through a sermon and were now on their way home to Sunday dinner. I may be misreading the expressions, especially of those who would rather have heard King Pleasure sing "Little Red Top." But at least I am sure of the fact that we are on the way to dinner, which consists of: Baked Honey-Glazed Ham, Scalloped Potatoes, Golden Corn Niblets.

1800   The barometer is on its way down in a long slide. The secret is out. There must be a low somewhere northwest of us and from the rate at which the wind is increasing in speed, it must be coming toward us rapidly. Our speed is 7.3 knots on a course of 095°.

Mike, whose seafaring heritage must number stalwarts who sailed with Drake, Nelson, and Irish smugglers, has gone on sick list. He came on board plagued by assorted miseries, brought on, no doubt, by a vigorous regime of shoreside living. He spent a lot of time visiting with friends on our side of the shiny great big water. From my own experience on his side of the great pond, I know how much one's well-being is impaired just through the simple act of responding to toasts of welcome. His recovery was not at all helped by the intransigence of the compass. It takes a while to recover from the effects of riotous living ashore. At sea, this low level of resistance erupts in many ways. In his case, the dissipation has gone to his feet. For any man, much less a navigator, the area in trouble is surely 180° out of phase. Other men get headaches, with Mike it's his feet. As a matter of fact, he has an infected toe which is already sending warning signals to a gland in the groin. He is shaken, he smiles, but for the moment is not overly communicative—even as to our position. Mike is relieved of all duties and has taken to the sack. The crew holds to the belief that it is sailing the great circle courses, those under Mike's eyes.

I am busy in my role of pharmacist's mate and dispenser of healing. Our senior officers seem to be caving in. (On the other hand, some younger men seem to improve with age. Cleody, who used to have a touchy stomach at sea, goes rampaging around the deck like a tiger now that he has attained his majority.) Mike is given an antibiotic, Tetracycline, and Buz is still being dosed with Chlortrimeton to clear his cluttered antrums. These prescriptions may be wrong, but they seem to be helping. For that matter, how do I know that the doctors from whom I sought advice and prescriptions did not slip me a bunch of placebos.

For a while I wondered if Mike's illness was psychosomatic; he had every reason for it to be so. He must have had it up to here, what with the planning for the traditional Fourth of July celebration. Mike is one of those Anglo-Irish characters who find it difficult to see virtues in the land of the Sassenachs until someone like an American comes along with an opinion or two. It is then that he reveals latent admiration for mad King George III, English weather, and English cooking. In this case, he finds our patrioitc enthusiasm shocking and uncontagious.

With so many scholars aboard, one of the ideas being bruited about for Mike's benefit is a project for group reading from something in the style of a mystery play (still to be written). After all, if such a mediaeval device is good enough for T. S. Eliot in celebration of Canterbury Cathedral, it ought to be good enough for FIGARO. Mike, the only lobsterback aboard, has been cast for all English parts. It is difficult to agree on a subject. Cleody, who went to a university in Boston, favors the Tea Party as a symbolic event. Skip, from a Vermont school, favors the Battle of Bennington. It is rejected as being too obscure. All we know of Bennington is girls with long, dank hair. I favor the Battle of Yorktown. It was not only the final victory, but Mike would make a splendid Lord Cornwallis and I fancy the nautical eminence of De Grasse. Mike knows nothing of the American Revolution, and cares less. His only contact is through a Shavian play he once saw, and therefore thinks General Gentleman Johnny Burgoyne would be a fat part. In that case, everyone else will be an Indian. All in all, this sort of talk has an appalling effect on Mike, who cannot whip up any enthusiasm for revolting colonials.

1900–2100   The barometer continues its downward slide. There is definitely a low in the northwest which is overtaking us at a great rate of speed. The wind in the southeast is still increasing. Our own speed is 7.3 knots.

The Genoa is handed, and we go to the big double head rig combination consisting of the big overlapping Yankee jib top set over a Genoa staysail. We are going like a train of cars. It is a marvelous feeling.

2300   The barometer is still going down. The bilges are pumped dry. All lashings and stowage are checked and re-examined. The ship is being made ready for a blow. This is the time to get ready.

2400   The barometer is at 29.80. The wind is in the south-southeast, blowing at about 25 to 30 m.p.h. The lee scuppers are awash. Below, you can feel her dip her rail into a sea, then hear the water go rushing aft in the waterway. She leaps from sea to sea, sometimes on the crests, at other times you can feel and hear her as she puts her shoulder into a sea, smashing through and sending the spray rattling diagonally across the deck, fetching up on spar, smokestack, and ventilators. We are snug and dry below, but sleeping is now an active sport. Every once in a while there is a bone-jarring bounce that reminds you that you are at sea. FIGARO goes on like the proper thoroughbred racer that she is.

XVII

THURSDAY, THE (GLORIOUS) FOURTH OF JULY

Three Cheers for the Red, White, and Blue!

0010   It is difficult to sleep in the weather berth. By tradition, the captain sleeps in a starboard berth, a tradition not suited to American eastern seaboard ocean racing. The prevailing wind in a trans-Atlantic race going east is from the southwest. In the Bermuda Race the wind is from southwest to southeast. As a result of all this, if the skipper sleeps in a starboard bunk he usually has a weather berth, which certainly cannot be what was originally intended. Come to think of it, there is another tradition which is difficult to escape and, while no longer a practice, leaves an indelible mark on the design and therefore the use of yachts. It is the fact that in the days of paid hands, the captain, officers, and their guests boarded a ship on its starboard side; the crew boarding to port. The same elite side was reserved for the guests' swimming and for the captain's walkway. For this reason, the heads usually were placed on the port side. That etiquette of boarding is almost abandoned now and there is no room to walk on a yacht, but the heads are still located on the port side. All that remains in use of the old tradition is that crew signals, such as crew mealtime, fly from the port spreader. In any case it is for such obscure reasons I usually wind up with a weather bunk; it's hard to fight the system.

FIGARO is heeled down and leaping. The bunk board cuts into one's side with sharp, unrelenting pressure. From time to time you are heaved into the air like a flapjack in the window of one of those Broadway eateries. The return to the bunk from being airborne is as trying to the soul as it is to the ribs. I have had enough of it and go up on deck to have a look around. Things have a different aspect up here. The cockpit has far less movement, which speaks volumes for the advantages of an after stateroom. FIGARO is on course and going well. The speedometer records 7.5 knots. There are numerous rain squalls about, each equipped with its own private gusts of wind at its front. Visibility is down to about one-half mile.

0130   It is raining very hard. The visibility has closed down to about 200 yards. The barograph is still on a ski slope going down; now at 29.70.

0200   The rest of Able watch leave the misery of the bunk for the trial by chill and damp on deck. We are steaming as before on a course of 095° at a speed of 7.5 knots.

0300   The same conditions hold. The wind, if anything, coming on a little harder. The boat is still moving well through the water, despite the bucking and leaping. Course still 095°; speed for the hour is an average of 7.6 knots.

0500   There are signs that the low has begun to pull abreast of us to the north, the wind slowly edging around to the south and it is blowing hard. We have lowered the mizzen to ease the steering. In a centerboard yawl of this design, a very severe weather helm develops when on a hard close reach. A second centerboard aft would help alleviate such a situation. It would move the center of lateral resistance of the hull aft to counteract the shift aft of the center of lateral effort of the sails in this point of sailing. However, FIGARO has only one board so we try to balance the boat by taking off the aftermost sail, the mizzen, and by easing the main.

0545   The wind is still farther aft now, enough to carry the bag. We take off the Yankee jib topsail and set the White Mist spinnaker. When this is up, we take off the Genoa staysail and trim the spinnaker to a better set. When the spinnaker and the main are drawing to our satisfaction, we reset the mizzen. I am not using a mizzen staysail this year because I do not believe the sail warrants the penalty in rating, and so I have been measured without it. It is questionable, in any case, whether I could carry it usefully at this time. I think I would just be lugging it. The White Mist bag is a sail which belongs to a sister yawl, WHITE MIST. We always borrowed this sail from Blunt White for our trans-Atlantic efforts, except for the year we both raced to Spain. It is a real bulletproof, cast-iron job, made of 3-ounce nylon, hand-sewn on the head, luff, and clews. Blunt, that magnificent sea dog and late friend, is gone now to join his seagoing forebears, but Melville Grosvenor, the new owner of WHITE MIST, did not break the tradition set by Blunt. He lent us the sail for this race. For this kind of going, it is a beauty. It has narrow girths, less than our regular C.C.A. sails, but in a hard blow it stands up there like the Rock of Gibraltar, does not oscillate and therefore is the helmsman's friend. It takes a pretty bad job of steering to break it. It's a marvelous feeling to have a sail on that you don't have to fight and at the same time know that it's pulling like a team of mules.

The Atlantic really looks like an ocean now, none of that millpond disguise. The waves are cold gray-green and crested with plumes. They come marching steadily toward, under and around us. In the cold light of dawn they impart a feeling of majesty and power and make us feel like true sailors of the deep.

Our course 095°. Speed 7.6 knots.

0630   Able watch is staggering for want of sleep. Its previous stint below in the rack was not blessed much with shut-eye. The boat was far too active. But now, with the sea on the beam and a little aft, the sleeping should be better.

Some forego breakfast in order to get into the rack sooner. It's hard to eat and go to sleep right after it, especially when you are that tuckered out. Now for six hours of sweet sacktime.

0650   Baker watch takes down the White Mist bag and resets the Number One Genoa. The wind is coming ahead. What the hell! Do we have to play tag with a low at this time, or is this a larger system made up of a number of cells? In any case, why do we have to go on the wind every time I go to bed? I'm not running for sainthood.

0730   THE MAIN BOOM IS BROKEN!! Of all the son-of-a-bitching luck. It's dispiriting to be brought out of sleep with this kind of news. It gave way under the strain caused by a makeshift vang strop. This probably means that our chances for winning this race are blown. It's pretty god-damned hard to recover from a lousy break like this one. DAMN IT TO HELL. And the worst of it is that the break was probably avoidable. We lost the regular, wide vang strop overboard in a fit of carelessness a day or so ago and have been using a doubled sail stop as a jury rig. It not only gave a narrower bearing surface, but worse than that, the strop was set over the part of the main boom where two pieces of sail track join. We not only lack the reinforcement that comes from an unbroken piece of metal, but as though this were not enough, this same area

Dragging the main boom

of the boom holds two fittings and a cleat. The perforations from so many screw holes have made this the tenderest part of the boom and we had to pick this place to hang a narrow vang strop.*

The first thing to do is to lower the sail carefully. For the moment at least, the sail is acting like a reinforcing member. Its foot is taut and rigid, helping to hold the boom together. We can't put too much strain on the main sheet which is attached near the outer end, this would bend the boom too much. On lowering, the sail must be quickly smothered, flogging will increase the damage. We get it down without further mishap, the sail is lowered quickly, all hands lay to and smother the main. The end of the boom is laid on the dodger which is acting like a gallows frame. Our boom is a squarish, hollow spar, made of four pieces of straight grained spruce—top, bottom, and two sides glued up over occasional blocking. A preliminary examination shows the top piece is broken, the bottom badly cracked and the two sides splintered and torn; but since it is good spruce, the long strands of the grain in the side pieces are, for the most part, unsheered, though splintered in longitudinal separations.

We decide that the boom can be fixed by putting splints on the sides and then fishing the whole thing with line which, in effect, means binding it with a continuous lashing. The sail is taken off the mast, but left on the boom sail track. In fishing we will have to take the line over the sail track, which would prevent getting the sail back if it were removed beforehand; and it is questionable whether we could use the sail as a loose-footed main with any efficacy. The boom is not built for that. The boom is removed from the forward gooseneck and the fittings are removed from the neighborhood of the break. While this is going on, Cleody dives into the forepeak and comes up with a number of long lengths of seasoned, straight-grained oak. I have been carrying this lumber with me on all major voyages almost from the time the boat was launched. The wood has gone to Bermuda several times and crossed the Atlantic three times and now the emergency so long-feared and anticipated is here. With the wood come drills, nails, and screws, and the repair crew is off and at it— like an auto crew during a pit stop in the Indianapolis 500.

After the fittings are removed, the slats are fitted in place along the side of the boom and tacked in place. Following this, they are drilled and affixed to the boom with screws. The screws are kept to the outer ends of the slats as the

---

* We use a vang (a line to hold the boom down) whenever we reach or run. The line, or vang, is hooked into a wide dacron sling, or strop, which goes around the boom. The vang must go down to the deck in a manner which will apply downward rather than angled pull, since a great part of the boom hangs over the water when reaching or running. Because of this, the strop is unavoidably placed somewhere from the middle of the boom forward. The vang, or line, attached to this strop leads down to the deck, passes through a block and then to a winch. The object in holding a boom down is to increase the exposed area of the sail because the boom will kick up as the sail is eased and balloons out. In addition, the vang takes the curve out of the leech and thereby reduces weather helm. For vangs we use stretchy, nylon line. We don't want to hold the boom rigid, for, in the case of a jerking lurch, or if the boom should dip in the sea when a pattern of rhythmic rolling occurs, the boom may break if held too rigidly. It needs some give, and here, in spite of our precautions in planning, but because of our careless application, the boom is busted.

The main boom with splints and bandage

wood fibre in the broken parts is too injured to give much holding quality. As the last screws are being driven home, the process of fishing the spar with dacron line begins. While the sail is down in this unfortunate emergency, other crew members are at work sewing up the main. We have been delaying repairs for the moment when the wind would become light and we could sew with less loss of speed to the boat. It is always a fine decision as to how long you dare carry along with trouble, taking the chance that you can effect repairs at a less important time. Naturally, if your judgment is wrong, then in your contrariness to normal practice you pile trouble on trouble—a veritable Ossa on Pelion. Now we fix two batten pockets and replace two reef points that have beaten themselves into useless, frayed fringe.

While all of this is going on, FIGARO is sailing on course under Number One Genoa and jigger. The yawl rig pays off again. She is nearly balanced and sailing without too much helm. During the time it takes to work on the boom, she is doing about 6 knots.

Curiously, with so much activity going on there is little time to do any Monday morning quarterbacking, or hold a wake. The thoughts of the disaster to our racing chances, while not brushed completely out of mind, are well back in the consciousness. The urgency is to get on with it. Hope is a tiny flame that will not go out.

0930   The boom is ready. Fittings are put back in new places. The boom is rehung and the main restrung on the mast. Up she goes, everyone looking hard at the jury rig. It looks sturdy enough. We trim the main properly and we are sailing with a main once more. The whole job, from the time we took off the sail until it was reset, took one hour and fifty minutes—although it seemed like eons. This is pretty gol-durned good! The crew did a magnificent job, especially Conn and Jon. It is this kind of spirit that wins races. We won't be counted out and are still in there pitching. The hope is that we haven't given up too much distance. It's not a bad-looking jury rig, but we are going to need some real good breaks to take us into Cowes a winner. So far, we have been getting the dirty end of the stick.

There is something peculiar about the Fourth of July and racing where we are concerned. Disasters seem to dog us on this date. We have had noteworthy happenings to remind us of the day. During the race to Sweden, by July 4 we had already suffered one important setback, having discovered more than half of our drinking water was gone. The discovery had been made the night before, a long night of tears. I was below in the early afternoon of the Glorious Fourth, trying to rebuild morale with a big holiday dinner. In the middle of constructing a magnificent sauce for roast turkey (canned whole), my attention was called to a very black squall line on the western horizon. It was pretty wide and looked desperate. At that moment, we were carrying everything we possibly could: spinnaker, spinnaker staysail, mizzen staysail, in addition to the main and jigger. I didn't take the squall line seriously, feeling that at the worst we would have five or ten vigorous minutes which we could jockey through and then go merrily on our way after the front of the squall had passed through. I knew something was brewing, but this looked like an outriding, isolated squall. After all, I reasoned in interior dialogue, this is how we did it on the Trans-Pacific. On that race, when you reach the region of the trade wind squalls some 400 miles east of Hawaii, the squalls come down on you at intervals about twenty to thirty minutes apart; and if you bothered to lower for each one you would make little forward progress; so you hang on to all of your go-fast and ride them out when they hit. Therefore, with the exception of taking down the spinnaker staysail in order to give the spinnaker freer air in whatever convolutions were about to occur, my order was to stay with it and I went back to the more important business of sauce-making.

Well, I misread that one for fair. That was no squall. That was the front of a depression that took about a week to go over us. When we heard it described much later on BBC we learned that at one time it extended from Iceland to the eastern shores of the Baltic—a pretty fair-sized depression. When that one hit, it was like a giant hand shoving over a toy boat. In an instant, the spinnaker and mizzen staysail exploded. Chaos reigned for a few moments. The wind howled, the air was filled with shards of nylon and what wasn't flying was snapping and crackling in the wind like a machine gun. I scrambled for the deck just as the sauce hit the cabin sole and as a deluge of rain came down. We conquered the fragmented sails and got the pieces on deck. The boat seemed to be riding all right with what was left so that we were faced with a snap decision. We desperately needed drinking water, and on the other hand we should get on with the race. Naturally, we decided to try to accomplish both. The crew was divided into work parties, one gang to put up the hard-weather spinnaker (the White Mist sail) and the other to capture water. The sail got up fine, but the water detail was a flop. Being prepared for almost anything, not including bad judgment, I had a special rain catcher made for the boat. It was a cleverly devised spread of cloth which could be hung under the boom and attached to the rail, thereby catching all of the water pouring off the mainsail, no mean rain catcher itself. The water was collected in a pocket at a lower end and controlled by a spout. The only catch in the catcher was that to insure the fact that the cloth was waterproof it was made of Fiberglas which, we discovered to our dismay, made the water taste like creosote. The water was collected in buckets, and any container we could find, against the day we would relish a creosoted drink. The tanks, meanwhile, had been opened to receive these new supplies and I believe we lost more fresh water than we collected when great spouts erupted from the openings as the boat threshed around in the sea. When peace was at last re-established and FIGARO was roaring along in a strong breeze, I went below to make a new sauce and kick myself in the ass for being so boneheaded. We had a spirit-rebuilding dinner and went on to win the race. So maybe it will happen again. Who says lightning never strikes the same boat twice?

One serious aspect to consider in our reconstructed boom is that we don't know how far to test its strength. We will constantly hold back from putting a heavy load on it with sheet, vang, or foreguy. We don't know what the accumulated result of being out of perfect trim may cost in time.

Mike is on deck with the rest of us during Operation Boom. He either has responded in true Hearts of Oak tradition to the emergency or is healing because of medication. He seems also to have composed himself to the idea of July 4. He just sighted a sail to leeward ahead of the beam. No positive identification is made. I hopefully judge it to be CARINA because of the real or imagined silhouette of the blur on the horizon. It seems to have an 85-percent forward triangle and looks large. But then, all competition looks large until it sails alongside and you find it is the bottom boat in division four. In the Bay of Biscay, when we first spied WHITE MIST, we thought she was CRIOLLO. In the North Sea ANITRA was first identified as HAMBURG V. But no matter who it is we get an overwhelming reassurance. In spite of all of Mike's splendid navigational skills, there is always the lurking suspicion that the compass may still be misleading. Here though, is a competitor in sight, after several days. He verifies our estimate of the deviation in the compass (unless this guy is a joker who decided to sail off with us). By the time we are squared away, our friend disappears in the muck to leeward.

1000   What a long morning! The fishing on the main boom looks good. If it goes again (heaven forfend), it will not be at the splints, we are sure. The barometer is rising to 29.8. Resetting the main increased our speed to 7.0 knots, a net gain of 1 knot. It is interesting to see the power in a big jib balanced by the jigger on a reach.

1330   The barometer continues to rise. The low is going off into the northeast. Barograph reading 29.90.

1500   The wind is slightly aft and is fresh. We take off the Genoa and put back the White Mist chute, but not without some fresh indication of trouble which lurks over us just looking for a chance. Again we see how dependent a racing boat is upon the continued working contribution of all of its skinned-down components. As soon as one thing goes awry, it leads to an accumulation of little disasters which sometimes lead up to a final major calamity. Hopefully, we see no reason for such a situation to arise, but the threat keeps us on edge.

A whole new series of mishaps began with the reluctance to put a load on the boom. It looked spongy between the splints and when the point of sailing required that the vang be put in the place where the break occurred, we were reluctant to do so. The same reasoning extends to the foreguy, which we no longer crank in too much. During the process of putting up the chute just now, FIGARO was going through a series of rolling gyrations. The particular part of the ocean in which we chose to put up the chute had a very irregular pattern to the sea. In fact, there were two seas running; the first a leftover swell from the old wind on the beam, and the second a new one now making up on the quarter. When they hit in one-two fashion, FIGARO would first be rolled down

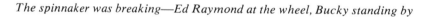

The spinnaker was breaking—Ed Raymond at the wheel, Bucky standing by

to leeward by the beam sea, then, while in that position, the new one on the quarter would get under her and start shoving her up to windward. I was at the wheel trying to keep her headed down. We put the spinnaker up under the Genoa so that the spinnaker was in the spoiled air under the Genoa and was diving all around. It threatened to foul at the head stay or else go into the water, but I had eyes only for the main boom which, being inefficiently vanged and held loosely by the foreguy, was swinging madly. The loose foreguy, inefficient as it was, still helped, for without it we would have had a Chinese jibe right then and there. The snapping of the boom was enough to make me worry about nothing but that. All this action didn't take long, just the time to get the Genoa down and temporarily lashed to the deck. However, no sooner was the spinnaker trimmed, then bang, the sheet let go and all hell broke loose once more. The chute streamed out ahead in the wind, snapping, whipping, and jerking the head of the mast like a terrier with a rat in his teeth.

The Genoa went back up and the boat was sailed downwind into the flapping chute. It was drawn into the quiet air behind the main and jib and taken down. We found the shackle on the sheet bent back and cracked. In all probability, it had opened during the process of diving around. It is extraordinary how often this happens. I have had shackles, and even snatch blocks, that you had to strain to open with your fingers, suddenly pop out when merely touching the deck, or even, at times (more inexplicably), shaking themselves loose. This one had most likely been hanging like an open hook after shaking loose, and when the pressure went on, it snapped.

A new sheet was rove. The whole process was re-instituted, this time without mishap, and the chute is pulling us along in its regular style. The wind is blowing about 30 m.p.h. and we are moving well, but it is a constant reminder to us how the old story of the want of a nail and the outcome of the battle applies at sea. Ours started with losing the vang strop, on to the breaking of the boom, and now we could have had a broken masthead fitting.

1600   We have finally settled down. There are no more impending disasters visible, or at least so we hope. It is time to look to the dinner. This was to have been our banquet celebration of our Independence from Mike and we stay with the plan. However, our energies and adrenalin are pretty well used up so that tonight's feast will be tempered to our condition.

Mike, to show that he is willing to enter in the spirit of our Independence which, after all, was bred out of men like Locke and other free English thinkers, comes below to help me. On the other hand, he may wish to protect himself against nefarious Yankee tricks (if you can't beat them, join them).

Our menu for tonight:

DEHYDRATED (OR REHYDRATED) STEAK

LYONNAISE POTATOES—NIBLETS

PEACHES IN SYRUP—CAKE

CHÂTEAU MARGAUX '55

(*very nice tipple according to Mike*)

Preparations were gotten under way by a very good jazz concert from our tape machine. This enlivened everything. Mike worked doggedly, determined to make the best of a bad lot. A naturally taciturn man, at least when his foot hurts or you ask about our position, he was heard to mutter a few isolated phrases now and then. On one occasion he was clearly heard to say, "Very interesting. Colonel Washington's birthday, you say. Very nice." His particular job was to rehydrate the quick-freeze-dried steaks, which he went at with such a dubious mien as to make his stiff upper lip practically rigid. His whole attitude, as he poured the melted enzymes (or whatever they are) back into the foil envelope, seemed to say, "If they eat it, then by the blood of Nelson, so will I."

The program for the dinner started very well indeed. I had been cherishing a mounting number of injuries to my racing spirit and finally gave way to my feelings during the grace and invocation. While calling maledictions down upon the gremlins who had played havoc with us, a reasonable prayer was made to all the gods, goddesses, demigods and demigoddesses, their hosts, minions, consorts, and allies who rule on this watery dominion. In their oceanic wisdom they were asked to bring us fair winds and kindly seas. Having run this off in nearly one breath, we then besought them to keep any decent conditions they could devise just for us. They were further asked to reserve the tribulations and trials for our competitors, who, we assured them, did not have our kind of allegiance to their oceanic majesties. If our prayers are granted, proper recognition of their collective might will be made in suitable alcoholic temples when reaching shore.

The dinner itself was surprisingly good for anything that is dehydrated and comes in a foil bag. It was followed by patriotic songs. "Columbia, the Gem of the Ocean" was featured, as was the last stanza of "The Star-Spangled Banner," no mean feat in itself. A box of favors, put on by the captain's splendid wife, was uncovered by Skip and as each favor was drawn, it provided an occasion for a spontaneous inanity. Certainly the most inane was the moment when, in an overly vigorous patriotic gesture, I plunged a toy dress sword into a pound cake, liberally spattering chocolate sauce. All of this was done to the accompaniment of a few short words reminding us all, once again, of the bloody massacre on Boston Common in 1770. Thus, another Independence Day celebration was brought to a close.

While I was recovering from the day's trials, and too much dinner, the sharpshooters on Baker watch put a hole in the Hood spinnaker. How, they refuse to say. It was repaired and reset in fifteen minutes.

2230   The navigator reports 245 miles made good in the last 32 hours. An average of approximately 7.7 knots, which is not bad, considering what we have been through. I wonder what the competition has done. They can't all have had bad luck. Their day must come, so saith the Great Equalizer.

2330   In the words of watch officer Buz Knowlton: "The Glorious Fourth of July was certainly a Banger!"

XVIII

A SERIES OF INGLORIOUS DAYS

FRIDAY, JULY 5

0100   We suffer a vexatious aftermath to the short-lived blow. During the night, the wind has been easing off. We are on our desired compass course of 100°—by our compass, that is—but the speed is down. It now stands at 3 knots and less seems indicated. The barograph is 30.05 and is rising.

0200   The Baker watch is called with sweet song and ribaldry. No one gets mad. The speed is up to 3.5 knots for a short time and then promptly falls off again. The wind is huffing and puffing, a very bad sign for those who are always looking for menaces under their clouds.

0600   For the past several hours, the wind had gone up sufficiently to warrant the replacement of the light Genoa with the Number One. The barograph is at 30.10 and still rising. The wind is getting shifty, now coming in from ahead! We can no longer hold to our desired course, but have been headed off to 080°.

A breakfast of French toast and bacon, and I am again reminded of our former navigator, Francis Chichester, on the Fastnet Race of '57 (to my mind, the ball-buster of ball-busters—the race, not Francis). As we started this race he had just completed his second singlehanded trans-Atlantic passage.

0800   I have the uncomfortable suspicion that a high must be about to descend upon us. One was indicated on the weather maps when we left. It was over the continental U.S. to the south of two lows and halfway between them. If, as it turns out, the entire pattern is to come over us, then I hope the high doesn't last too long. There is nothing more trying or exasperating than the flukey light airs one gets under a high cell. We have just felt the winds generated by the first low. Let's get to the next one. We hacked this last one up pretty grievously with carelessness. In the next one we will act a little more professionally, or we deserve to be down amongst the also-rans. Lows and depressions are for yacht racers. Highs are for swimmers, horsemen, and picnickers.

0830   A curious physiological phenomenon is observed. As the wind lessens in speed, the crew members become involved in protracted periods of fixed staring. Their eyes, in a somewhat opaque and glazed scrutiny, are riveted on certain pages of "Playboy." There is a zombie-like rigidity to their bodies. The only way you can tell they are in a state of animation is that their lips purse from time to time in a silent whistle. I wonder if there is any direct relationship between high-pressure atmospheres and the libido?

In order that we do not degenerate into lassitude, I order a swift series of sail changes. It is down Number One light Genoa, up the ghoster—down the ghoster, up light Genoa—all with attendant changes of running, rigging, at one point using a line no thicker than flag halyard. Perhaps, as a reward for all of this industry, we get a little more breeze and we make one more change to the Number One Genoa. Our speed has gone from 1.5 knots to 4.5 knots. The gods reward those who try.

0900   The increased breeze lifts our hearts and at least one of us to song. Freddy, the playboy of the Western World, gives us his version of "Ciao-Ciao, Bambino." We wonder how he keeps up with contemporary Italian culture in the mountain fastness of Denver.

1000   The ready locker, that which is normally our ice chest and is now used to store perishables and things to eat next, is being cleaned out. It's a vigil one must maintain or else the smell of rotting vegetables can put you off the ship. The vegetables are now being cleaned, rotten leaves taken off the outside of the lettuce, carrots peeled, and celery clipped. Skip offers the sea-gods some rotting lettuce, a dangerous by-play!

1200   The watch is called and our position at noon is declared to be 43° 02′ N 55° 35′ W. We are on the latitude of Charlie.

1300   A wearying calm. There can be no doubt that we are fouled up with a high, the center of which is southwest of us. The barograph continues to rise, now at 30.2 and still on the escalator.

Conn and the navigator respond to swimming call. After a brief and shocking immersion, Mike reports the water to be colder than a vestal in Vergil. I am mystified by the phrase. I cannot for the life of me see why a vestal in Vergil is colder than a vestal in anyone else, or vice versa. As a matter of fact, if memory serves, I believe Vergil found more favor in the Asiatic arts of love and, therefore, would have little response to a vestal, hot or cold. I can only assume this is university slang, or reluctance to say virgin for ritual reasons, or that virgin and Vergil in one breath would make quite a mouthful.

1600   I rise from a troubled sleep, troubled more by the on watch than by niceties of conscience. Cleody, ever the racing man, blow foul, blow fair, is on the foredeck raising sail after sail in a moderately loud voice. If the gods won't provide a wind, then he will do so by his own exertions. Since it is difficult to go back to sleep and one must be positive in all actions, I seek to maintain *mens sana in corpore sano* through the agency of washing my drawers. Since one must be self-conscious about using fresh water too frequently for the arts of hygiene while at sea, they are washed in salt water and rinsed in fresh. May they dry in one piece.

The glass continues to rise, 30.25. The speed is plus or minus 1 knot. The wind is mostly up and down the mast. We need the help of Aeolus in the worst, or better yet, in the best way.

1800 In an absolute and utter calm, not a breath of wind to ruffle the face of the sea, which reflects the sky like a mirror. For some time, the navigator and the Baker watch officer have been discussing the necessity of swinging the ship to find what the deviations on the other headings can be. Constant azimuth readings have more or less verified that we had an 8° divergence on an eastward heading, but we don't know what the other deviation can be, and as we approach soundings this may create a clear and present danger.

For that reason, we contemplate turning on the engine for the purpose of swinging the ship. The conditions of the race say that the engine cannot be used for any forward propulsion; the engine can only be used in case of an emergency. This is an emergency about to happen and we will take great care that no forward propulsion will result from anything we do.

The operation is to be run under the direction of the navigator and port watch officer, who will sign the certificate of compliance which will contain the report of the action. The engine is started, the wheel put hard over, and the boat kept in constant slow rotation from E to ENE, NNE, and N in a left rotation. The boat returns to the eastward heading, it is put through a right rotation from E to ESE, SE, SSE, S, SSW, SW, WSW, W, and WNW. The procedure finished, the engine is secured. A stop watch was held on the whole action. The entire operation took twelve minutes and fifteen seconds. The engine was engaged for less than one-half minute during the entire sequence, since with the wheel over she was just given a shot and then permitted to coast.

The following deviations showed up and a Napier chart was constructed, which looks like this:

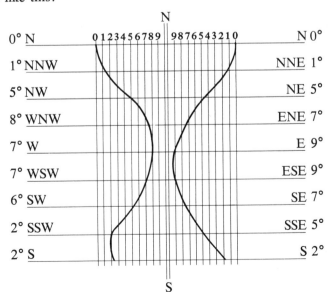

This whole operation will be reported to the committee when we file the affidavit of compliance. I have never before gone to sea with such a wild deviation card.

1900   No wind, no forward movement. It is difficult to maintain steerageway. In this kind of weather it should make little difference which way we are heading. You don't go anywhere and that very fast. But it's a point of honor to keep her pointing toward the objective, at least we fight like hell to do it. All of this is bad for our fighting spirit. It's hard to keep a stiff upper denture. We never move with any authority, when we do move, we crawl.

2100   Occasionally, a little zephyr comes in and lifts our speed and spirit. There are little whirly vortexes within this big nothing. The boat that carries the blessings of the fates will whip from one of these to another, never going fast, but never stopping. That boat does not seem to be us. Unhappy day.

Our speed is 3.7 knots as of now, on a course of 78°. The desired course is 105°, but at least we are not diverging very fast.

2300   Up until a while ago, we were steering a course of 70° at a speed of 3.0 knots, when the wind went up the flue once more. Now we are sailing on a heading of 30° at a dizzying 0.5 to 1.0 knots.

It has been an *amerdement* sort of day. We have tried everything and worked heartbreakingly. The sails were changed every hour on the half hour. You could run a radio commercial on our timing. But all to no avail.

> Whene the winde dothe notte blowe
> We dothe notte goe.
> —Anon (circa 1963)

SATURDAY, THE INGLORIOUS JULY 6

0001   The fog descends on its little skunk feet; an odd and rather unpleasant smell, more likely to be encountered in the environs of Fulton Fish Market than out here. In this wet, gray invisibility, the air is heavy with what I think is the odor of schooling bluefish.

The race is not going well. If the God of Racing is in his heaven, then the blinds are drawn in the porthole looking out at these sparrows. The minions governing his world of wind and wave are at it again, testing us. The secret inner assurance that only the brave deserve the fair is wearing thin, and yet we must secretly believe it or else why do we keep trying? On the other hand, do we have any other option?

The wind comes and goes, never settling into a good fair breeze. We manage to hold within striking distance of our desired course, now averaging between 095° and 100°, the desirable course being 105°, and our speed ranges between 2.5 and 3.5 knots.

0330   Whatever wind was, is not. Our speed forward is scarcely perceptible, the only measurable tests are on the occasions when someone makes water overside. We can then see if we are leaving the bubbles.

The navigator left word for a shout at this time, in order to get morning stars. There are no stars. Sleep on, Canopus, there will be other mornings.

0700   To vary our routine, we have taken to rousing the oncoming watch with taped music. It has removed the personal touch, but this automated electronic cockcrow is equally effective. If, in the future, we miss the more imaginative, personal approach, we can always go back. Everyone has his own way of waking the opposite watch when employing non-mechanical methods. A few go at the task with evident relish, especially if it is cold and wet on deck. It is not necessarily the compulsion of a sadistic instinct but rather a release for the feeling of outrage against the fates which divided the world into those who are wet and cold and those who are dry and warm. Another kind of waker-upper is always thinking up gags, sure to put those who are waiting to go to sleep in stitches but falling flatter than stale beer on those who are still numbed with sleep, or the efforts to get some. Then there are the gentle needlers, who bring the sad news from Aix to Ghent with sympathetic tones but insistent voices. The tape recorder, on the other hand, gives us a wide spectrum of choices— from a Handel chorale to Ray Charles' hollering. They may be put out of sorts with the shock of Charles at first, but are snapping their fingers before long. It has the advantage of getting a watch on deck with fully opened eyes.

In terms of percentage, we have just had an enormous increase, going from nil to 2 knots. It would look great on a graph. But if it looks good on a graph, it looks like hell on a plotting sheet. We are averaging a course of 150° to 160°, headed for the Azores, but not very fast. The wind is variable in constancy, speed and direction.

0930   The speed at this moment is 5.0 knots, but we are still headed off course. By this time, the high has us so besotted and bedeviled that we don't seem to care where we go, as long as we keep moving.

1200   The noon position showed:
82 miles made good since yesterday!

We knew we were not doing well, but it's a shock to the eyeball when you see the numbers in the deck log. This is true misery making. Somehow or other, it doesn't seem right. In our racing careers, all of us have been becalmed while racing in Long Island Sound or Chesapeake Bay. You sort of expect it there. However, at that time you can generally see your competition sitting it out with you (except for that son-of-a-gun sneaking up along the beach). But we have come out here in the great wide ocean where the wind is free and we do the same kind of sitting, fretting and staring out across the waste of water looking for signs of a breeze. And what about the competition?

1300   Things are a little better now, maybe you just have to keep beefing. We have the Number One Genoa up. Speed is 3.8 knots on a course of 115°.

1600   The wind has been holding its weight, but the direction is slightly more adverse. The boat speed is a respectable 5.8 knots. We have been headed to a course of 125°.

It is a good sleeping watch and a time for ridding ourselves of the accumulated tensions which pile up in light- or no-wind sailing. For that matter, we could accommodate ourselves to these conditions if we were not haunted by the idea that other boats have been romping toward the goal on the wings of a private breeze. No matter how we try to reassure ourselves of the fact that what is happening to us must be happening to the others as well, past experience has shown that this is not the case. Somebody always seems to be moving along while you sit it out. However, for the moment we have made our peace with this idea. Skip, occasionally scratching his emerging beard, is buried once more in "Playboy," finding interesting details that escaped his notice before. Ciao-Ciao Freddy is off on some exotic adventure with 007. Conn is below, puttering. Our Olympic champ is a great shipmate and ship's husband. He puts things to rights below decks. A small yacht on an ocean crossing with a boatload of crew can turn into a slum in short order if the crew is careless. When such a situation develops, it can have disastrous effects on crew morale, despite meals, entertainment, and pranks. Conn's activities go a long way toward keeping this a happy ship.

As a matter of fact, the entire crew has been very good at shipkeeping chores. On their watch, Cleody and Jon, in a burst of advance Sunday spit and polish (it is only Saturday), not only washed down below, removing the salt and grime from the cabin sole and bulkheads, but bronze-wooled the teak in the cockpit and on the decks flanking the cockpit. These areas, which comprise the wash-up scullery, were getting grease-stained with table scrapings. In order to save fresh water, we wash everything in sea water. The new detergents make this possible, although I must say that at times the coffee tastes of a perfume that is remarkably close to that of the detergent. We don't want to splash all that salt below, so we do it on deck. After an outstanding meal, the deck and cockpit look like the back side of a greasy spoon.

It is cold, and below decks gets a lot of attention. It is extraordinary, the degree to which one finds important things to do below in such weather. Freddy endlessly fixes the barograph. If, for the moment, it does not need fixing, he just stares at it. The navigator is constantly going below to navigate, despite the fact that we have not moved very far from the point at which he placed us just a while ago. And I, naturally, go below to check on the navigator. The best deck holders we have are Cleody, Jon, and Skip. Cleody and Jon, in the best racing tradition, restlessly fiddle with the set of the sails, and Skip, when his chores are done, wraps a towel around his head, shutting himself off from the unfriendly world, and settles into a corner under the dodger. What with his beard and general beat attitude toward dress, if he were to wrap a towel around his feet as well he would look like a figure out of "War and Peace"—the retreat of the Imperial Guard from Moscow—or perhaps one of our own ragged veterans who saluted George Washington at Valley Forge.

Conn dives below as soon as he finishes a wheel trick. He will do anything rather than put on pants and shoes. However, his determination to sail across barefoot and in shorts has built-in advantages, since he spends so much time shipkeeping below. His dress, after our thoughts about the competition, is the second most active speculation on board. Every evening when the sinking sun opens the refrigerator door, we think this is it. But he manages to survive and get below just before he congeals. He would have made a great shipmate for Shackleton.

1830   It will be a good night for penguins, if not for Conn—fog and chill light wind from the northeast with a freight of arctic air. Cleody has a cold, but is so conscientious that he will take no treatment. He says it will make him sleepy on watch. He settles for blowing his nose and complaining. It does not seem to have impaired his effectiveness.

Course is now 138°. The speed is up and down, ranging from a high of 6.2 to 2.5 knots.

2200   The breeze has freshened once more in this cat-and-mouse game that is being played with us. I don't enjoy being a mouse. This was an unhappy day for a racing man. It does seem the height of indecency to inveigle a man out into an adventure like this under the grand illusion that he is a member of that select company of sailors who have adorned story and history from Vikings to the lonely heroes of Conrad, only to find that he "bloweth where the wind listeth." We are not the masters of our fate, but have been reduced to worrying whether the drifter sheet (which is the size of flag halyard) is too heavy. We wonder whether its weight drains the sail of kinetic energy before that force is transferred to the hull. It's pretty bad when there isn't enough wind to support the weight of flag halyard. Of such is the kingdom of our heaven and watery world. But one thing we have learned on the Atlantic: it will change! It will change!

SUNDAY, THE EVEN LESS GLORIOUS JULY 7

0001   The second week of the race is ushered in with an active and foreboding omen. A bird, a red-eyed straggler from the Hitchcock movie, makes threatening gestures. Harsh-voiced and malevolent, it circles my head, calling down what are presumed to be maledictions. Its intonation is vaguely Danish. Can this be a familiar from WINDROSE? At one time, it was clearly heard to say, "Tuborg," although Skip insists that Heineken tastes better.

The barograph is at 30.35. Could it at last be heading down? If this is so, is it the diurnal dip (when does that occur?), or is it for real?

Course 105°. Speed (for want of another name) 1.5 knots.

0200   The course still 105°; speed up somewhat, 2.5 knots. No progress to speak of, but whatever there is, is all ours.

0400   The wind is now completely up the mast. It is almost nonexistent. What there is comes from aft. We move with all of the spirit of a man going to his hanging.

At one time or another we try every light sail in our complement, to no avail. When the wind she do not blow, we do not go.

0700   Our unfortunate situation persisted until just a while ago when a light breeze came in. Our speed is 3.5 knots. Our course, 110°.

It has been a dull sailing morning. The wind was scarce and, with the exception of fighting a light sail from time to time, most of the ship's activities were below decks. Somehow or other, we have to last out this protracted calm without going nuts. It being Sunday morning, many of the things we find ourselves doing, here adrift, southeast of Newfoundland, are not unlike those of a Sunday at home. To start off the day, and just like home, we were wakened by a racing motorcycle charging up the cabin. After composure was re-established and the tape recording of Cleody's Honda turned off, the ship returned to its routine. On a few, the effect was electric. Buz figuratively leaned out of a window, ready to throw a bottle. At times he sleeps in a bedroom whose window faces a street which has been converted to a drag strip.

After breakfast, there being no ardent claim for attention from the deck, a long chin-wag between captain, navigator, and watch captain—ethics, esthetics, ministers of God we have known. The atmosphere being left with an unresolved ecclesiastical aura, we played the "B-Minor Mass" of J.S.B. To give equal time to the younger contingent, this was followed by a jazz concert, with illuminating commentary from Skip as to the merits of various sidemen.

1000   The clocks are advanced one hour. There is no fuss. The crew is beaten into submission.

1200   Our position at noon is 42° 44′ N 52° 48′ W.

The run for twenty-three hours is 58 miles!!!

There is no comment adequate to describe the dumps which prevails behind brave talk. What a heartbreaking series of day's runs during a race. Nobody but nobody can be doing this badly. It requires deep faith in the Great Equalizer in order for us to maintain any fighting spirit.

The new position makes it necessary to establish a new desired course—100°. We are sailing that course at 2.2 knots in a light wind from the WNW. The sky is low, with a solid overcast. We have fair visibility.

To keep mind and hands busy and away from the glooms, we indulge in a spate of Sunday spun yarn work. Cleaning, bosun repairs, and the like. Bosun Rohde goes to the masthead for a tour of inspection of tangs, pins, shackles, turnbuckles, etc. All gear and fittings reported doing well. No ships or sails in sight. It would have been comforting to see a big fellow roosting in the calm with us.

2000–2400   The wind still light and unsettled. It keeps moving around the compass with no recognizable pattern. Our speed is very, very sad.

The night is still, little to break the dispiriting monotony. The only activity to break the quiet is the sudden eruption of a school of tuna, probably migrating eastward. The sea was suddenly broken with great splashings and leapings and then settled back to a black, oily hush. This day ends—no bangs, no whimpers, no wind.

MONDAY, JULY 8

0001   The new day begins, ingloriously and with small promise. No wind and Bonnie Charlie still lies over the ocean. We are barely able to move under the light blue-top spinnaker. We change sails with backbreaking regularity in the old-fashioned, if mistaken, belief that you have to fight hard to win. But our battle is with a feather-stuffed pillow. No mark is left, no advance made, nothing happens. It is doubtful whether all of our struggles have added anything significant in the way of increased distance, yet that is why we are here—to race. In a calm, at the finish, 100 yards' lead has meant as much as two hours.

0200   Our desired course is still 100°, but in order to make any reasonable headway, we must take a better sailing angle. The wind is from dead aft and very light. We steer 90° at about 2.0 knots.

0300   The wind is going even lighter. We go through a wearying series of sail drills. There is much up and down of the blue-top to the drifter to the blue-top, to the etc., etc. The task is not simply one of lowering a sail and raising another. The running rigging changes and has different leads each time. To reduce some of the labor, the spinnaker pole is rigged and kept in position and as each sail is dropped to the deck, it is immediatley flaked out, ready for quick hoisting. Light sheets are rove and kept in place in the quarter blocks and through a block in the end of the main boom. All of the work is done in the dark and as quietly as we can in order not to disturb the watch below, which adds to the problem for, on occasion, a wrong lead is grabbed or a foul-up aloft is not seen in time, to say nothing of snarls of wet line on deck.

But this part of the work is the easiest of the whole detail. The most heartbreaking is to try and get whatever sail is up to draw. The air is heavy with dampness. The light sails are wet with dew. The folds of the nylon cloth cling like a brassière to Brigitte Bardot but without the lift to flesh and spirit. As the foredeck man grabs the clew and shakes the sail, hoping to free the folds so that whatever wind there is can fill the sail, a shower of raindrops falls from the sail to the deck and into his upturned eyes. (I have often thought that a spin dryer would be an important addition to yacht racing equipment.)

As the sail is shaken, it wraps around any convenient piece of standing rigging and perversely assumes the stance of a furled umbrella. It then takes minutes to clear the sail, sometimes even requiring that it be eased down on the halyard.

After all this has been accomplished the sail, freed, hangs out there, barely able to maintain its own increased wet weight, much less impart any thrust to the boat. Suddenly the wind changes and the whole procedure is repeated with another sail. It is discouraging work.

0400   The ultimate insult! For the love of Pete! We are heading west. There is no steerageway and we are rolling in a sea without wind.

The main has been taken down to prevent it from slatting itself to tatters. The blue-top came down with difficulty; it was grabbing at anything aloft like a drunk at a cocktail party. The drifter is up and sheeted tightly to the boom. The boom itself is strapped down with vang and sheet to keep it immobile. The object in this, beyond the desire to prevent damage, is to see whether the light drifter can fan us along. As the boat rolls, the pendulum motion artificially creates a series of alternating beam winds by the action of the sail rolling through the heavy air—just like a giant punkah. It is a question whether we will do more damage to the sail with the shock of each reversal than any good it will do us. But in extremes you try anything under the name of racing.

We seem to have slowed the period of rolling, but with only little discernible forward progress. At least we have turned the boat around. Our Hearts of Oak threaten to turn into poison oak.

0600   The Baker watch, not to be outdone, tries a couple of 360° turns by itself. All complete with the buckling and unbuckling of go-fast, leading sheets around, untangling snarls, and the exasperating trimmings that go with such sailing.

Course 140° at 1.5 knots.

0745   The roll became so bad that we tacked to 35° to make some headway and, if possible, to ease the boat, which is straining in each swing. The jerk on the lower shrouds at the tangs, turnbuckles, and chain plates is fearsome. We have turned up the turnbuckles to take as much slack out of the rigging as we can, but it is impossible to take it all out without putting an unnatural compression strain on the spar.

Down below, the bunk watch has created engineering marvels in the way of buffers to reduce the impact of each sideway thrust. I think we gave up the idea of hammocks at sea too soon without thinking it through.

0815   We have tacked back to 150°. In this kind of going, FIGARO tacks like a square-rigger. Her head comes around with agonizing slowness and once she starts to swing, there is difficulty in stopping her. She doesn't point at all. I am reminded of the Conrad story of the old barque that spent a week in St. George's Channel tacking from Ireland to Wales with no forward progress, finally going into port and waiting for a wind shift.

The wind is freshening briefly, 090° is the great circle course now to Eddystone Light, leaving Point Able to port.

As a fresh treat, we have heavy fog and cold.

1030 The only happy man on board is Rohde. He was having seagoing alimentary problems and has been eating his weight in laxatives; after eight days he labored and brought forth.

With this, the sun, in all its radiant glory, burst through. Can this have been our albatross? We have everything now but the celestial choir.

1200 Our noon position is 42° 50′ N 51° 48′ W. A day's run, in terms of forward progress—44 MILES. It's so bad it's hard to believe. While it is true that we haven't been sailing anywhere very fast, we didn't think that in twenty-four hours it could be this bad. After all, there were times when we had a bow wave, but we have been staggering all over the ocean. It all adds up to tough titty. When I get back, I can look forward to winning the yellow-water medal from the lee-rail Vikings. Alf Loomis, please note.

1300 Our speed and spirits sink. We are lost in aimlessness. Skipper is putting Turk's-heads on everything that comes to hand. Cleody, seeking to re-inspirit me, puts on a selection of Bach, Handel, and Purcell. It does a little for me, but doesn't change the wind. However, when King Pleasure sings out "Little Red Top," there are notable changes.

Can it be that Poseidon, Aeolus, *et al.,* are jazz buffs? In any case, the wind is up and our speed reaches astounding heights, 6 knots—and King Pleasure sings on and on.

1500 We are sailing a course of 25° on a desired course of 80° at a speed of 5.5 knots. The reason that our desired course changes so often is that, while our great circle course to Eddystone is hardly affected by our blind staggers over the sea, Charlie (Point Able) is close enough to require these adjustments. We must leave it on our port hand, but we want to be in the north and going north when we do. Sometimes a sea condition makes us take a longer tack as well.

1630 Afternoon tea to warm up the deck gang. It is sunny now and warm out of the breeze, but the breeze has some tooth, feeling as though it has just come off of Greenland's icy mountains.

1700 Fog banks are on the horizon. With any luck, they will hold off until the next watch. I stand up to have a look around and am sure that I see the icy mountains, but am willing to settle for a hot grog at one more Happy Hour.

1930 The barograph registers 30.55. We have come over from 45° to a course of 145°. We are beating to pass south of Charlie, as per instructions. Of all the ridiculous things I have ever experienced, this takes the cake. Here, far out in the Atlantic, we are going in for round-the-buoy racing, beating up to round a nonexistent marker buoy so that we can continue on in the Atlantic. I'll bet the race committee never thought of this and, if they did, may their whiskey turn to water.

Sundown brings with it the cold and damp. Fog, which we pass through, in a mixture of light and heavy sectors. Conn is still making the scene in the same zoot and barefooted. He does occasionally fasten the top button of his shirt and at times laconically admits it to be nippy.

2300   A ship is blowing its foghorn to windward. We blow back. Gloves are making their first appearance, along with woolen watch caps. It is cold.

You want to know what kind of a day this was? It was this kind of a day:

It was a day in which Cleody said, "Captain, we are sailing clear of our urine."

It was a day in which the captain trimmed Skip's beard.

It was a day in which Cleody recorded Jon's travail in an epic called: "A Krapp's Last Tape."

It was a day in which Skipper said Conn was trying to write a book called: "Bare-assed to Britain."

It was a day in which we made dishearteningly little forward progress.

XIX

THAT OLD BLACK MAGIC

TUESDAY, JULY 9

0001   This day has all the earmarks of its forerunners. The fog bank hangs over us, holding little cheer, no wind, and less promise of good things to come.

0140   From a course of 148°, tacked briefly on a wind shift to 65° and held it for fifteen minutes.

0400   Struck the Number One Genoa and set the light one. We had been moving well for a while, but now the wind is acting up again and we find ourselves sailing south on a course of 170° at 3.0 knots.

0800   The course is now 142° at 3.8 knots.

Pumped the bilges; we seem to be making water at an increased rate. What now? Is there still another cross to bear? We are caught betwixt wind and water. We catch it from on high, or else it tries to get at us from the deep.

0930   We are being headed by the perverse wind again. The wind not only refuses to blow with any force, but even when its pallid breath is felt, it comes from the wrong direction. A trying time.

1030   At last it has come to this—SORCERY! Put on your seat belt! Our lives and racing fortunes have been committed to the black science. The lack of wind finally got to me, and so, without thought of apostasy or whether it makes me out a warlock, heresiarch, or some kind of nut, I have tried my hand at witchcraft. It all began as a lark, but lurking in the atavistic recesses of the mind are a host of sneaking, subliminal beliefs. Who dares scoff at Hamlet's warning to Horatio about things in heaven and earth other than dreamt of in his philosophy? The ethos and mythos of civilized life must be very thin veneers indeed. When faced with adverse elemental problems, unbelievers beseech a god, churchgoers rub a rabbit's foot, and there is an increased consciousness of black cats, ladders, and hats on the bed. Locked inside of each man is a Kurtz lost in his own mysterious heart of darkness.

Superstitition runs close to the surface at sea. Now, in a moment when the frustrations of no wind make us feel like eight mariners in search of Coleridge, I have turned to the black arts. Up to now my experiments in sorcery have been restrained mostly to calling timidly on certain demigods for help. At that, there were times when I have been shaken by the results. Now I was about to take the step into the big time.

My sorcerer's apprentice, Skipper, had been deep in researches all morning. He brought my attention to a section in Sir James Frazer's "Golden Bough" having to do with the subject of summoning wind. Up until then I had been toying with the idea of using the device know as the centered tetrahedron, a most powerful instrument of necromancy. The trouble was, I didn't know much about it except the name, having seen it once in a rousing TV outer-fringe sort of play. It was strong stuff and looked a mite uncontrollable. You never can tell about these things, sometimes they work. Even in the face of the long chance that it would come off, I was unsure of the amount of wind which would be released. After protracted calms, a gale would be a most unkind blow, and so I chickened out. I decided instead to use the three-knot supplication mentioned by Frazer.

It went like this. Taking up the mainsheet, I tied three overhand knots in the end of the run and then, pointing the bitter end of the line in the direction from which the wind was to be called, I made long and varied incantations and supplications (a ship's secret). Then I untied one knot! It would have been foolhardy to untie more than one at the start, probably an invitation to disaster. The sheet then was placed on deck with warnings to the crew not to tamper with the other knots—if they valued their lives. Just in case we had not propitiated all of the gods, and to leave no stone unturned, we played "Little Red Top" for Poseidon. He liked it so much before.

And so, with this seemingly innocent business of tying and untying a knot, we have crossed the dark line into the realm of their satanic majesties.

1200   IT IS HERE! THE WIND IS HERE!

Whether you believe in the working of the black sciences or choose to set it down to coincidence, one piece of evidence is incontrovertible. The wind is here! Even those strong-minded souls on board who could not get themselves to believe but went along with the gag (what could they lose?) are rather subdued. They gingerly step around the bitter end of the mainsheet like civilized visitors to an ancient shrine. It lies there, inanimate, inert, but pregnant with reserve strength. There are two knots to go. I congratulate myself on resisting the impulse to use the untamed centered tetrahedron.

Our position at noon is 42° 51′ N 50° 21′ W. The day's run is recorded as 70 miles. Another gruesome milestone in a procession of inglorious days. The last, we hope, now that the wind comes when we beckon. We are now sailing toward Charlie at a respectable speed, 5.8 knots on a course of 76°.

1400   To add to our mounting joys, the fog is lifting, there is a bite to the air, but it is sunny and our spirits respond to the brightness of the world and the new pulse and energy of our craft.

1430   At last, we have passed the first sea mark. We went by Point Able 43N–50W at a distance of 99.9 yards, although I swear I could feel us go right through it. This arbitrary check point, which has for so long haunted our thoughts, is now behind us. The next mandatory mark is Bishop Rock, which we hope to reach without bumping into Brittany or Ireland.

1630 A large freighter, followed by a large whale, pass. We have no reason to think there is any connection.

1700 The bilges are pumped, they keep making water. We will have to start looking around for the reason.

1830 The sorcerer's apprentice, his nose buried in Frazer and animated by the success of his last suggestion, is burrowing for more kernels. In his studies, he encounters and reports on fertility goddesses other than those he has been seeing in "Playboy." With such an opening, I can scarcely restrain reminiscing of goddesses I have known and, for one reason or another, am reminded that the Diana of the Ephesians had nine breasts. The odd one, I like to believe, in the middle of her back, which would have made her a most interesting dancing partner. FIGARO, unconcerned with such idle conversation, sails on at a speed of 5.5 knots, course 060°.

2130 A beautiful night. High, hazy clouds, waning full moon and an easy sea. We are moving, not very fast, but moving steadily, which is a change. Those on watch talk in subdued voices. Those below make sleeping sounds, dreaming of other and perhaps better worlds. They should be dreaming about Lucullan feasts, for that's what they are sleeping off. In honor of the return of wind, I took special care with the dinner. While it is true that the basic commodity of the repast was canned hamburgers, still there are possibilities, even with such a mundane base. To begin with, I threw away all the gravy that came in the can and created a whole new sauce for the occasion. By and large, it was treated with respect, but I still cherish a few wounds such as must be shared by all chefs when a culinary triumph is greeted by one or two unfeeling requests for catsup, the opiate of the masses.

The navigator comes on deck for twilight stars. Evening twilight comes late in these latitudes and at this time of the year. It is brisk and cold and he is sleepy and warm, fresh from the sack, but even this shock to his nervous system does not alter his normally quiet intoning of "hup," his own almost whispered variant to the loud staccato "mark" more usual to this vessel. Normally, when they have brought the sun or star to the dip on the horizon, our navigators have given us a "mark" so ringing as to make the deck carlins quiver. Whether they do this to make it sound more authoritative—or perhaps to give them reassurance in a chancy sight, one in which at the last moment the star sank completely in the sea or leaped degrees high above the horizon—is a secret locked in their own breasts. Whatever the case, Mike's style is entirely his own. It gives even more reassurance by its quiet and makes his time-taker stay on the *qui vive*. One little lapse and the man on the chronometer has missed that important moment in eternity. Mike's hushed signal is all in one with this peaceful and beautiful night. *In dulce jubilo.*

2330   The night ends with Cleody's admonition to one of Mother Carey's restless, following chickens, illuminated momentarily by our stern light, to go back and round Point Able or be protested.

Wind SE, force 3, barometer 30.5.

Course is 64° on a desired course of 80°, speed 4.8 knots.

WEDNESDAY, JULY 10

0001   Eight bells have gone and the new day begins. It holds more promise in the way of wind and of pleasanter weather to come. For one thing, the fog which has been a regular nightly companion, did not show up last night. 'Tis true 'tis cold, but at least 'tis dry. The wind we summoned stays, faithful to its masters. It poops the boat along at a moderate speed. While the direction is not quite that which was asked for, still it allows us to go within 15° of our desired course. After what we have been through, any quibbling about minutiae would be like examining a gift horse for pyorrhea. Maybe I put a few words out of their proper sequence during the incantation. It will be easy enough to straighten out when the time comes.

Course 65°. Speed 5.0 knots although it appears faster, looking overside.

0200   Able watch takes over. Conn makes the scene in the same working clothes. I have wrung a promise from him that he will put on boots or shoes in the event that the weather turns bad. Other men's safety may well depend on his sure-footedness. When the going is bad, any man fighting to hold his own balance must rely on a mate to carry out his share of the work. The main or spinnaker booms have a nasty way of drawing a bead on a fellow's back or head when a friend has momentarily lost his grip on a sheet, lift, or halyard while in the course of fighting for balance. Conn's internal freon system is working fine. Or maybe his thermostat is stuck.

0430   Conn goes below to get things ready for breakfast. He cannot draw water from the port tank. We have run out one tank. A few gallons are left, but out of reach of the take-off line at this angle of heel.

0500   The wind has eased a bit. We are able to come to our course, 80° at a speed of 5.7 knots. We are not quite hard on the wind. FIGARO is kept driving as best we can manage with the winds available. We hope this favorable shift is a happy augury of better times to come.

0715   A pristine and empty Tru Heet bottle (alcohol stove fuel—popular on yachts) sighted, under a full head proceeding west. Now we know that we have a competitor ahead and to the south and, we hope, near us. It is reasonable to assume that Mr. X's stove's fuel tank needed to be replenished this morning in order to make breakfast and that, having emptied the bottle, he heaved it

Coming back from the Rock, with ANITRA *in hot pursuit*

overboard. He sailed away from it, we sailed toward it, and the wind carried it up from the southeast, but not too far. But we reason she must be a small boat, or near our size, for, as the ancient runic verse has it:

> The big boats cook with gas
> And little boats cook with alcohol.

It can be CARINA or WINDROSE, since both are definitely known to use alcohol-fueled Heritage stoves.

0800   Baker watch has just finished examining and retaping many sections of the running and standing rigging.

0810   The Number One Genoa is lowered briefly in order to clear a halyard wrap visible from deck. The cross was all the way up near the truck. Spun yarn work continues with oiling of shackles and overhaul of spinnaker gear.

1030   The wind has slackened a bit and gone slightly ahead. We are on a course of 60° at a speed of 3.5 knots.

1200   The noon fix gives us a position of 47° 30′ N 47° 30′ W. Sounds like a broken record, or maybe the computer is stuck.

A day's run of 155 miles, more than we expected and certaintly wonderful after the days we have been getting up until now. Our hearts are once more young and gay.

With this fix we begin to suspect that our port Kenyon speedometer is under-reading.

1330   Bathing in the scuddy up on the foredeck, Conn, Mike, and Buz bring up buckets of icy water and throw it over one another, all the while roaring like walruses in rut. Their goose bumps stand out like mosquito welts. They strut back to the cockpit toweling their crotches and wearing self-righteous smirks, enough to sicken the rest of us grubby bastards.

1430   Off-watch members of the crew abandon their bunks in a body to sleep on deck in the sun. If this were a trans-Atlantic cruise, it would be perfect. But we are racing, at least that's what it says in the circular. We could use more speed, at the expense of comfort if it need be.

1500   Eight gallons of water taken out of the bilge—pumped out, that is. In my role of taster of the bilge (a division of the Chevalier Tastevin called *Goûter de l'Eau Bas*), I sample the water. It tastes horrible—thank God. It could not have come from a fresh-water tank.

1600   Conn, who has asked for the privilege (he is either cold or he really wants to cook), has gone below to make a Shepperd's Pie. He says this one is named for Skip, not sheep. Heavenly aromas come from the galley.

1700   Bilges are pumped again, another eight gallons are taken out. We know how much water we made. We are not sure where it is coming from, but that's a helluva lot of water. At a steep angle of heel it would get up into the turn of the bilge, out of reach of our pump and get into lockers and drawers. We have to find the leak.

2000 The Baker watch captain, in a fit of self-flagellation, has counted up the hours sailed under 3 knots. The dismal count comes to 64 hours—how to win a race!

2100 The wind is fairing; we are able to steer course 082° at 5.0 knots. In my role of haruspex and familiar of the winds, I detect a low southwest of us and moving in a northeasterly direction. Despite my analysis, the barograph perversely continues to rise.

2130 Our observed position at this time is 45° 10′ N 47° 12′ W.

2230 The captain, at the wheel and sucking on a wet cigar, tells his younger mates about the perils of Paris. A note in the deck log sneeringly reads: "Oh Youth, Oh Folly"; but then, "those who disregard history are doomed to make the same errors" (more or less Santayana).

2330 The wind eases, giving us a fright, and then comes back.

This day ends a little better. It gives promise of being a long, slow, if pleasant trip.

THURSDAY, JULY 11

0100 At last, a day that begins with most happy signs. The wind is picking up in speed and freeing us. Despite the fact that the barograph seems stubbornly set on withholding the information, it seems abundantly clear to me that there is a low behind us coming across our stern. The barograph tells us what we are in; it takes interpretation to know what we will get—the lonely role of the wind reader.

0200 At the turn of the watch, the speed is 7.0 knots on the Kenyon. It appears definite that it underreads. What's more, at the higher speed range it seems dampened, so that it registers no surges. It may cut into some of the fun and thrill when the time comes to skiball down the face of the following wave. At that time you get a great charge as you watch the needle climb up to 13–14 knots. Now this, too, is denied us.

FIGARO, being a shallow, beamy boat, tends to roll up high when at a big angle of heel. Her garboard strake at times can clearly be seen below the surface. In order to get structural strength in a centerboarder, the mother keel is fairly wide and heavy and, because it is above the lead, generally high in the hull. This forces the location of the speedometer to be high up as well. When the boat is at a steep angle of heel the speedometer tends to roll near the surface. When it is that high, it becomes inaccurate. For that reason, we installed two speedometers in FIGARO, so that we could always have one deeply immersed, but we never could get them to agree with one another at all speeds. The starboard speedometer always read lower. It was called the pessimist. Our optimist was fairly accurate until now, but it, too, seems to have joined the war between man and inanimate objects.

0600   A very pleasant morning. A tanker close aboard and to leeward.

Breakfast was a culinary triumph, enjoyed by all—by all but Skip, of course. He has brought his own shoreside food preferences with him—a steady diet of peanut butter, cheese, and bread—the despair of his mother and other conscientious dieticians. But despite this odd diet, he is cheerful and abounds with his own brand of humor.

1200   Our noon position gives us a run of 165 miles. Things are getting a little better. The position is 45° 58′ N 44° 40′ W.

1400   The wind is picking up, even more air up high. Mare's-tails going to the southeast, the wind on the surface from the southeast—an under and over flow of air.

Barometer 30.53, wind SSE, course 085°, speed 7.8 knots.

1500   The lighting batteries are getting low and this seems the opportune moment to throw a charge into them. The engine, upon which exhaustive funds have been spent in various shipyards all spring, now, naturally, refuses to run. The admirable Conn, our own favorite gold-medal winner, goes to work. I suppose if you are going to be that big, you've got to be patient, just to keep yourself in scale with the ordinary-sized world. In some way, known heretofore only to Houdini, he folds his entire 6′ 10″ (or is it 10′ 6″?) into a cubbyhole under the sink in order to get at the carburetor. (In building an auxiliary yacht, they place the engine in the middle of the floor and then proceed to build a boat around it. That's the last time you ever see it; from then on you just feel around in the dark, hoping that you remember what a distributor feels like.) Conn gets the carburetor off, cleans it, puts it back and the engine still won't run. It is decided that the trouble lies with the high-speed framish which comes off the auberge of the carburetor. They bindle the framish, but the engine still won't run.

In the time and state of the science of mechanics when I was introduced to naphtha engines, I developed two classic nostrums for recalcitrant motors. The first is to hit the offending engine with a hammer and then push the starter button. (This method can be usefully employed for radios and television sets as well, but the stroke has to be somewhat softer.) Failing the opportunity to apply this method, because of the absence of a hammer or some other oversight, the second approach is to put lighter fuel into the cylinder heads and let her buck. We use the latter method and, naturally, the engine starts. But the water pump won't. Two more attempts are made. The captain, not as tall as Conn and therefore perhaps lacking his infinite patience, says screw it and goes back to his rack for twenty minutes. Exercise Engine Starting is secured—let 'em use candles!

2130   The wind has finally pulled aft, far enough to require a spinnaker. The White Mist, galvanized iron, bulletproof, nonpareil, is put up. It draws! It draws!

The captain, not an easy man to please, who but a short several hours ago, was tearing his hair over the lack of wind, now bemoans the speed at which the low is overtaking and passing. He wants nothing less than to carry it into Cowes.

Course 085°, speed 7.1 knots.

2330   The day ends at speed, the ship's company bubbling over with fine spirits. A pleasant night, but gradually clouding over. A promise of wind tomorrow.

XX

WE HOLD THE BREEZE

FRIDAY, JULY 12

0300   The entry of the date into the log of a new day makes one realize that it begins with a hairbreadth escape—we miss the ominous confluence of Friday and of 13. Our speed is over 8 knots. (The Kenyon speedometer no help.) Course 085°.

0200   It is raining hard, and miserable weather is our lot once more. The watch changes. Baker watch captain, Buz Knowlton, is suddenly doubled up with a sciatic spasm. He is eased to the leeward settee, covered with a blanket and given medication. It is a muscle-dilator, relaxer, and painkiller. The drug enables him to sleep.

0400   We are booming along, our course 090° speed is 7.6 knots.

0600   It is time for the change of the watch, although both watches are tired. During the early hours, the wind kept shifting around from slightly ahead to slightly aft, which made for much spinnaker drill. Finally, we took it down and set the double head rig: Yankee jib top over Genoa staysail.

0700   Wind is increasing in weight and the sea becoming more rambunctious. The Kenyon speedometer has the willies for fair. It freezes absolutely when it reaches 8 knots and it can only reach that when we are at a breakneck surge of speed. The Kenyon does not recognize surges, which is disappointing. It's a thrill to see the needle reach 10 and start climbing again.

0900   A high and confused sea is running. One sea rolling in on the quarter and the other coming in abeam. It makes carrying the spinnaker a hairy deal, especially when a beam sea has just rolled the boat down and suddenly the quarter sea gets under her and starts shoving her bow up to weather. The bag goes through turbulent gyrations. It momentarily collapses and then fills out with a bang. During one deep plunge, a shackle on the spinnaker sheet rings explodes with the sound of a gunshot. The spinnaker flogs out ahead, shaking the whole rig. We get it down and set the Yankee and Genoa staysail. A new sheet is rove on the spinnaker and it is reset, and off we are again, roll and go. Our bandaged boom occasionally dips into the water, plowing up great harrowing

176

streams. It is "nervous"-making. The sea, if anything, is more confused, and after a series of desperate lunges, we hand the spinnaker once more. The Yankee and staysail are reset. The boat is quieter and the boom stays out of the water. The speed seems to drop a bit, although it is hard to tell how much, for it is still beyond the range of the speedometer. This is one of the times that total performance becomes hard to estimate. You don't know whether, by easing the steering and keeping her tracking in a line, the boat makes good more miles along her course than staggering along with her spinnaker. It is tiring work. We seem to be doing well, but we are oppressed with the idea that someone, somewhere, is successfully carrying a bag.

1030   Course ordered 088°. Steered 090° at 8+ knots.

1200   Our position at noon: 47° 06′ N 40° 20′ W.
   The run for the day, 192 miles—pretty good, eh?
   Barometer 30.25, wind force 7–8.

1400   Wind right over the ass. Running off with main, mizzen; Yankee wung out on spinnaker pole.

1500   Skipper, who has his heart set on achieving a beard, indulges in a bit of whisker trimming. His adviser in matters of hair styling is the captain, who never advanced his own ambition beyond a mustache. But between the two, something fairly creditable is managed.

1615   We have jibed to the starboard tack, a most delicate maneuver, because of the broken boom. The wind is very fresh. The jibe is successfully carried out, nary a splinter from the bandaged boom.

1730   She's a rippin' and a snortin', wind force 7. Main, Yankee wung out.

2000   Course 082°, 8+ knots, steaming as before.

2100   Position by star fix 47° 45′ N 38° 14′ W.

2200   Old bulletproof up—the galvanized White Mist spinnaker is a magnificent sail for this kind of going, steady and strong, any other sail would have been flogged to bits by now. In addition to her strength, she is docile and the most willing of her species.

2330   A magnificent night—just pouring down the surges, skiballing along. This is most exhilarating sailing. It makes all the other crap we have been taking worthwhile and, from the shape of the sky, it looks even better, with more wind for tomorrow. FIGARO the beauty! She was made for big seas and strong winds like this. I'm for sleep, but she goes on and on.

SATURDAY, JULY 13

0100   She is boiling along, carrying old galvanized. FIGARO is making noises like a clipper. The water hisses by at an inspiring rate.

The boat is making a little more water than I can accept with equanimity. The water seems to be coming from aft. Progressively, we blocked off all forward limber holes and have at least isolated the area. Skip crawls into the windward sail locker and burrows aft. He finds the leak. He reports that considerable water wells up through the rudder gland, especially when a wave comes up under her and several sharp, corrective twists of the rudder ensue. He also reports that the rudder gland wrench, a special one kept near the rudder head, is nowhere in sight. There begins a frantic, midnight search for the wrench. Conn the Admirable Crichton finds it, right where it was supposed to be, but buried under a spare coil of Genoa and spinnaker sheet line. The gland is taken up, the flow lessens, and the bilges are pumped. Old yawl FIGARO just keeps rolling along.

0200   The wind is still freshening. Our speed indicator says 7.9 knots, but that's meaningless. At the rate that our quarter waves well up it would seem that we are flat out at near hull speed.

0300   The wind coming on even more. FIGARO strains and strains, but cannot break through the sound barrier of the indicator. The barometer has started down again. The wind is in the north-northwest. I reason that one of two things has happened, perhaps even both. (1) The depression which had galloped through us like a dose of salts has been slowed down to a walk by that creeping high up ahead. But where before we were in the southern limits of the low, now we are overtaking it and sailing toward its center. OR (2) The low, in going eastward, is not taking a straight line, but rather taking a sinuous course. Its first direction was toward the northeast and now it is going southeast. In that case, our easterly course would intercept it on its southerly dive.

0600   The rising sun silhouettes the spinnaker and its filtering rays reveal a slight opening in the seam of the White Mist bag which has been up all night, pulling like the proverbial team of mules. A remarkable sail, it tears up wire rigging, expodes shackles and rings, wears down blocks, and settles for just a little repair for itself now and then. This seam separation doesn't seem to be in a place that will spread, so we will leave the sail up for the time being.

The wind, if anything, is increasing. The barometer is still on a downward trend. Steering is an active sport as of now. The pole is well forward and the seas want to shove the boat into a roundup.

0700   The wind feels heavier, although its actual speed may not have increased. As the apparent wind moves steadily ahead because of our changing relationship to the center of the depression, the forward speed of the boat, added to the true wind, gives us a greater apparent wind. In addition, as we get closer to the center, the winds increase. The old indestructible finally had to come off, but not until both the sail and I were given a test of strength. A fair-sized sea rolled the boat down just as a gust of wind hit her. She was knocked down with the spinnaker straining and hovering a few feet off the surface of the water. The leeward deck disappeared like a half-tide rock at the flood, the water foaming up to the deckhouse; the stanchions just showing their tops. The winch holding the spinnaker sheet was on the verge of going under water, which would make the sheet hard to get at if we had to in a hurry. I had the wheel down, but at that angle of heel the rudder was acting more like an aileron, and she was slow in recovery. But the most alarming thing was the situation of the injured main boom, which was dragging through the water with great and evident strain on the broken part. The after part of the boom was immersed and was held there by the foreguy as the boat charged uphill. The wheel must have been down for about forty-five seconds before there was any response, but with ease on the sheet we finally got her up on her feet and she was off again, going like a train of cars. We are too far away from a shipyard to play these kinds of games; and since the wind is on the edge of going abeam, I call for a sail change. All hands lay to in order to make it light work.

The Yankee jib top is set, and we go racing on beyond the ability of our speedo to record the amount. We think there is a noticeable drop in speed, but she is steadier and has given up the business of charging upwind, so we believe that to all intents and purposes we are making better speed toward Bishop Rock.

1130   We pass the American troopship GENERAL MAURICE ROSE. She is homeward bound, loaded with GI's, probably from Germany. The soldiers line the rail in order to see the madmen who trust their lives to cockleshells. They are so thick at the rail as to give GENERAL MAURICE ROSE a decided list. She alters course to pass us close aboard. There is much shouting and waving, but nothing can be heard in the wind. The troopship salutes us with three blasts of the horn. (As a past commodore, I should have gotten at least thirteen guns.) We run up and dip our ensign in return. The skipper of the ship must be a former small-boat sailor and a gent. He altered course to pass us to leeward. We hope they took pictures so that we can get some.

Which reminds me of a story of several years ago when a boat which seemingly had done well in a race was disqualified because a picture taken from a steamer showed her carrying a sail sheeted in an illegal manner—that is, illegal in terms of racing conditions. A glance around shows us to be as legal as income tax—the kind that hurts. We are real sportsmen; yes, sir.

1200   Our noon position reveals a truly magnificent day's run. Either FIGARO or Mike has outdone himself. 220 miles—how about that? An average speed for the twenty-four-hour period of 9.125 knots, way beyond her ultimate hull speed.*

* Ultimate hull speed is either a fact or a product of professional imagination. The formula states that a boat's potential is 1.4 times the square root of its waterline length. FIGARO is designed at a 32.5 D.W.L.; if we assume that, due to her overhangs, her heeled waterline is 36 ft., the square root of this is 6 ft. 0 ins. If we multiply that by 1.4, it gives us a potential hull speed of 8.4 knots, and we have averaged 9.125 for the twenty-four

Either the immutable law is a bust, or what is likeliest is that something else happens to the wave-making potential of the hull in surfing down the seas.

Up until this day's run, FIGARO's two high-run days were a 218-mile day during the race to Sweden in 1960 and a 232-mile day during the '62 Bermuda, but that day we estimate that we got a near 70-mile lift from a favorable Gulf Stream meander. (The biggest boost I ever experienced, shared by several boats.) In this case, we may have received a favorable lift from the Atlantic drift; if so, it may amount to about 10 or 15 miles at best. *Quién sabe?* In any case, lift or no, it is a magnificent day's run for a boat her size.

It all demonstrates the importance of being able to control the boat in going downhill in strong breezes and a running sea. Before FIGARO's keel was deepened and her rudder extended, she was a lively handful in such conditions. The net result was that in the struggle to straighten her out after a big rush and a threat of rounding up, the next wave would be missed, sometimes two in a row. This kind of miss reduces the number of surges by at least one-third and consequently reduces the averages of speed over her potential by one-third. In twenty-four hours, it mounts up. After she was changed, we rarely missed a surge. The best demonstration of this ability came during the race to Sweden. For five days, four boats were clearly in sight of one another. Each morning, on getting up, the first look around would show the sails of the same competition: Tom Watson's PALAWAN, Jake Isbrandtsen's WINDROSE, and Hank du Pont's CYANE. One morning a boat would be off to starboard, the next morning the same boat would be off to port, having worked her way across the bow or stern during the night. It stayed that way for five days, almost as though they were attached to the same towline. It's hard to do extra well in moderate downwind sailing; all boats seem to go about the same speed. The old saying is, "A stern chase is a long chase." So it remained that way until the front of a depression came through. After we had recovered from some grievous wounds to our sail complement, we settled down to hard racing downwind. That day we outdistanced our competition and in the next several days opened steadily on them, going on to win. I have always considered the ability to control a boat in strong, downwind conditions a most important quality for racing in the open ocean (as against the needs of a boat that races mainly around the buoys), and one must not discount the safety factor which is the result of control.

1230   Sighted a liner going east. Looks Italian. We are in the great circle steamer lanes for fair.

1400   The wind is strong, about force 7 out of the NNW. Changed the Yankee from a normal to a goose wing set. It is now wung out to weather at the end of the spinnaker pole. A snatch block is rigged on the end of the pole and the sheet run through it and then led aft through the footblocks.

FIGARO is rushing along as if her throttle were floored. We estimate her speed to be 10 or 11 knots in the surges on the slalom side of the waves.

---

hours, which certainly means that we were doing well over 10 knots for much of the time in order to get such a high average.

1615   I have been looking at an increasingly dour sky in the NW and finally decide it is time for a reef. The reef in the main is handily tied. In order to take off the vang, which is still made fast to the bale on the end boom, Conn does a layout on the mainsheet while the boat is rolling heavily. He is stretched out over the water, lying on the lines, and, with each roll of the boat, dips down toward the fast-rushing sea. It is a dangerous perch, so I reach out to hold onto his belt. I am not certain of how much reassurance I give him, but I succeed in getting icy cold water up to my armpit through the oilskin sleeve, and filling my boots.

This is a first-class crew—experienced, calm, determined, and cheerful. They tie in a reef so smoothly and quickly that it makes roller reefing gear seem ridiculous. The only value I can see to that patent gear is that you can take out inches at a time, instead of the big bites determined by the location of reef points. With the patent gear, you adjust the amount of reef to the needs of the moment.

1700   Wind still increasing. We are scooting on a course of 080°.
The speedometer indicates 7.7 knots, but it lies in its teeth.

1730   Cleody has been carrying on the abominable game first introduced on board by that abominable seaman The Simple Island Boy, known in his own preserves as the Honorable Robert Symonette. The object of the game, played by the helmsman, is to dampen a shipmate with a boarding sea or with spray, to fill his boots, sleeves, or neck openings without wetting oneself or one's belongings. It results, therefore, in a great deal of sharpshooting, especially when a shipmate attempts to relieve himself at the mizzen lee shrouds—the game here being to fill his boots if possible. The simple rules of this simple game set forth by Simple have as their basis a system of scoring points, the scale and numbers of which increase in direct ratio to the difficulty of the shot and the higher rank of the target. Cleody, as historian of memorable shots, keeps this repellent pastime alive, despite the fact that most of us have retired from the field of battle long since (with wet feet).

This afternoon, Cleody racked up a whole poolroom full of points; more than Minnesota Fats scored in a lifetime. With one boarding sea coming off our quarter wave, he was able (1) to knock Buz and Mike off their feet, as they were standing in the forward part of the cockpit near the dodger; (2) to fill the navigation drawer in the chart table, wetting all the charts; (3) to get under the glass case of the chronometer; and lastly (4) to fill my bunk (it is mid-ships!) with buckets and buckets of sea water. The horror of this is that I had just retired to it with the loud-spoken conviction that it was the only warm and dry spot left on the entire boat.

No matter how much my spluttering and swearing, added to that of Buz and Mike, increased the decibel value, the reaction was brushed off as normal to a target of the game. In reality, the white heat of the comments only succeeded in increasing the point score. There seems to be little defense against anything done as a game. I will have to devise a punishment to fit the score and see if I can introduce gentler pastimes.

2100   We have just spent considerable time in exchanging lamp signals with a freighter nearby. He was most solicitous, needing to be assured that we were all right and in command of our situation, and not a group of Sunday sailors blown offshore by adverse tides and winds.

He came plunging by in a moderately heavy sea that let even him know he was out on the North Atlantic. Suddenly a flurry of light signals burst from his bridge. He was a strange sort of alien, for he appeared to be signaling with a heavy middle-European accent. After much hemming, hawing, and consultation amongst ourselves, we finally determined that he was asking us if we were all right. Since he was so considerate in asking after our health and well-being, we could do little else but reassure him. We have no signal lamp (something I keep promising myself), and so, after much rooting about, we came up with the half-mile ray, but we couldn't get it to work at first. When it finally began to put out light, we were far from him and out of sight when we went down in the trough, so we could only send signals when riding on the crests. It took us a long time to say, "Thank you, mysterious stranger, we are okay."

2200   The sea continues to be fairly heavy. While I was standing at the wheel, steering, I was knocked off my feet by a lurch of the boat, accompanied by the scurf off a wave. It was a cold, wet, unrefreshing dip. Since I was doing my own steering, nobody got points. We have been wearing life belts hooked onto the boat for the last several hours. Walking around and working on deck require careful footing, and the application of the old rule of the sea, "One hand for the boat and one hand for Johnny."

2330   The wind is growing heavier from the NNW, the barometer continues to fall. The sea, which was heavy before, is now something to behold. We should have a good day's run to show in another twelve hours. The crew, unmindful of any personal discomfort, is bucked up by our splendid runs, since the weather went bad. Blow high, blow low, as long as we move. We'll take it as it comes.

The two knots in the end of the mainsheet lie in a little puddle, separated from the rest of the coil. I wonder if there is anything in that malarkey?

BASTILLE DAY—SUNDAY, JULY 14

0200   The first new watch of the day is stirred into action by the singing of the "Marseillaise." Buz knows most of the words, which makes a pleasant change from the normal pah-rumps, dee-das, and at-rahs in which it is usually sung.

Our course 085°, speed well up. The wind from the NNW and colder, barograph 29.85, barometer 29.5.

0500   Sailing on a course of 090°. Speed 7.0+. Low on the horizon, flying at about 200 to 300 feet above the water, we see a four-engine plane. They buzz us twice, first coming in from the NW. The plane has military markings, either RAF or RCAF; we cannot determine which. We judge them to be on either submarine patrol or weather reconnaissance; they can't be thinking of little us.

0530   More trouble!

We were shaking out the reef and ran into a foul-up. The two middle reef points did not come out in a hurry and there was insufficient strain taken up on the topping left, so that the resulting load on the sail at the leech reefing cringle was too much for the sail. The sail promptly tore. It had to be taken down. Bosun Jon Rohde retacked the sail in its original position, then made a patch of doubled sail cloth to be sewn over the torn area. While he was doing this, I made two new reef points and sewed those in. Two broken battens were replaced. FIGARO is sailing along on head sail and jigger. I happen to remember that it was only yesterday that I was putting the brag on our reefing drill. At sea, it's best not to throw out your chest in any self-esteem. The fates have a way of shooting you down in flames.

0730   Our position, by a cross of the sun and the moon, at 0700 48° 53′ N 31° 16′ W. Mike keeps taking sights whenever they present themselves.

0930   A Danish freighter heading west passes us two miles abeam to starboard.

We enjoy intermittent rain squalls. The barometer is rising, 29.80, wind NW.

0945   The torn main is at last fully repaired and put up again. The patch, with its new cringle, holds well. Extra stitching has been put along all strain lines. The sail is not deformed in shape, but we have been four hours without its services. We create our own handicaps. That's ocean racing for you. Your own unhandiness stands ready to snatch defeat out of a victory.

1200   Another great day's run—212 miles. Position at noon 48° 57′ N 30° 48′ W. If only this kind of day's run could be continued, it would make up for those three inglorious days sitting under the high. We are at last under the 1000-miles-to-go mark—985 miles to Eddystone Light.

1400   Clocks are moved ahead once more, and once more questioning looks from the crew, but what can they do about it? It's the only game in town.

1500   Course 093°, speed 7.5+ knots. The mainsail is holding its shape well, as is the wounded boom. Looking at our injured tactical weapons, I am moved to quote Napoleon (only proper on Bastille Day): "My right is crushed, the left in retreat; I will attack with the center."

1730   A cry from the crow's nest (figurative). "Thar she blows!" A whole gam?—pod?—of whales. They come closer and are identified as black fish. Does this make them a school?

1900   Course 095°, speed 7.2+ knots.

2230   On course and moving very well. It has been a good day's sailing, with some bad handling thrown in to keep us humble.

We are sailing on the back side of the depression, which is moving off from us. At the height of the blow, it reached about 40 m.p.h. The waves were 18 to 20 feet crest to trough (captain's estimate); 20 to 25 feet (first watch officer's estimate). They were breaking on the crest, the top blowing off and gray foam streaking down the watery hillsides. It was an awesome and beautiful show of force—that is, when you could remove yourself enough to think of the waves objectively and not be conscious of their striking power. Happily, one feels safe in FIGARO, so that it is possible to view these waves with some dispassion.

She sails these seas magnificently, lifting to an oncoming comber and then surging down its side with a breathtaking rush and swoop. At the moment when the crest comes up to her, the bow hangs over a sloping chasm some twenty feet deep. It is a most extraordinary feeling, while standing forward of the mast, to see her bow pointing at the leaden gray sky while she is poised on the brink of a steep valley. Then, suddenly, her stern lifts, her bow turns down as the sea passes under her and she goes rushing downhill at anywhere from 10 to 14 knots. She throws two high waves from her bows like a destroyer. They arc well over the height of the deck, throwing frothy white water to the sides. Her quarter wave comes welling up, dark green marked with ridges of swiftly rushing flow lines. Sometimes they curl back on board into both quarter waterways, occasionally breaking back in over the transom. Freddie Hibberd had a prize rush. I have never seen one like it before. It was made of twin quarter waves rushing back in a symmetrical flow. They met at the stern and the result was a high arcing rooster tail. A number of us saw it and rushed for cameras, waiting for another such phenomenon, but none came. I suppose it can come only at the rare moment when the boat is absolutely perpendicular to her line of flow or else one quarter wave becomes more dominant than the other and you get a breaking wave rather than a rooster tail.

This kind of sailing is a warm and exhilarating exercise. For the helmsman it is exciting. He watches the wave come down on him (and with practice he need not look, he feels it in the boat's rhythm); at the moment the boat begins its lift to the onrushing sea, he gives the wheel a slight, quick turn, slanting her head slightly across the slope like a surf rider. Looking forward, he sees her bow momentarily hanging over nothing and then, suddenly, she is off. The sound of the bow and the quarter wave mix with the hiss of the foaming crest. The rudder becomes frozen midships with the power of the water running by both of its sides. Finally, she slows down. He can pull her out of her charge and he prepares her for the next rush. What sailor wouldn't put up with getting wet, cold, and seasick if he can get sailing like this?

XXI

SOME FINE RUNS

MONDAY, JULY 15

0100   We are sailing under the double head rig, Yankee jib top over Genoa staysail. The course is 095° and our speed is now frozen on the Kenyon speedometer at a constant 7.2 knots. Both Kenyons are giving trouble. Porpoises managed to injure the starboard speedometer strut so that it is kaput. The port Kenyon has developed a wheeze. It may even be its death rattle, for it gives off such weird sounds. The needle appears stuck at 7.2 knots. Jon says it will neither go up nor down. Michael looks worried in a gentlemanly English manner. He is being put upon. So far, he has had to suffer with an inaccurate compass, jazz music, aspersions on England, and now, the final indignity that a Grade A, one-hundred-percent ocean racer can heap on its navigator, the inability to determine distance run. How is he to establish a dead reckoning position? He asked me to stream a recording log, but I told him I no longer carry it, as towing a log slows a boat down, a practice to be frowned on by racing men.

0200   The wind has just begun to edge forward. I say there, what the hell goes on?

    Course still maintained, 095°; speed 7.2 knots (naturally). The wind is NNE, barometer 30.20, bilges are pumped.

0400   The wind is going into the NE and freshening. Barometer is the same, but something is definitely going on. Course 088°, speed 7.2 (you bet).

0530   The Kenyon with a new series of quirks and wheezes changes its reading from 7.2 to 6.9 knots, confounding everyone. It's still alive, but not well.

0730   The wind has gone back, speed 7.3 on a course of 093°.

0900   Mike appears on deck to take a morning sun line. Our speed and the course still maintained.

1000   Old Indestructible is up. I offer loud gratitude to Mel Grosvenor for his sporting decision to carry on the tradition of lending us this wonderful sail. Grosvenor is WHITE MIST's new owner. May she serve him as splendidly as she did Blunt.

Conn, our patient and temperate ship's husband, has been working on the engine for more than an hour. Still no luck. He is meticulously checking and drying each part in the oven. He has put on a new coil, but all attempts to start have failed, and now the starting battery shows signs of giving up its ghost.

1130   Blessed omens! Porpy, the playful friends of mariners, come sporting under our bow. At the same moment, from the radio (whose dials were being twisted by Cleody in his perennial search for unsquare music) comes that splendid aria by Rossini—FIGARO.

As an amateur diviner, I interpret this doubling of events as holding the most favorable of omens, equal to finding a shiny pin or a new penny, and certainly better than a poke in the eye with a sharp stick. The crew is not only ready but eager to accept these judgments. I have the crew cowed with my occult knowledge. Meanwhile, the engine no tickee, no runnee, allee same quit.

1200   Noon position 49° 56′ N 26° 15′ W. Since the clocks were set ahead one hour, this represents a run for 23 hours, and in 23 hours we did 175 miles. If our speed will hold, we will have a 24-hour run of 183.5 miles, not as great as the last couple of days, but still damned good. We have 795 miles to go.

1400   We have struck Old Indestructible in favor of the Hood spinnaker. The wind was growing a little lighter, so we put up a larger spinnaker. Course 095°, speed 7.0+ knots.

1430   After long, patient hours—like a Chinese artisan cutting ivory balls inside of ivory balls—our admirable ship's husband, Conn, got the engine running. Fortunate boats get a great ship's husband and in Conn we have a beauty. This last job was a most difficult and frustrating one, since the engine in FIGARO is almost inaccessible and hedged in with odd bits of plumbing and construction.

In this case, he baked out every part and laboriously reassembled them. Then, putting lighter fuel in the cylinders, he tried once more. Again no luck, and this time the starting motor sounded sick. The starting battery was serving notice that as far as it was concerned, "To hell with it." But this did not daunt our beauty. Unflustered, unflurried, and unflapped, he resoused the cylinders with tiger juice and pressed the starter once more. Hosanna, miracles and wonders, with its dying spasm, the engine caught! Bucking, snorting, the firing at first halting and irregular—not all cylinders were co-operating. Clearly, the engine did not believe in itself, but under Conn's masterful influence the engine became re-acquainted with the idea of running again and, slowly gaining confidence, it settled down, becoming smoother and stronger until it was purring merrily. A burst of spontaneous applause; the crew was too choked up with grateful emotion to be able to cheer. We had been facing the probability of continuing without a binnacle light and with troublesome navigation lights. A chilling prospect for the Channel sailing bit, certainly not of the finest kind.

1545   The wind is coming ahead N to NE. It is light and brings with it occasional sprinkles of rain. Course 095° and speed 5.8 knots. Engine is secured, we have had four hours of battery charging. Let there be light!

1600   Again we come knocking at the portals of the dark world! It's that old black magic once again. I have permitted the Young Turks in the crew to make me act against prudent judgment. However, the gravity of the situation requires some sort of action. At their urging I have untied the second of the two knots originally tied in the mainsheet, all according to the rules and instructions as rediscovered by Sir James Gordon Frazer. Untying the first knot brought a half gale, just as he said; in the second knot lies the power of a whole gale. If we weren't all so brave, it would be scary. I must say that I put on a rather wheedling performance, asking their oceanic majesties and friends in the wind regions to restrict their normally boisterous responses to measures more adaptable to our uses. Perhaps they will listen to us and oblige. In any case, we need more wind and the fair goes to the brave. Older heads in the crew incline in grave concern. This is screwing around with unnatural things, best left outside of man's domain. There are uneasy flickering glances at the sky. An entry in the deck log, written in a firm hand, reads, "Hold onto your hats."

1700   Supper music tonight pours out of the valiant little tape recorder. The Young Turks play "Little Red Top" once more. The beauties of this song, if any, have long since palled on certain square members of the crew, but the Young Turks insist the selection is not so much for their enjoyment as it is for the pleasures of Poseidon, who has shown pleasure with King Pleasure before.

1730   We take down the light Genoa as the wind goes from light to pale. The ballooner is put up to take advantage of the barely breathing northerly wind. The barograph is going up in a steep slope. But then, their dark lordships need time to marshal their forces.

2305   The wind has gone aft. It is still light, but enough to fill the .75-ounce blue-top spinnaker. Wind NW, barometer 30.5 steady, course 085°, speed 3.5 knots.

Today produced a mixed bag. I sense that the crew needs to be re-inspired, but I am unprepared to offer them either Bunnies or Playmates. We will settle for a party. I have therefore once again resorted to the powers invested in me to declare that Michael Richey's birthday stands in need of a replay and to that end have decreed tomorrow as his re-birthday. Everyone is to bring a present. Anything will be acceptable, unless it smells or ticks. An entertainment of banquet, music, and the spoken word is promised.

TUESDAY, JULY 16
Michael W. Richey's Birthday—Opus No. 2

0300   I always am ready to discourse with the crew on the vagaries of the weather and have still another theory about what is happening to us. I believe that a vagrant high-pressure cell has been overtaking us and it is going south and crossing our stern. It will pass us on the starboard beam and draw slowly ahead. Should this be the case (and who on board dares refute me? There are certain perquisites of rank), then we are fortunate in that for once the dome of the high is nowhere near us. (Those three awful days still haunt us.) And further, should this be so, the wind will continue to back around from the NW to the SW through W and increase. It should bring a descending barometer and fresher winds.

Our course now 085° at a speed of 5.6 knots.

0330   We replace the blue-top with the Hood spinnaker and, in preparation for the sport of the wind and the waves to be provided by their oceanic majesties, we stop up Old Indestructible.

Our course 085°, speed 6.0 knots.

0700   Course 100°, speed 6.7 knots.

1000   Weather analysis and second knot operative. All systems are go. It is breezier than before, wind fairer. Course 085°, speed 7.5 knots.

1200   Our noon position 50° 16′ N 22° 12′ W.

The day's run, despite the lamentable influence of the suspected high cell, a respectable 158 miles. We have 655 miles left to go. Course 092°, speed 7.3 knots.

1400   The preparation for *La Fête Galante* in progress. The second coming this year of Michael William Richey, the authority on matters navigatorial and on Arab music. It is to be celebrated with fife, cymbal, and drum, with frankincense and myrrh. The captain starts it in the pastry kitchen and constructs a commendable apple pie. Buz and Freddy, in charge of decoration, prepare rude phallic fetishes from twisted balloons. Skipper, having tied a Turk's-head as pretty as you please on a Havana cigar from my fast-dwindling supply, is going to offer this to Michael in memory of a great race he never made—the St. Pete–Havana. Besides, he likes cigars, especially mine. Having finished this, Skip is on to a more important project, the construction of a sidereal computer, course-analyzer, and helmsman's friend—a most ingenious device of his own constructing. He hopes it will help Mike out of his troubles. Conn has prepared a navigator's night kit, replete with a flask of gin. Jon has sewed up a peter-heater. The fly on Mike's sailing trousers is broken and some mornings he comes on deck for his morning sight, waist high in the matinal dews and damps, with his carronade threatening to run out of the gun port.

Meanwhile, FIGARO, uninvolved with the scatological play of her caretakers, goes roaring downhill in a strong wind, shooting down the waves on a course of 100° while the Kenyon strains to stay 8 knots.

1700–1830   The re-celebration of Mike's natal day takes place with all due pomp and ceremony. A wide variety of fertility fetishes are handed over to the navigator. His mien changes in rapid series as each gift brings thoughts to his mind, either of glories past or of glories to come. He has lent himself to this

occasion with all of the relaxation and inner calm of a Christian walking toward a waiting lion in the Colosseum. All hands declare this to be a most successful *fête*.

2000   For nonbelievers in the power of incantation and sorcery, I can only offer what is taking place. Observe and be not quick in judgment. Since untying the second knot, the wind has changed its direction and increased in speed. It is now blowing force 6. FIGARO is scooting. Her barometer is falling and she shoots rapidly through her dead reckoning, which is estimated to be 50° 21′ N 20° 34′ W.

2130   Black squalls in the fading light. FIGARO is plunging wildly in an angry and broken sea, whipped up by the series of squalls. I called all hands some time ago. They are suited up, awaiting my decision to take off the spinnaker, or perhaps the boat will make my mind up for me, in which case they will have to do it in a hurry. While they wait the boat staggers along as we are struck by gust after gust of harsh wind.

I finally decide to take off the spinnaker and put up the Yankee, wung out to the pole.

2330   It is two hours since the bag came off and now I know it was the right move to make. The wind increased, the sea became higher and wilder with angry, breaking crests. By now, the boat would be absolutely unmanageable under the spinnaker and sail handling would be difficult. The sail came off none too soon.

It was a hard decision to make. The whole crew sat awaiting the order, dressed in their oilskins, ready to go at a moment's notice. The off watch dozed on the settees. I spent two hours in uneasy study of the sail, the spars, the boat, the sea, and the helmsmen. She was going so fast, I was reluctant to change. She raced through the water like a destroyer, but in the rain squalls and wind gusts she was difficult to handle. FIGARO was alternately being rolled down by the sea or blown down by the wind so that her patched-up boom was half buried in the sea, plowing a great white furrow, the water backing way up the main. Each time she dipped we waited with bated breath, expecting to hear the cracking sound that would herald disaster. The mast fitting, spinnaker poles, and pole fittings were all straining with the jerk and slam. I tried several changes of helmsman to see if anyone could hold her upright. The Young Turks kept assuring me that they could. They would keep her up for seven or eight minutes and then, off she would go in a series of lunges and roll-downs. Finally, I gave the order to take the spinnaker off, and down came Old Indestructible. If we had not been racing, I would never have dreamt of carrying the sail as long as this. But at any rate we are too far offshore to play ducks and drakes with our safety and a broken boom.

Now that we are settled down, we have a chance to look around. Even in the dark we can make out the graybeard tops as they come near the boat. They are high and are moving swiftly. Scud is being picked off the breaking tops and is

Taking out a wrap in the halyards

being blown at us. It's the North Atlantic all right. The boat is in fine control, the crew is at ease. We hope that the sleeping will not be too bad. The crew deserves a rest after a fine day crowned with nerve-tingling, hard sailing. Good night, sweet princes.

WEDNESDAY, JULY 17

0001   Our new day begins with a continuation of the hard sailing. It is uncomfortable, but not as uncomfortable as if we were still hanging onto the spinnaker, which we could not be carrying in any case. The wind squalls are more frequent and the sea seems more menacing. I am fully satisfied that I made the right move at the right time. If it had been delayed much longer we would have been forced to make the sail change and reset in the dark and in a wilder sea. As it is, we just caught the end of the daylight.

It is even uncomfortable below, which is not normally the case when running down wind. The boat is rolling and darting and those *trying* to sleep are rolled from side to side, occasionally being thrown. Dressing for the deck is a miserable bit of business, as is trying to hold one's seat on the head.

What we really need in this kind of sailing is an old-type, triangular, flat-cut spinnaker instead of a make-do jib, wung out. The jib we have up cannot be trimmed to keep the boat's head down at all times; consequently, when a sea and a gust conspire to make her charge up wind, the jib becomes even less effective, since it presents the leach to the wind. The sea and the push of the mainsail, in tandem, pull mightily at the helmsman's arms. The jib is not effective enough to offset the thrust.

The courses are varied and rapidly changing, approximately 110°, the speed very much upwards of 8 knots.

0200   Baker watch takes over. I am aware of a noticeable drop in the sort of banter sacred to this hour. The watch going off is intent on getting out of the rain squalls and wooing rest, if not sleep. Those coming on are grim at the prospect of the next four hours.

0300   Mike reaches the nadir of his spirit. He has taken the deep plunge. He is heard to be muttering: "God-damned trip, no compass, lousy Kenyon, lousy meatheads, no co-operation, why don't they keep up the deck log?" He is a most unhappy feller and steers with a vengeance. However, there is a bright side. His spirit, having plumbed the depths, has no place to go but up.

Wind still in southwest, force 6, intermittent rain squalls, course 115°, speed 8 knots plus. Estimated position 50° 04′N 19° 08′ W. 545 miles to go.

0400   Course 095°, speed 8 knots plus.

Big seas ran down upon us

0600   The wind is abating, but the seas are still wild. Jon does a wonderful job in the galley, putting a breakfast together in this rolling, heaving, and pitching boat. It's just as hard to eat as it was to make, but we get most of it down.

0800   Wind right up the butt; by the lee at 105°.

0900   Jibed and reset Old Indestructible. We are on a course for the stable once more, 095°, 7 knots.

1100   Clocks set ahead. I am loath to do it, not for the crew's sake, but for the sake of the record. I'd like another day's run of more than 200 miles and moving the clock gives us a 23-hour day. The overcast sky gives little promise of a noon sight and we will be forced to stay with the Kenyon, which underreads.

1130   The deck log reads, "Mike gets a sun line." How do you like that for timing? An uneasy note—an onion is thrown overboard. Evidently some member of the crew is rebelling against the steady diet of this *roi des légumes*. A mutinous and foolhardy act. Haven't they ever heard of scurvy? Captain James Cook, R.N., would never have stood for this. To the gratings!

1200   Our noon position 50°12′ N 16° 54′ W, a run of 202 miles in 23 hours, which probably means 210 plus in 24 hours. Another great day's run.

FIGARO loves this hard running and reaching. She shoots down the waves like a skier in a long glissade. She is beautiful and most times relatively easy to handle, although at rare instances the going gets hairy, especially when two seas are running on the quarter and on the beam.

Distance to go, 440 miles.

1300   The wind is easing a bit. We take down the White Mist bulletproof and put up the Hood. We are carrying everything that is legal. Course 095°, speed 7.0 knots.

Whatever untying the second knot brought is now leaving. We hope it does not go too fast and too far.

1500   The course is 098°, speed at 5.7 knots. The bilges are pumped dry. We make a pass at battery-charging and the *engine starts promptly*. Now we believe anything can happen. After Conn ministered to the engine he covered it with aluminum foil, just like a Thanksgiving turkey; in this case it was to keep the moisture out rather than in. His care and foresight pays off. We switch back to the other water tank. Now that we are on the port tack we can get at the remaining supply left in the near-empty tank. It comes out the color of China tea—rich in iron. Iron water for iron men.

1600   Cleody is cleaning up the cookstove, which sorely needs it. It is bedabbed with the remainder of many meals; general housecleaning sets in. Nothing like quieter weather to make a man long for a cleaner nest.

Course 095°, speed 6.5 knots.

1800   Dinner is served on deck to everyone, at a single sitting. It is our first pleasant evening in a long while and the crew is in fine spirits. Song, stories, cigars.

Course 095°, speed 6.2 knots.

2000   The wind bloweth in and it bloweth out. We maintain an average speed of 5.6 knots.

2330   The wind is from the NNW and the barometer, at 30.35, still rising. We carry on with the Hood and keep hoping for more wind. It is a pleasant, dry, and warm night. We would settle for more speed.

XXII

ANOTHER HIGH?

THURSDAY, JULY 18

0100   We start the 19th day of the race. It certainly is going to take longer than we hoped. The breakdown days early in the voyage may be our sad story —unless, of course, everyone else had the same experiences. Since then, we have been doing rather well. I am glad now that I refused to join any compact in regard to communication between boats. Beyond the fact that the isolation at sea is a healing experience, especially for urbanites, we now savor the tingle of long-drawn-out suspense. We do not know how badly or how well we are doing and will have little chance of finding out until we are near, or at, the finish line. Perhaps we will not be able to find out until we get to Cowes. This ability to maintain hope is good for morale. It keeps the crew up to a fighting edge. Naturally, if we knew we were doing well, it would be splendid. However, we'll play it this way.

Ocean and passage races are an off-beat way to engage in competitive sports. Calling anything a competitive sport in which you cannot tell whether you've lost or won at the end seems odd, and yet that's precisely what happens in this kind of racing. There are times when the outcome is quite clear. All you have to do is see a smaller boat which has already finished or is near finishing, and you know you've had it. Or you can ask the committee boat what time the larger boats came in and you know whether you have saved your time or not. That's if they will tell you. But to win from the middle of the fleet, as we are trying to do, is the hard way. The longer the race, the longer you wait to find out. In the Swedish Race, we knew we had everyone beaten who had finished ahead of us. We heard that over the Swedish Radio while roaring by Jutland. But we had to wait four or five days on the beach, until the time ran out on the smallest boat. I once had the Bermuda won for nine solid hours, only to lose it fourteen minutes before the time ran out on the smallest boat. The same sort of thing happened to us on the St. Pete–Havana and other unsplendid times. Inshore passage racing, especially as run on our own eastern seaboard, is the oddest kind of contest in terms of a known conclusion at the end. Let's say your boat finishes Sunday morning, having started Friday night. You take your boat across the finish line, identify yourself to the committee, and if you think you are doing well you ask for the finish time of certain boats. If not, you turn around immediately and sail for your home port; you must get your crew home, ready to go to work the following morning. You get home and your wife asks you how you did and you say, "I dunno." (She didn't use to believe you, but now she does.) The next morning you buy a newspaper and, if the race finished early enough to phone the results in, you find out you snatched a second or third in your class. If it's not there, then you call up the sponsoring club. Sometimes there is no one around to give you the information, so you call up a friend who knows somebody, and gradually the best-kept secret in the world unfolds. At last, you find out what happened. Now isn't that one hell of a competitive sport?

0130   Course steered 065° on a desired course of 095°. Speed is 4.5 knots. The wind has gone around west and is very light. Something new is happening! But what?

0200   Barograph starts a downward slope. Is a new low coming, or is the high going off? With the passing of the high, we will go back to normal weather. Course 065° at 4.5 knots.

0230   Exasperating steering and sailing. A short, lumpy sea is coming in from the direction of the wind. It is dead aft. FIGARO rocks and twists, shaking the wind out of her sails. We have put go-fast on everything, trying to keep quiet, but it's damn near impossible.

0330   Barograph still sliding down. Course 070° at 4.0 knots. It is almost time to gybe.

0415   Gybed and on a course for the barn, 095° at 5.0 knots. As the song has it, "The wind at southwest, boys." It's roll and go.

0500   Barograph continues down. Is there a new low to the north, or is it the same old one playing tag with us?

0600   A very large breakfast. Buckwheat cakes, syrup, Canadian bacon, coffee.

All of the meals have been wonderful. Due, mostly, to the magnificent planning and organization on the part of my wife, who, in addition to being an understanding and loving helpmate, is the finest ship's chandler on the eastern seaboard. Our meals are planned and packed by the week, recorded, tested, and accompanied by instructions. It makes cooking easy. Many thinks to you, Betty!

Mike attends breakfast, bringing with him a supremely stiff upper lip. Very little conversation out of him. He is locked into an interior dialogue. In an entirely British way, he is registering landfallitis, an affliction that hits all navigators when approaching soundings. It is a point of pride for any navigator to make his landfall right on the nose. But the state of our boat's gear and the casual attitude of the crew have given him only a modicum of help toward making a pinpoint landing. He is given to muttering in his beer (not having a beard) for the edification of the crew on his various and sundry opinions on the state of the world around us. Of late, the most recurrent theme is his wonder at why people have taken the trouble to invent new instruments of navigation when we cannot seem to keep our simple units operative. As a navigator, Mike is a classicist. He has an inborn disrespect for that electronic aid, the radio direction finder. When I point out to him that it offers less drag than a taffrail log, his answer is, "Yes, there is that to say for it." He keeps looking hungrily at the sky for a shot of the sun, but as of now there seems to be little chance of that, what with the heavy cover of clouds and drizzle.

However, he does warm up now and then in response to his mates in the exchange of banter and pleasantries. He is resigned to the proposition that where there is no sense there can be no feeling. He is experiencing his passion by himself.

0700   Bosun Jon up the mast for a check of gear and fittings. All is well aloft, except for a seam in the top panel of the mainsail. He sews that up while sitting in the bosun's chair aloft. He is a gallant young man, in love with the sea and its traditions.

The main has been subjected to a lot of hard usage during our running, more so than is usual. As the boom is squared, the sail lies against the upper spreaders and shrouds. Usually we vang it down hard which flattens the sail, giving us more projected area and, in taking out the belly, tends to reduce the rubbing of the sail against the standing rigging. We dare not do this now, because of the broken boom. There is that accumulating price we pay for a single failure.

The report from the masthead is as follows:

1. Shackle for port spinnaker halyard block shows some wear—not bad or dangerous, just keep an eye on it.
2. All pins are checked and taped.
3. The pin in the main headboard shackle is digging into the mast, because of its position while running. No worry—just remember to fill and varnish the spot when we reach Cowes so that it won't rot.
4. Keep an eye on the top batten pocket and the top four or five seams in the main. Watch for chafe.
5. No boats in sight.

1000   We shift from the Hood spinnaker to the Number One Genoa. Our coures is altered to 100°, the wind is coming slightly ahead from the south.

1100   Intermittent rain, fog, heavy overcast. *Hélas!* No sights. Course 100°, speed 7.0 knots.

1130   An unreliable cross of consol bearings from Bushmill on Northern Ireland and Plonéis in the northwest corner of France. It verifies our dead reckoning to the best of our ability at this distance.

1200   Our noon dead reckoning position: 50° 28′ N 13° 06′ W. Day's run 145 miles—no so good. We have 290 miles to go for Eddystone Light, 200 miles to the first landfall, which should be Round Island in the Scilly Isles.

1430   The wind is fairing, not yet enough to carry the spinnaker. Our course 098° at 7.0 knots, barometer still down. There is a low evidently moving down across our bow. We are closing with it very slowly. It means that any boats ahead, most likely the big ones, are getting a sleigh ride. Maybe we can hold onto it too, an urgent hope.

1530   The wind has faired enough to take down the Number One Genoa and run up Old Indestructible, which gives us a slight increase in speed. All is quiet. The watch below is softly snoring, lost in separate dreams.

For that matter, the boat is very peaceful. Little is said. The sounds are those of the water rushing by, the protracted death rattle of the Kenyon, still clinging to life, and the creaking and churning of the mast.

The creaking noise from the mast is a worrying sound, but there is nothing really wrong with it. But the noises do give you the willies; it sounds as though the whole rig were about to come down around your ears. It's not the mast giving out with the screeches, but the wedges in the partners around the mast. Early this year, I was having trouble getting a good set to the jibs. I had them recut and pulled up on the luff wire in order to move the draft forward. They were still not right. In addition, they had stretched along the foot and leech so that I could not sheet them properly. I therefore took all the rake out of the mast, even giving it a wee bit of forward rake in order to lift the clews. It was do this or buy new sails and, since the boat was sold, I couldn't get myself to spend the money. In order to move the mast forward enough, I took out the forward wedges in the partners and put ordinary wood shingles in their place. By and large, however, I was sailing with a loose mast, and as it is compressed under a load and the rigging slacks, the mast tends to raise hell amongst the shingles. At times, when the mast jumped in a sea, the shingles fell to the cabin sole with a frightening clatter. I keep them in so that the mast won't rub itself against the abrasive partners. The shingles now have been taped in and Conn has even put butter on them to reduce the intensity of the creaks, but nothing we have done seems to have alleviated the horrible noise.

In the first days of the race, what with the compass going out and the boom breaking, the crew was gun-shy. Each man kept jumping at every loud squeal from the stick, expecting to see it go over the side at any moment. I took them on a personally conducted tour of inspection at the partners, explained what had happened, and tried to give reassurance that the stick was okay, but those noises are hard to reason against. However, the sounds either have become so usual as to become acceptable (the human ear has extraordinary adaptability), or they are taken for granted as a proof that we are pushing the boat to the point of discomfort.

And talking of discomfort, the crew seems to go out of its way to keep itself uncomfortable in the matters of dress and hygiene. In dress, each crew member effects his own personal version of sackcloth and ashes, perhaps as propitiating symbols in a offering to the gods, or the dress can really be interpreted as a set of virility fetishes, the kind which convince the wearers that they are natural men in combat with elements and not rarefied products of an effete civilization.

Skip, Cleody, and Jon have all grown beards. They tug at them, look abstractedly off into space, and scratch. In an effort to reduce the scratching, I try to convince them that a trim is needed. They can now begin to shape their adornments, but it would help most to get their hair shaved off the throat, where it doesn't help appearance and is the major focus for scratching.

Conn is now completely dedicated to making it bare-assed to Britain. Before, it was a gag, but now he has a real chance of making it and he hangs on. His shorts have failed in a few places, but he throws a few stitches into them and hauls them back on his frame. By agreement, he puts on his German foulweather gear and boots so that he will not stumble at an inopportune time and endanger his mates.

Michael takes off his socks when he goes on deck in order to have dry socks below. There seems to be some mad inverse logic in this that almost makes sense, but for the moment it eludes me. He does not wear a hat in any weather as he feels it is unbecoming to an outdoors man.

And so we drive along on this gray afternoon. Each man armed with his own quirks—noticeable, but not necessarily obtrusive to his fellow voyagers.

1630   The wind is going aft. We square the pole and trim all around. The Kenyon keeps reading between 6 and 6.5 knots, but the boat looks and feels faster than that. We have begun to keep a double entry system for the deck log in terms of speed. One entry, for instance, reads 6.3 knots, which is what we take off the Kenyon. The other column reads 7.0 knots, which is what we think we are doing by looking overside. All this on a course of 098°.

2200   At the break of the watch, the deck gang came below, but held off hitting the rack. They were fascinated, listening to sea stories, especially about Mike's adventures in the late war.

2330   The wind holds, but our course is now 105° at a speed of 6.2 knots.

All in all, this has not been a particularly distinguished day; however, steady progress was made. The wind has been holding fairly level, blowing from aft. The weather has been sloppy with rain coming in and out. All hands are cheerful and in good health. At the start of the voyage we had some troubles—Cleody and Skip had colds, which they threw off; Mike had an infected toe which started to raise hell, running up to a gland in the groin, but Tetracycline caught that in time; Conn had an infection in a foot, same treatment; and Buz had had troubles with his sinuses and then a sciatic spasm. I have dosed him at separate intervals with Chlortrimeton, with codein and a muscle-relaxer with a long, unpronounceable name. Doctor Kildare, you'd better watch out!

FRIDAY, JULY 19

0100 Our twentieth day began with a fair wind, although its strength and promise is uncertain, it is puffy and irregular. Nevertheless, we are on a course of 105° at 6.3 knots. The wind's direction is SW by W.

0130 Freddy hears cow bells. There is a suggestion of peat smoke in the air. We can get ourselves to believe anything. If wishes would put us there, we would be sweeping past Eddystone right now. But we have a fur piece to go.

0200 We see trawlers, a pair working on our port beam. Our course still 105° and speed 6.0 knots.

0500 The course is changed to 115°

0700 We pass a Russian trawler close aboard. He is hauling his gear. It's a large, handsome boat. They have a fine-looking fishing fleet. We show the flag, hurl imprecations with smiling faces. The captain of the trawler waves back, friendly like. The thaw must be in again.

0800 Our neverguesser is restless. He changes the course once more—115°. The speed, according to the diseased Kenyon, is 6.3 knots. A look overside is more like 7.0 knots, or maybe even better.

We have made 92 miles in twelve hours. It is better than expected.

An unidentified seer makes a note in the log. It reads: "Bishop Rock at 2300—Eddystone 0800 tomorrow."

1200 Our noon position 50° 04′ N 8° 03′ W. A day's run of 162 miles and 155 miles to go!

1300 BBC weather on 200 kilocycles coming in. We read it loud and clear and tape it for future reference. The rig works very well.

It tells us of a large, high ridge from Biscay to the Baltic. It is expected to center in the section called Biscay on the British weather maps. This is a scary prospect. If we can't beat this high to Eddystone, we may suffer the unfortunate fate visited upon us so many times before. We may find ourselves rolling around helplessly several miles from the finish. Please, please don't do that to us, not again.

1600 I have decided that there has been too much of song and story in the pungent Saxon idiom and lead the crew toward better things. A more genteel mood is sought in group a-cappella singing of auld Englishe rounde songes. The quality of the output did not match its power, but the results were taped to the delighted astonishment of all participants. This led to some solo extravaganzas. One particularly fetching one was a song by Hibberd to the tune of "Hark, the Herald Angels Sing." In effect, it told that Uncle John and Auntie Mabel no longer faint at the breakfast table.

Course 107°, speed 5.9 knots.

2000   The weather gets even thicker. Fog and no visibility, a traditional English greeting. We shall have to make our landfall by braille, unless the thickness lifts. Mike has been diddling the dials and having a countdown of Plonéis and some sharpshooting at Round Island. He informs us that Bishop Rock, a turning point of the course, is but eight miles away. The deck watch is told to keep a sharp watch forward. This is normally a congested traffic point.

2100   LAND HEAR!! Or some other suitable expression. In the fog and in the mist, we hear Bishop Rock. It has a warning signal of the most romantic sort. A gun is fired every five minutes. That is the sound we hear.

2135   Gybed for the Lizard. Our course is 075°, speed 5.2 knots.

2145   We set the blue-top spinnaker as the wind goes aft. The wind is getting lighter and the fickle finger of fate seems about to goose us one more time.

2200   We try to get Land's End on the radiotelephone, as per race instructions. No soap, there is too much radio traffic.

2225   The centerboard is on the fritz, the lifting pennant seems to be broken. The board is down and no way to get it back.

2330   The barometer at 30.5 and still going up.

The normally surcharged atmosphere that hangs over a boat about to make a landfall is freighted with sad electric right now. We have 90 miles to go after making our way across the North Atlantic. We must sail through current-troubled waters on a dying wind. The race has narrowed down to us and a gigantic high, which is dominating the continent of Europe. If the wind peters out entirely, it will be as unfair a turn as is possible to conceive. We have suffered overly much from calms, but to have one now is the height of indecency. When we were all out on the ocean, the chances were fair that a big calm hit everyone equally, although sometimes a lucky Joe does keep moving. But now, when the big boats either have finished or are about to, they can win the race drinking toasts at anchor, while we wallow on a windless sea so near and yet so far. We might as well not have started.

XXIII

WHERE'S EDDYSTONE?

SATURDAY, JULY 20

0015   This new day has all of the earmarks of a ballbuster to be. Considering that this should be, by rights, our last day and that we are sailing into a big nothing, the signs are bad. For one thing, we can't see. There are ships all around. Some pass so closely in the fog, we can hear the thump-thump of their engines. There is real danger of being run down and, after the ANDREA DORIA, who can trust radar? In spite of this lack of confidence, we have put the radar reflector up. But that's only one thing. The other is the wind. It is puffy, weak, and unwilling. We can only hope it lasts. Course 075°, speed 3.5 knots.

0200   At the break of the watch, Freddy reports ill. He is dosed with Bufferin and Tetracycline, because he is running a temperature slightly over 101° and has an ague. I tell him to sleep out the watch, but before he can make it to the sack, he throws up the medication. In a short while, he is redosed and sleeps soundly. We hope it's not serious. On the surface, it looks like some little bug got to him, but the crew knows better. IT'S THE CURSE OF THE WHITE PORPOISE. It has struck swiftly.

Yesterday, we saw an example of how sailors' beliefs and superstitions come into being and join the other legends in the mythology of the sea. This is what happened. I'll tell you the story. You make your own judgment.

A school of twenty or so porpoises came charging down on FIGARO. It was a bigger school than I had ever seen before. There they were, sporting, snorting, and gallivanting around our boat. The crew members, those up and about and those below who came tumbling on deck, all were upon the foredeck jumping and shouting in extra loud good spirits. Porpoises always seem to infect people with the need to shout and laugh. Hibberd was at the wheel and asked my permission to go forward to join the fun. Since he is a young fellow and I have seen lots of porpoises, I relieved him and he joined the foredeck gang. But the unfeeling bastard picked up the boathook as he ran forward. That should have been the tip-off.

In the school was a rare sight—a white porpoise, shades of Moby Dick, Timor Tim, and Mocha Jack. And of all the playful animals, he paid us the most attention, darting diagonally under our bows and leaping alongside. There was all kinds of talk about the peculiar gifts inherent in this mystical beast. Someone even offered the suggestion that it is second only to the unicorn in magical powers. But this didn't faze our unrepentant Freddy. He made like Queequeg; taking aim with the boathook, he let fly a healthy stab at the white porpoise. (Later, at an arraignment before the captain's mast, I described his thrust as burying the point and half the shaft right up the porpoise's ass—not that I am sure that a porpoise has an ass, or where it is if he has, but this seemed the only way to describe the heinous crime.)

No sooner was the beast struck, than we heard clearly uttered cries (imprecations?) and, with that, the whole herd vanished as one.

To a man, the crew turned on Freddy and asked him if he had lost his marbles. Was he trying to jinx the boat, right at the end of the race? But Freddy the unabashed said he had heard they were good eating and that he was only trying to get us some fresh whale veal. The crew, however, sensing the enormity of the act, refused to be put off and called for a hearing. In their minds, they knew Freddy was going to catch hell from on high, or maybe low, but they didn't want to go down with him; and besides, they wanted to win the race and they didn't sign on the PEQUOD, and maybe he ought to be thrown overboard, and where the hell did he get off, anyway?

So it was agreed to have a hearing that evening during Happy Hour before holding a formal captain's mast. As the captain, I naturally was the presiding judge. Freddy was asked to choose someone to defend him and he promptly chose me. He's a good kid and I couldn't let him down, so I took on the defense as well and, with some wily legal shenanigans, won a postponement. And there the matter stands. Certain zealot members of the crew feel that Freddy, like Jonah, must be cast into the sea so that the ship can win her race. Others are willing to wait and see what happens. As for me, I am torn, but then I told Lorna and Fred (his mother and father), and his new bride, Lucy, that I would see he got back in one piece and, despite the fact that they are ardent racers, I might have trouble with explanations if he goes missing. So there the matter stands and now Freddy is sick and what do you think?

0230   We finally got through to Land's End signal station and reported ourselves ten miles east of Bishop's Rock. In answer to our questions, we were told that BOLERO had finished first, then CORSARO and next in order ONDINE, DYNA, and BACCARAT. In some cases, we were unclear as to whether the times given us were for finish at Eddystone, or for reporting at Land's End. So they had coasted in on the tail of the low, the undeserving bastards. But it seems to us that we still have a chance if only the wind would pipe up a bit.

0400   So, of course, the winds crap out altogether—barely making steerageway, on a course of 088°.

0500   No forward progress. It's the curse! the curse! Of all the stupid ways to finish an indifferent race, this is it. We struggle across 2800 miles of alternating blow and calm and now we run into this feather pillow. What a way to struggle up to the line, no banners or pennants, no trumpets, drums, or cymbals. We are dying with Roland at Roncesvalles. But life goes on and we can't give up yet. We keep working the ship.

0600   Course 095°, speed 1.0 knots?

Freddy shows up for breakfast and to go on watch. He is weak and tired, but whatever he had is thrown off. He is definitely on the mend. Some halfhearted chatter is started about the curse, but no one has too much stomach for this kind of banter, besides Hibberd is still not well enough to hit back. There is no fun in a poste unless you can get a riposte.

0930   Course 075°, speed 2.7 knots.

We cannot see England, but we are surrounded by the sounds of the approaches to British waters. We hear the diaphone on Wolf Rock, the siren on Runnelstone, and two shots from Longships. They all come to us through the fog, rainy mist, and drear.

1200   Our position is east of Land's End, not too far off. I'm going to close with the beach in the hope that something will be happening there. The difference in temperatures between the land and sea should create some thermals, and in this high we should soon have some sunshine. It seems ridiculous to finish a trans-Atlantic race with the same strategy and tactics we use in Block Island races. Long Island Sound has become the new horse latitudes. When racing there, you never use the middle of the Sound—that's for steamers. We always sneak up one beach or another. Once, as a matter of fact, in this kind of condition I did the same thing on a Havana-Veradero race and did well for myself. In any case, we haven't given up the fight. We are switching to American-water, guerrilla-type tactics.

1300   Into Mount's Bay, past Asparagus Island, and pointing at the Mulvin at the end of Lizard Head. The sun is out and we have a land-made thermal. We are sailing with fair speed in a great arc, hugging the shore.

1330   As we come to the end of the bay and turn into the Channel, the wind dies. If there is a thermal on this stretch of shore, we don't feel it. It is not leapfrogging over us, for there is not a sign of wind ruffling on the water anywhere. This is a very bold headland and with the heave and roll of the Channel, a surf is breaking on the rocks. The tide is favorable, running about 1.4 knots, but it is setting northeasterly and pushing us into the surf. We are helpless and without steerageway. What to do? But there is a way. We turn the boat so that she is heading south, toward France. We then put up our 1.5-ounce nylon ballooner. We are making a 1.4-knot sideways drift, which is enough to inflate the ballooner. With this sail filled by the boat's movement, FIGARO slowly but surely is edging off the cliff and going into deeper water, while at the same time drifting toward the Lizard. This is inelegant and totally lacking in dignity. Imagine finishing a race sideways. The trouble is that soon the tide will start the other way. However, for the moment it takes us out of trouble and toward our goal.

1630   The tide is still favorable, but there is not a breath of air. We are making slow drifting progress toward the Lizard. What lack of style!

1650   Buz exchanges signals with Lloyd's station at the Lizard. They acknowledge and will report us. Buz asks, "Have you seen WINDROSE?" Lizard to Buz, "No." But what of it, they could be on the other side of the Channel.

1800   Very little forward progress. We are beset by indifferent winds, variable in speed and direction, although the variations in speed go from slow to slower and the direction is always from ahead. We keep tacking in and offshore, but mainly trying to hold away from the strong tidal areas.

2000   Very little forward progress.

2100   V.L.F.P.

2330   A light breeze from ahead. Course 128°, speed 2.0 knots. This has been a day to forget. It's almost as if we had been set up for the *coup de grâce* by the Chairman of the Racing Division (Heavenly Affairs—Maritime Section). We fought our way out of a hole and almost made it, only to be shoved back into a hole again. This sounds like a plot line for a race described by Beckett or Ionesco. To think that nature in all its power, splendor, and majesty can stoop to being so mean. That's what puts ground glass into your guts. "Why me?" is the question, but there is no one around to say.

SUNDAY, JULY 21

0001   This must be the last day. They can't drag it out much more. It's a for-the-birds day. Now we are told that there is an advancing cold front. How about that? They throw wind, rain, and miserable weather at us after the finish when we must make the run to Cowes. Just rub our noses in it, that's what. Not that we have anything decent to work with yet. There are gales to the north of us and rain and fog here in the south, with built-in head winds.

The wind constantly shifts; we tack on most of the headers to try to take advantage of any lead on the wind.

0200–5030   In these past few hours we have been suffering from lousy racing conditions. It is foggy and wet. A lumpy head sea is building up. The wind keeps veering. We make innumerable shifts and tacks as a sampling taken the deck log shows: 032° at 4.0 knots—010° at 3.5 knots—355° at 3.0 knots —125° at 5.5 knots—135° at 5.2 knots.

0600   The watch changes. It is a gray, foggy morning. We have only limited visibility. Eddystone Light should be near, but where?

0615   Finish line in sight!!
SKIP SIGHTS THE EDDYSTONE!!

Eddystone at last

It is about 2.5 miles to the south of us. In this thick, gray morning it was a difficult target to hit. We are lucky we did not sail past and then have to find our way back. Eddystone has no radio beacon and stands well off from the land; according to the racing circular we must leave it to port at a distance not to exceed 1000 feet. In this kind of weather, with visibility so low, it was not easy to hit on the nose. A *Cordon Bleu* to Mike for putting us so close and to Skip for finding it in the brief break in the fog curtain. We have been sailing on a course of 042°. We tack to 135° and make for the Light.

Up to the mark at long last, we turn it close aboard, everyone staring hungrily at the blank windows of the lighthouse. Maybe the lightkeeper is asleep. That would be a payoff—sail all the way across, then not have our time taken. We will take our time in any case, but it is more official if they do. Finally, an answering pennant flutters weakly out on the roof of the lighthouse. We are not alone. We are observed. The keeper of the Eddystone Light—or his son, fathered out of the mermaid—has seen us. We wave back. Our finish time is 07 hrs. 03 min. 20 sec. G.M.T.

A great deal of handshaking and a few raucous cheers, now that the frustratting trial is over. Despite the unseasonable hour, we prepare and down a bumper of grog.

It is over, racing discipline falls apart. Picture-taking breaks out in a rash. And then all of the company witness a final ceremony. Our admirable Conn has made it across bare-assed to Britain in one pair of shorts and one shirt, although at times his knees turned blue. In slow and studied gestures, he divests himself of all of his garments. Standing, balls naked, on the after deck, as a last defiant gesture in this cold, drizzly fog he consigns his rags to the deep off Eddystone. The cameras clack and record his goose pimples. He goes down to don new garb. Up he comes all togged out. In what? Shorts and shirt, of course, but this time he is wearing tennis shoes and socks.

Conn's change is symbolic of our feelings now. It is the same, and yet it is different. The sea is still lumpy and nasty. The cold front is still coming on with its advance curtain of fog and rain. And we still have a long way to go. But the anticlimax has set in. The boat is sailed less sharply. Sails are no longer watched like hawks for perfect trim and helmsmanship becomes a little sloppier. We have crossed the invisible line from racing to cruising. All we have to do now is get to Cowes in one piece. But we miss the demanding discipline of racing, somehow or other getting there in a hurry now seems less important.

THE NEXT DAY

It was rainy and cold all the way to Cowes. The wind was not helpful, but then we did not care. After all, it would have been the insult supreme to give us fair breezes after the race was over.

Conn gives his shorts the deep 6

The historic headlands of the Channel coast of England are ticked off as we sail past Start Point, Portland Bill, and finally, in the gray dawn, past the dramatic chalk Needles into Needles Channel and the Solent itself.

We reach Cowes on a cold and rainy morning, but are warmed by a salute from Sir Max at the Prospect. He stayed over a day to greet us.

We sail up to a trot, tie on, and lower all sails. FIGARO is suddenly still, but now by intention. We have a round of drinks, and some moderate clean-up starts while I hie over to the Island Sailing Club to file my certificate of compliance. Finally found the chap in charge of the Finish Committee and filed our statement and bona fides. "FIGARO?" said he. "Oh yes, it looks like you won Class B."

THE RESULTS

Class	Boat	Elapsed Time				Corrected Time			
		dy	hr	mn	sc	dy	hr	mn	sc
	ONDINE	18	07	46	29	12	13	40	56
A	CORSARO	17	22	12	29	13	11	15	13
	BOLERO	17	07	24	29	13	14	17	52
	DYNA	19	05	14	29	13	23	26	53
	FIGARO	20	15	03	29	14	05	56	44
	WINDROSE	21	02	13	29	14	11	50	44
B	CYANE	21	02	41	29	14	11	51	31
	CARINA	20	10	27	29	14	12	38	04
	BACCARAT	20	10	50	29	14	13	01	04
	GUINEVERE	22	11	31	29	14	11	16	15
	KATAMA	22	06	03	29	14	12	27	18
C	SITZMARK	22	09	47	29	15	03	18	37
	CHINA BIRD	23	07	16	29	15	07	38	29
	EN RAPPORT	23	07	27	29	15	16	44	34

Over-all winner: ONDINE
Distance: 3000 miles
June 30–July 23, 1963

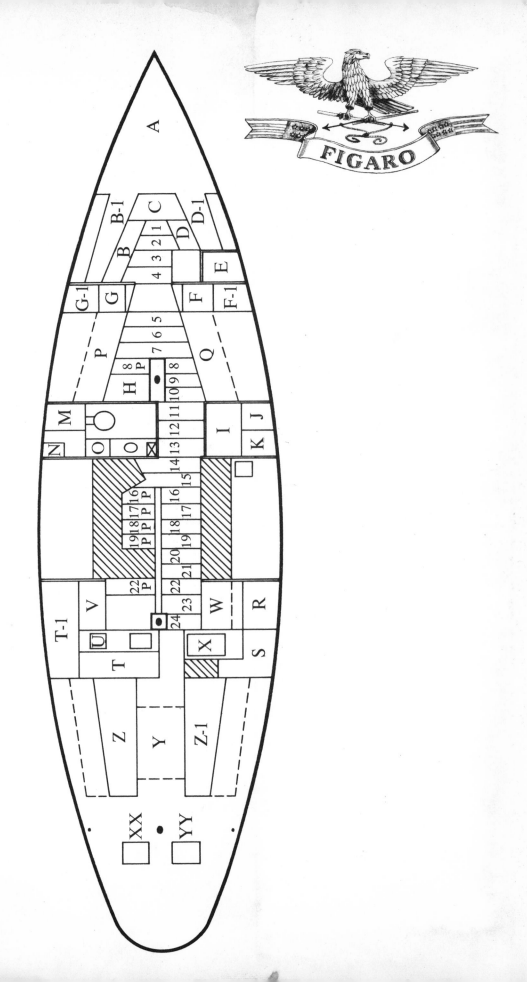

FIGARO